LITERARY GEOGRAPHY

ON THE MEDWAY. (THE DICKENS COUNTRY.)

From a drawing by William Hyde.

Literary Geography

By

WILLIAM SHARP

LONDON : " PALL MALL " PRESS, HOLBORN, W.C.

1907.

FOREWORD.

THE following papers on the distinctive features of the actual
or delineated country of certain famous writers, and on certain
regions which have many literary associations, now collectively
grouped under the title *Literary Geography*, have appeared at
intervals during 1903 and 1904 in *The Pall Mall Magazine*.
The order in which they appeared there has not been adhered
to, and here and there a few passages or quotations or illustrations have been cancelled ; otherwise, save for the correction of
one or two slips in nomenclature or other misstatements, the
articles appear as they were written. It has been thought better
to keep the illustrations apart from the text, hence the arrange-
ment by which they now stand by themselves.

It is obvious that the choice of theme has been arbitrary.
Where, for instance, is " The Country of Thomas Hardy " ?
But 'Wessex' has been so exploited that further writing on the
subject seemed to be superfluous. It is, however, equally obvious
that, to be adequately inclusive, not a single volume but a
Cyclopædia of Literary Geography would be necessary. The
present volume aims at nothing more than to be a readable
companion in times of leisure for those who are in sympathy
with the author's choice of writers and localities ; and if they
share his own pleasure in wandering through these ' literary
lands ' he on his part will be well content.

To GEORGE R. HALKETT.

My Dear Halkett,

More years ago now than either of us cares to recall, we were both, and in the same dismal autumn for us, sent wandering from our native lands in Scotland to the ends of the earth. I remember that each commiserated the other because of that doctor's-doom in which we both, being young and foolish, believed. Since then we have sailed many seas and traversed many lands, and I, at least, have the wayfaring fever too strong upon me ever to be cured now. At times, however, one not only returns to one's own country, but to the familiar lands of literary geography where, since we were boys, we have so often fared with never-failing gladness and content. Some of these wayfarings, set in the steadfastness of print, are now chronicled in this book : and to whom better could I dedicate it than to you, who are at once editorially its godfather and the old-time and valued friend of

THE AUTHOR.

CONTENTS.

INDEX

THE COUNTRY OF GEORGE MEREDITH.

The day was a van-bird of summer ; the robin still piped, but the blue,
A warm and dreamy palace with voices of larks ringing through,
Looked down as if wistfully eyeing the blossoms that fell from its lap ;
A day to sweeten the juices,—a day to quicken the sap !
All round the shadowy orchard sloped meadows in gold, and the dear
Shy violets breathed their hearts out—the maiden breath of the year !

 N just such a van-bird day as sung in those lines of the poet-romancist himself I take up my pen to write of "The Country of George Meredith." The Country of George Meredith : a fascinating theme indeed ! For the true Meredithian, there is no living writer so saturated with the spirit of nature in England as this rare poet. What other has sung with so vibrant and exultant a note as this great analyst and portrayer of men and women ? —who with all his Aristophanic laughter and keen Voltairian spirit feels to the core what he has himself so finely expressed . . . that nothing but poetry makes romances passable, "for poetry is the everlastingly and embracingly human ; without it, your fictions are flat foolishness." But what a country it is—how wide its domain, how evasive its frontiers ! I doubt if any living writer is as intimate with nature-life, with what we mean by 'country-life.' Certainly none can so flash manifold aspect into sudden revelation. Not even Richard Jefferies knew nature more intimately, though he gave his whole thought to what with Mr. Meredith is but a beautiful and ever-varying background. I recollect Grant Allen, himself as keen a lover and accomplished a student of nature as England could show, speaking of this singular intimacy in one who had no pretension to be a man of science And that recalls to me a delightful afternoon illustrative of what has just been said.

c

Some twelve or fourteen years ago, when Grant Allen (whom
I did not then know) was residing at The Nook, Dorking, I
happened to be on a few days' visit to Mr. Meredith at his
cottage-home near Burford Bridge, a few miles away.   On the
Sunday morning I walked over the field - ways to Dorking,
and found Grant Allen at home.   It was a pleasant meeting.
We had friends in common, were colleagues on the staff of
two London literary ' weeklies,' and I had recently enjoyed
favourably reviewing a new book by this prolific and always
interesting and delightful writer.   So, with these ' credentials,'
enhanced by the fact that I came as a guest of his friend Mr.
Meredith, I found a cordial welcome, and began there and
then with that most winsome personality a friendship which I
have always accounted one of the best things that literary life
has brought me.   After luncheon, Grant Allen said he would
accompany me back by Box Hill; as, apart from the pleasure
of seeing Mr. Meredith, he particularly wanted to ask him
about some disputed point in natural history (a botanical point
of some kind, in connection, I think, with the lovely spring
flower ' Love-in-a-Mist ' — for which Mr. Meredith has a
special affection, and had and still has fine slips of it in his
garden) which he had not been able to observe satisfactorily for
himself.   I frankly expressed my surprise that a specialist such
as my host should wish to consult any other than a colleague
on a matter of intimate knowledge and observation ; but
was assured that there were " not half a dozen men living to
whom I would go in preference to Meredith on a point of this
kind.   He knows the intimate facts of countryside life as very
few of us do after the most specific training.   I don't know
whether he could describe that greenfinch in the wild cherry
yonder in the terms of an ornithologist and botanist—in fact,
I'm pretty sure he couldn't.   But you may rest assured there
is no ornithologist living who knows more about the finch of

real life than George Meredith does—its appearance, male and female, its song, its habits, its dates of coming and going, the places where it builds, how its nest is made, how many eggs it lays and what-like they are, what it feeds on, what its song is like before and after mating, and when and where it may best be heard, and so forth. As for the wild cherry . . . perhaps he doesn't know much about it technically (very likely he does, I may add! . . . it's never safe with ' our wily friend ' to take for granted that he doesn't know more about *any* subject than any one else does !) . . . but if any one could say when the first blossoms will appear and how long they will last, how many petals each blossom has, what variations in colour and what kind of smell they have, then it's he and no other better. And as for *how* he would describe that cherry-tree . . . well, you've read *Richard Feverel* and ' Love in a Valley,' and that should tell you everything ! "

But before we come to Mr. Meredith's own particular country—the home-country so intimately described in much of his most distinctive poetry and prose, and endeared to all who love both by his long residence in its midst—let us turn first to the wider aspects implied in the title of this article of our ' Literary Geography ' series.

Mr. Meredith as a writer of romance has annexed no particular region, as Mr. Hardy has annexed Wessex, as, among younger men, Mr. Eden Phillpotts has restricted his scope to the Devon wilds, or Mr. Murray Gilchrist to the Peakland region. In truth, he has no territorial acquisitiveness : it would matter nothing to him, I fancy, whether Richard Feverel, or Nevil Beauchamp, or Evan Harrington, or Rhoda or Dahlia Fleming, or Clara Middleton, or ' Browny ' Farrell, or any other of his men and women, played their parts in this or that country, in southern England or western or eastern, in Bath or Berlin, in London or Limburg. Although the natural background of his English stories is ever subtly used by him, it is only occasionally the background of specific geographical region or of locality ; though at times we may find ourselves for a while at Bath, or Tunbridge Wells, or Wimbledon (if Wimbledon it be where General Ople had his ' gentlemanly residence ' and was appropriated out of widowerhood by the redoubtable Lady Camper), or by Thames-side, or at Felixstowe, or anywhere east or south of Waterloo Bridge as far as the dancing tide of that unforgettable off-Harwich swim in *Lord Ormont and his Aminta*, or that particular reach of ' blue water' of the Channel betwixt the Isle of Wight and the coast of France where Jenny Denham, on board the *Esperanza*, wakes to the truth that she is to be the crowning personal factor in Nevil Beauchamp's diversified amorous career.

In this series of ' Literary Geography ' it has ever been a puzzle how to treat specifically the country of a famous writer when that writer has wandered far afield, as Scott did, or as Stevenson did. It is rare that one finds a novelist so restricted in locality as George Eliot or Mr. Thomas Hardy. The former made one great and unconvincing venture abroad ; but in connection with the titular phrase "The Country of George Eliot " the Florence of *Romola* would not naturally be thought of. George Eliot made photographic Florentine studies : she did not herself re-create for us the country of Romola, as she re-created her own home-land for us in *Adam Bede*, or *Silas Marner*, or *The Mill on the Floss*. And Mr. Hardy is Wessex to the core. Little beyond is of account in what he has done, and we can no more readily imagine him writing a tale of Venice or of Switzerland than we could readily imagine Dostoievsky or Maxim Gorki emulating Samuel Lover or Charles Lever.

But Mr. Meredith leaves one in face of an acuter difficulty. In a sense, he is English of the English : there is none living who more swiftly and poignantly conveys the very breath and bloom of nature as we know it in England—above all in Surrey and the long continuous vale of the Thames. The titles of one or two books of his verse are significant: *Poems of the English Roadside, Poems and Lyrics of the Joy of Earth.* He is, before all, the poet of the joy of life, and none has more intimately brought us nearer in delight to the countryside. I know no more winsome book of verse, for the truly in love with nature, than *The Nature Poems of George Meredith*, with Mr. William Hyde's wholly delightful drawings: a volume containing little in quantity, but superlatively rich in quality. It is enough to add that its contents include the noble 'Hymn to Colour,' the 'Woods of Westermain,' 'Love in a Valley,' 'The South-Wester,' 'The Thrush in February,' 'The Lark Ascending,' 'Night of Frost in May,' the 'Dirge in Woods.' Yet, while this is obvious, any lover of his writings will recall that much of what is most beautiful in description—rather in evocation, for anything of detailed description, save on the broadest canvas with a swift and burning brush, is rare with this master of English prose—is in connection with Italian, or French, or German, or Austrian, or Swiss scenery. He has made Venice and the Alpine regions more alive with unforgettable light and magic touch than any other has done since Ruskin, and in a way wholly his own, supremely the Tintoretto of the pen as he is. How, then, in speaking of "The Country of George Meredith," are we to limit ourselves to Surrey or the home-counties? The most English of his novels is held to be *The Ordeal of Richard Feverel;* but the finest piece of descriptive writing of nature in that book (and, as it happens, the longest of any in the books of Mr. Meredith) is not of nature as we know it on the Surrey downs or by the banks o' Thames, but among the hills of Nassau in Rhineland and by the clear flood of the Lahn where it calls to the forest not far from that old bridge at Limburg, "where the shadow of a stone bishop is thrown by the moonlight on the water crawling over slabs of slate." No one who has read (how many there must be who know it almost by heart !) the forty-second chapter of this book—the chapter so aptly named, though with double meaning, ' Nature speaks '—will be ready to forego the author's right to have this riverland and forestland of Nassau included in his ' Country.' If one of the most deep, vivid, and beautiful pieces of writing in modern literature is not to bring the region limned within the frontier of the author's literary geography, what value in the designation remains ?   It is not isolated in beauty, that unforgettable scene   .   .   .   not even when set with its compeer in the same book, the familiar but never staled beauty of that finest prose-poem in English fiction, the famous ' Enchanted Islands ' chapter, or wooing of Richard Feverel and Lucy Desborough (with characteristic irony entitled " A Diversion Played on a Penny Whistle "), or with the brief but mordant passage given to the tragically ineffective meeting of married Richard and Lucy in Kensington Gardens, " when the round of the red winter sun was behind the bare chestnuts." One could companion these with a score, with a hundred passages, from the Rhineland of the early *Farina* to the Alps of the recent *Amazing Marriage.*

The literary geography of George Meredith, then, cannot be confined to a region or scattered regions with definite frontiers, still less to a mere county or two with adjustable boundaries : it must be constructed, say, like the shire of Cromarty, which one finds in bits about the north of Scotland, or like that familiar ' Empire ' map where the red flaunt of our kinship is scattered over the world with what a famous humourist has called an impartial and inveterate zest for ' dumping ' on all the desirable and soft spots.

Switzerland, from the Bernese Oberland to Monte Generoso; Italy, from the Lombard Plain below Monte Motterone to Verona and Venice; Austria, from the upper waters of Lago di Maggiore or from Friulian or Carinthian Alp, to hill-set Meran and imperial Vienna; Germany, from the Harz to the hills of Nassau and the Rhinelands of Cologne [of the thousands who invest there in the 'Farina' of commerce, one wonders how many indulge in or recall the 'Farina' of literature, wherein the Triumph of Odour is so picturesquely set forth !]; France, from the pleasant Vosges or old Touraine to the not unguessable 'Tourdestelle' of the Norman coast—are not these, with Solent waters and the open Channel and the Breton reaches of La Manche and 'the blue' west and south of Ushant, even to distant Madeira . . . are not all these to be brought within the compass of the literary geographer?

True, it may be urged, these are but swallow-flights into poetry. "A series of kaleidoscopic views, however beautiful, is not enough to justify the claim of the literary geographer to this or that region," or words to that effect, might be adduced. But the secret of the vivid and abiding charm of Mr. Meredith's backgrounds to the tragi-comedy of his outstanding men and women is just in their aloofness from anything 'kaleidoscopic,' with its implication of the arbitrary and the accidental. He does not go to Venice or to Limburg to write about these places, or to note the bloom of local colour for literary decoration; nor does he diverge by the Adriatic or by the winding ways of Lahn, so as to introduce this gondola-view of the sea-set city or that forest-vision which for English folk has given a touch of beauty to Nassau which before it hardly owned in literary remembrance. His men and women *are* there, for a time, or passingly; and so the beauty that is in the background closes round and upon them, or is flashed out for a moment, through the magic of the same power which gave themselves

the breath of life. The same vision which has seen into a
Renée's heart or the life-springs of a Nevil Beauchamp, or
pierced the veils of personality in a Cecilia Halkett (or any of
the long unequalled 'studies' from Lucy Desborough to
beautiful Carinthia, from Rosamund Romfrey—perhaps Mr.
Meredith's subtlest portrait—to Mrs. Berry) or in men of
passionate life and action such as Richard Feverel, or 'Matey'
Weyburn, or the great Alvan [and here, too, what a gallery of
living natures, between the almost grotesque extremes of Sir
Willoughby Patterne of one great novel and the Dr. Shrapnel of
another!]—the same vision has noted the determining features and
outstanding aspects of this or that scene, and, in flashing a single
ray or flooding a long continuous beam, has revealed to us more
than the most conscientious photographic or 'pre-Raphaelite'
method could accomplish in ten times the space, or in ten times
ten.   It is, indeed, pre-eminently in these brief outlines of the
country in which his imagination temporarily pursues its
creative way that Mr. Meredith excels. A score of instances will
doubtless occur to the reader, but here are one or two chosen
almost at random.   I do not allude to those, and they are many,
which convey solely by awakening an emotion in the mind of
the reader—not by description but by a sudden terse expression
of deep feeling in the midst of dialogue or direct narrative : as,
for example, a couple of lines in that delightful romance *Lord
Ormont and his Aminta*, which so charmed readers of the *Pall
Mall Magazine* in the numbers issued from December 1893 to
July 1894 :   \

>   " Thus it happened that Lord Ormont and Philippa
> " were on the famous Bernese Terrace, grandest of terrestrial
> " theatres, where soul of man has fronting him earth's
> " utmost majesty. . . ."

I allude, rather, to vivid 'asides' such as—

>   " . . . poor Blackburn Tuckham descended greenish to his

"The Woods of Westermain," near Wooton, Surrey.
A drawing by William Hyde.]

FLINT COTTAGE, BOX HILL. (The home of Mr. Meredith.)

BOX HILL, DORKING. (The view from Mr. Meredith's house.)

Sunlit Slopes. (Looking towards Leith Hill.)

A drawing by W. Hyde.]

The châlet in the woods, in which most of Mr. Meredith's works have been written.

" cabin as soon as (the yacht) had crashed on the first wall-
" waves of the chalk-race, a throw beyond the peaked cliffs
" edged with cormorants, and were really tasting sea. . . ."
(*Beauchamp's Career.*)

or,

"Thames played round them on his pastoral pipes.
" Bee-note and woodside blackbird, and meadow cow, and the
" leap of the fish in the silver rolling rings composed the
" music "—(*Lord Ormont.*)

or that rapid impression of Venice, by Renée, in her brief
Adriatic flight romance-ward with Nevil Beauchamp—

". . . Green shutters, wet steps, barcaroli, brown
" women, striped posts, a scarlet night-cap, a sick fig-tree, an
" old shawl, faded spots of colour, peeling walls. . . ."

or, and finally, for one must make an end to what might be
indefinitely prolonged—and for the same reason, still to keep to
Beauchamp's Career—this of the fading of Venice from the
gaze of Renée and Nevil—

". . . [Leaning thus], with Nevil she said adieu to
" Venice, where the faint red Doge's palace was like the
" fading of another sunset north-westward of the glory along
" the hills. Venice dropped lower and lower, breasting the
" waters, until it was a thin line in air. The line was broken,
" and ran in dots, with here and there a pillar standing on
" opal sky. At last the topmost campanile sank. Renée
" looked up at the sails, and back for the submerged city. ' It
" is gone,' she said, as though a marvel had been worked ;
" and swiftly."

As for more detailed description of those regions—Venetian,
Lombardian, Alpine, Swiss, French, German, Austrian—which

must be included by the literary geographer of the country of
George Meredith, that too might be made the pleasant task of a
volume rather than the difficult *coup d'œil* and impossible adequate representation of a magazine article.   From *Richard
Feverel* and *Beauchamp's Career*, the two deepest and tenderest
and most winsome of the author's books, to the superb *Vittoria*,
the brilliant and fascinating *Diana of the Crossways* : from that
intense study of the Teuton nature aflame, *The Tragic Comedians*,
to *Lord Ormont and his Aminta*, and the best loved and most
lovable of Mr. Meredith's later romances, *The Amazing Marriage*,
there is not one which would not yield some long excerpt of
treasurable beauty and distinction.   Which would it be, if but
a quotation or two at most could be given ?   Shall it be just
across the Channel, at Renée's Tourdestelle in Normandy,
hidden behind that coast of interminable dunes, that coast seen
by Nevil Beauchamp on his fateful visit " dashed in rain-lines
across a weed-strewn sea ? "   Or at Baden Baden and the high
Alps with Carinthia ?   Or with Richard Feverel in the woods
at Nassau on the day when that ' tragic failure ' learns suddenly
what has happened to poor Lucy . . . that he is a father ?   Or
with beautiful and radiant Diana at Monte Generoso ?   Or with
superb Vittoria at Monte Motterone, overlooking Lombardy
and Italy ?   Or the Adriatic by night—or the Alps beyond
Venice at dawn—or . . . but an end !

    ' The woman guides us.'   But which of the many beautiful
women of Mr. Meredith's 'House of Life' shall it be ?   All are
unforgettable portraits, from Lucy Desborough and Renée de
Croisnel to Clara Middleton, to Diana, to Carinthia ; all are of
vital womanly nature at its vividest, from Vittoria to Clotilde,
from Cecilia Halkett to ' Browny ' Aminta (perhaps, of all, the
nearest to the most modern ideal of woman, she who of all this
author's women-characters appeals most to men and women
jointly, . . . and has not he who knows her best written of

her, " All women were eclipsed by her. She was that fire in the night which lights the night and draws the night to look at it " ?)

But let us choose another and less bewildering method. Nature is nature, whether viewed among the Alps, in Nassau forests, in Surrey woods or wealds. Mr. Meredith writes with his bewitching mastery, not because he has travelled widely and seen much, but because from his cottage-home in the heart of Surrey, or wherever else he has lived, briefly or for long, he has observed with insatiable love and eagerness—because he has the transmuting mind and the instinct of interpretation. "How did he learn to read at any moment right to the soul of a woman? It must be because of his being in heart and mind the brother to the sister with women." So, if not thus articulately, thought ' Browny ' of ' Matey ' Weyburn in that keen-eyed and perturbing chapter, ' Lovers Mated.' And, it might be added of their creator, how did he learn to read at any moment right to the soul of any aspect of nature? . . . it must be because of his being heart and mind the brother to the living soul that breathes and reveals itself in ' the everything and the all ' of Nature. Hidden in the midst of the two hundred and ninetieth page of *The Ordeal of Richard Feverel* is the clue-word of that book—of all his work. The ' auroral ' air is that wherein his genius takes wing, whence it comes, whither it soars, though its pastures are of earth, and oftenest indeed of the earth earthy. This is the secret of his magnificent sanity : this undying youth with the wisdom of the sage and the auroral joy of life.

What a wealth to draw from ! One need not turn to the more familiar scenes, and can find the unsurpassable by the sand country, marsh, and meadow of Bevisham, or by sea-set Felixstowe, as well as among the high Alps or where Venice lies ' like a sleeping queen ' on the Adriatic. What pictures innumerable, besides these the better known of Lucy and Renée,

Sandra and Clotilde, Diana and Clara, Aminta and Carinthia,
and their eager lovers . . . as, for example, that of the lovely
episode of Cecilia Halkett's voiceless wooing in the dawn " of a
splendid day of the young Spring."

So saturated with the sense of nature is all Mr. Meredith's
work in prose or verse, so continually illumined is it with vivid
allusion or revealing glance that—notwithstanding the innumerable pages given to nature-background in foreign lands, from
Norman Tourdestelle to Adriatic Chioggia, from Madeira in
the Canary Sea to Meran in the Austrian Tyrol—the prevailing
impression on the habitual reader of his writings is that his
' country ' is our own familiar English country, and pre-eminently Surrey and Hants and Dorset, or all from Felixstowe (of
the immortal swim) to Bevisham, south-west of the Isle of
Wight and the dancing Solent.

It is in his verse, however, that Mr. Meredith has given
most intimate and poignant as well as most personal expression
to his deep love of and exceptional intimacy with nature.   If
we must make exception, let it be such a passage as that where
Richard Feverel first sees Lucy Desborough, when on the
dream-quest after his ideal ' Clare Doria Forey ' . . . " (name
of) perfect melody ! . . . sliding with the tide, he heard it
fluting in the bosom of the hills ; " or that ever-lifting passage
beginning, " Above green-flashing plunges of a weir, and shaken
by the thunder below, lilies, golden and white, were swaying at
anchor among the reeds.   Meadow-sweet hung from the banks
thick with weed and trailing bramble, and there also hung a
daughter of earth ; " . . . or that (since Richard's romance
holds one spell-bound) where Sir Austin Feverel and his son are
together in a railway-carriage, as they approach Bellingham at
sundown, and the young man looks out over the pine-hills
beyond to the last rosy streak in a green sky, and sees in " the
sad beauty of that one spot in the heavens " the very symbol of

the ache and wonder in his heart. For in these things is the very breath of poetry, if not the metrical semblance.

But to begin now and quote from the poetry of George Meredith would keep us indefinitely. It is led to, often, by rough roads, and not infrequently rude and even unsightly and unwelcome banks, obscure dew-wet pasture and moonlit glade. But his 'country' is always the country of Beauty, of the poet. One ever looks back across 'the twilight wave,' and sees there, as in a dream, remembered images of what has impassioned and inspired.

> We saw the swallows gathering in the sky,
> And in the osier-isle we heard their noise.
> We had not to look back on summer joys,
> Or forward to a summer of bright dye.
> But in the largeness of the evening earth
> Our spirits grew as we went side by side.
> The hour became her husband, and my bride.
> Love that had robbed us so, thus bless'd our dearth!
> The pilgrims of the year wax'd very loud
> In multitudinous chatterings, as the flood
> Full brown came from the west, and like pale blood
> Expanded to the upper crimson cloud.
> Love that had robbed us of immortal things,
> This little moment mercifully gave,
> And still I see across the twilight wave
> The swan sail with her young beneath her wings.

Those who would be in closest touch with the veritable 'country of George Meredith' will find it in his poetry. It is the country of that Surrey where he has so long lived, so long watched the wild cherry in the hollow behind Box Hill blossom anew at the clarions of Spring, or the nightjar 'spin his dark monotony' from the moonlit pine-branch each recurrent June; where he has so often rejoiced in the south-west wind leaping bacchanalian across the hills and vales, or seen winter silence fall upon that winding Mole by whose still stream he has so often dreamed, or watched the reds and yellows of autumn glorify the woodland fastness behind the inn at Burford Bridge—that inn of many memories, where Keats

wrote part of his ' Endymion,' which for Robert Louis Stevenson
had so great a fascination (and has by him been snatched out
of the dusk of passing things), where first the two greatest
romancists of to-day met, " in the fellowship of Omar."   In
one or other of the small editions of the *Selected Poems* the
reader will find the 'life' of the author, as he lives it, and has
for so long lived it, in his quiet home.   This lies but a
stone's-throw from what was till recently a lonely country road,
though now a thoroughfare almost metropolitan in its continual
business of coach and motor.   It has still, however, at times,
much of its old fascination for the diminishing few who go
afoot, and the still rarer folk of the yellow van.   'The Lark
Ascending,' ' Woodland Peace,' ' Seed-time,' ' The South-
Wester,' 'The Thrush in February,' ' Breath of the Briar,'
' Love in a Valley,' ' Hymn to Colour,' ' Night of Frost in
May,' 'The Woods of Westermain '—the very names are
' breaths of the briar.'   Who has not thrilled over ' Love in a
Valley,' and to its lilting music ? . . . perhaps also to those four
lines which Rossetti once quoted to the present writer as the
most beautiful of their kind in the language, adding, " if
whiteness be the colour of poetry, then here is virgin
whiteness "—

> When from bed she rises, clothed from neck to ankle
>   In her long nightgown sweet as boughs of May,
> Beauteous she looks! like a tall garden lily
>   Pure from the night and perfect for the day!

There are such material differences in the two extant
versions (' Love in a Valley ') as to constitute them two poems
rather than variants of one.   In that of 1851 there are eleven
stanzas ; in that, thirty-two years later, of *Poems and Lyrics of
the Joy of Earth* (or, rather, that of *Macmillan's Magazine* in
1878, twenty-seven years later), there are more than half as
many again—in all, twenty-six.   Of the eleven stanzas of the

earlier version only the first, second, fourth, eighth, and ninth reappear, though through the fourteenth of the later version rises the phantom of the original fifth stanza. In rhythmic beauty this fourteenth stanza is finer, but in the earlier the poetic note is as authentic, and one misses the lovely line (following the " white-necked swallows twittering of summer," and the jasmine and woodbine ' breathing sweet '),

Fill her with balm and nested peace from head to feet.

Another lost beautiful line is that missing in the altered second stanza,

Full of all the wildness of the woodland creatures.

To the cancelled stanzas one can but say ' Ave atque vale,' since the author's mature judgment wills them away ; and yet it is with reluctance we lose the lines just quoted, or these :

. . . On a dewy eve-tide
Whispering together beneath the listening moon
I prayed till her cheek flush'd. . . .

. . . Show the bridal Heavens but one star?
Is she a nightingale that will not be nested
Till the April woodland has built her bridal bower ?

April . . with thy crescent brows . .
Come, merry month of cuckoo and the violet!
Come, weeping Loveliness in all thy blue delight !

Surely that exquisite last line might have been saved ! On the other hand, there is no music in the earlier to equal that of certain stanzas of the later version. . . .

Lovely are the curves of the white owl sweeping
Wavy in the dusk lit by one large star
Lone on the fir-branch, his rattle-note unvaried,
Brooding o'er the gloom, spins the brown eve-jar.
Darker grows the valley . . . .

or the lovely ' swaying whitebeam ' music of the twenty-sixth stanza, or that even lovelier twenty-fourth stanza, beginning, " Soon will she lie like a white-frost sunrise," and closing with

green-winged Spring,
Nightingale and swallow, song and dipping wing.

In the retained stanzas the alterations are generally, but by no means always, to the good, both poetically and metrically. A single instance, that of the second stanza of each version, will suffice.

(1851)

Shy as the squirrel, and wayward as the swallow,
    Swift as the swallow when athwart the western flood
Circleting the surface, he meets his mirror'd winglets,—
    Is that dear one in her maiden bud.
Shy as the squirrel whose nest is in the pine-tops;
    Gentle—ah! that she were jealous as the dove!
Full of all the wildness of the woodland creatures,
    Happy in herself is the maiden that I love!

(1878—1883)

Shy as the squirrel and wayward as the swallow,
    Swift as the swallow along the river's light
Circleting the surface to meet his mirrored winglets,
    Fleeter she seems in her stay than in her flight.
Shy as the squirrel that leaps among the pine-tops,
    Wayward as the swallow overhead at set of sun,
She whom I love is hard to catch and conquer,
    Hard, but O the glory of the winning were she won!

This oral citation of the poem by Rossetti must have been from two to three years before the publication of the revised and amplified 'Love in a Valley' in book-form (*Poems and Lyrics of the Joy of Earth*, 1883). The poem as it is now known first appeared in *Macmillan's Magazine* (October 1878); but when Rossetti quoted the lines to me it was out of old remembrance . . . hence the epithet 'perfect' for 'splendid' in the last line. On the same occasion he showed me (after some search) a manuscript copy of it made—if I remember his words exactly—"more than twenty years ago": and added that it was written in "Meredith's 'George Meredith Feverel' days." I had not seen the poem in *Macmillan's*, and did not then know of the *Poems* of 1851 ; and am not likely to forget the impression of its beauty as read by Rossetti from the MS., or the delight I had in making a copy of it. Years afterwards I had the deeper pleasure of hearing Mr. Meredith himself read the later and nobler version, in that little Swiss chalet of his above Flint Cottage and its gardens, where so much of his later work in prose and verse has been written—a little brown wooden house of the simplest, but to many friends richer in ardent memories than any palace in treasures . . . with its outlook down grassy terraces and pansied garden-rows across to the green thorn-stunted slope of Box Hill, and its glimpse left-ward up that valley where still in nightingale-weather may be seen in a snow of bloom the wild white cherry which inspired the lines—

> Fairer than the lily, than the wild white cherry:
> Fair as an image my seraph love appears.

One wishes that, in his later poetry, Mr. Meredith had oftener sounded the simple and beautiful pastoral note which gave so lovely a beauty to his first volume of verse. We miss the music of the scenery and nature-life of his beloved Surrey ; the lilt of songs such as the Autumn Song, beginning—

> When nuts behind the hazel leaf
>   Are brown as the squirrel that hunts them free,
> And the fields are rich with the sunburnt sheaf,
>   'Mid the blue cornflower and the yellowing tree . .

or this " Spring Song " :

> When buds of palm do burst and spread
>   Their downy feathers in the lane,
> And orchard blossoms, white and red,
>   Breathe Spring delight and Autumn gain,
>   And the skylark shakes his wings in the rain;
>
> Oh! then is the season to look for a bride!
>   Choose her warily, woo her unseen,
> For the choicest maids are those that hide
>   Like dewy violets under the green.

And, too, since he has proved himself of the few who can use

D

the hexameter with effect, we lament that he has not again given us summer-music such as inhabits Pastoral VII.—

Summer glows warm on the meadows, and speedwell and goldcups and daisies
Darken 'mid deepening masses of sorrel, and shadowy grasses
Show the ripe hue to the farmer, and summon the scythe and the haymakers
Down from the village; and now, even now, the air smells of the mowing,
And the sharp song of the scythe whistles daily, from dawn till the gloaming
Wears its cool star . .   .

        *   *   *   *   *   *   *   *

Heavily weighs the hot season, and drowses the darkening foliage,
Drooping with languor, the white cloud floats, but sails not, for windless
The blue heaven tents it, no lark singing up in its fleecy white valleys. . . .

And would that he would sing again and oftener of the great Surrey rolling slopes he knows so well, and most his own close by, up and down and along which he has walked at all hours in all seasons for so many years—

    All day into the open sky,
    All night to the eternal stars,
    For ever both at morn and eve
    When mellow distances draw near,
    And shadows lengthen in the dusk,
Athwart the heavens it rolls its glimmering line!

Among the ignorant and uncritical claims made for the poetry of the late W. E. Henley is that of his pioneer-use of unrhymed lyrical verse, or, it may be, with admission of Matthew Arnold's priority. But other writers preceded Mr. Henley, and, as I think, with a mastery beyond his (as again I think) overrated rhythmical experiments. At his best he never approaches the dignity of Arnold's unrhymed lyrical verse, or the suave and supple loveliness of Coventry Patmore's. Nor do I recollect any rhymeless lyrical verse of his finer in emotion

and touch than the unrhymed stanza just quoted; or than this,
from the unrhymed lyric of Nightfall (Pastoral No. V.)—

> Three short songs gives the clear-voiced throstle,
> Sweetening the twilight ere he fills the nest;
> While the little bird upon the leafless branches
> Tweets to its mate a tiny loving note.
>
> Deeper the stillness hangs on every motion;
> Calmer the silence follows every call:
> Now all is quiet save the roosting pheasant,
> The bell-wether tinkle and the watchdog's bark.
>
> Softly shine the lights from the silent kindling homestead,
> Stars of the hearth to the shepherd in the fold. . . .

In these and all such as these we have the true country of
George Meredith—that which is part of his daily life, which
is morning and noon and evening comrade, in whose companion-
ship all his work has grown and every poem taken wing, whose
solace has been his deepest comfort in long seasons of sorrow,
and is still his deepest happiness in the long days of old age—if
one can think of this blithe spirit other than as eternally young.

" *O joy thus to revel all day in the grass of our own beloved
country!* " he sang, as a youth; and to-day the solitary old poet,
looking out still on his 'beloved country' of mid-Surrey, finds
the same joy, if sobered to the deeper emotion of happiness, in
the warmth of human life around and human love radiating
from near and far.

> How barren would this valley be
> Without the golden orb that gazes
> On it, broadening to hues
> Of rose, and spreading wings of amber,
> Blessing it before it falls asleep!
>
> How barren would this valley be
> Without the human lives now beating
> In it, or the throbbing hearts
> Far distant, who their flower of childhood
> Cherish here, and water it with tears!

THE COUNTRY OF STEVENSON.

HE first time I saw Robert Louis Stevenson was at Waterloo Station. I did not at that time know him even by sight, and there was no speculation as to identity in my mind when my attention was attracted by a passenger, of a strangeness of appearance almost grotesque, emerging from a compartment in the Bournemouth train which had just arrived. I was at the station to meet a French friend coming by the Southampton route, but as I did not expect his arrival till by the express due some twenty minutes later, I allowed myself an idle and amused interest in the traveller who had just stepped on to the platform close by me. He was tall, thin, spare—indeed, he struck me as almost fantastically spare: I remember thinking that the station draught caught him like a torn leaf flowing at the end of a branch. His clothes hung about him, as the clothes of a convalescent who has lost bulk and weight after long fever. He had on a jacket of black velveteen—I cannot swear to the colour, but that detail always comes back in the recalled picture —a flannel shirt with a loose necktie negligently bundled into a sailor's-knot, somewhat fantastical trousers, though no doubt this effect was due in part to their limp amplitude about what seemed rather the thin green poles familiar in dahlia-pots than the legs of a human creature. He wore a straw hat, that in its rear rim suggested forgetfulness on the part of its wearer, who had apparently, in sleep or heedlessness, treated it as a cloth cap. These, however, were details in themselves trivial, and were not consciously noted till later. The long, narrow face, then almost sallow, with somewhat long, loose, dark hair, that draggled from beneath the yellow straw hat well over the ears, along the dusky hollows of temple and cheek, was what immediately attracted attention. But the extraordinariness of the impression was of a man who had just been rescued from the sea or a river. Except for the fact that his clothes did not drip, that the long black locks hung limp but not moist, and that the short velveteen jacket was disreputable but not damp, this impression of a man just come or taken from the water was overwhelming. That it was not merely an impression of my own was proved by the exclamation of a cabman, who was standing beside me expectant of a 'fare' who had gone to look after his luggage : "Looks like a sooercide, don't he, sir? one o' them chaps as takes their down-on-their-luck 'eaders inter the Thimes!" And, truth to tell, my fancy was somewhat to the same measure. I looked again, seriously wondering if the unknown had really suffered a recent submersion, voluntary or involuntary.

Meanwhile he had stepped back into the compartment, and was now emerging again with a travelling rug and a book he had obviously forgotten. Our eyes met. I was struck by their dark luminousness below the peculiar eyebrows; and, if not startled, which is perhaps too exaggerated a term, was certainly impressed by their sombre melancholy. Some poor fellow, I thought, on the last coasts of consumption, with Shadow-Ferry almost within hail.

The next moment another and more pleasing variant of the Dr. Jekyll and Mr. Hyde mystery was enacted. The stranger, who had been standing as if bewildered, certainly irresolute, had dropped his book, and with long, white, nervous fingers was with one hand crumpling and twisting the loose ends of his plaid or rug. Suddenly the friend whom he was expecting came forward. The whole man seemed to change. The impression of emaciation faded ; the 'drowned' look passed ; even the damaged straw hat and the short velveteen jacket and the shank-inhabited wilderness of trouser shared in this unique 'literary renascence.'   But the supreme change was in the face.   The dark locks apparently receded, like weedy tangle in the ebb; the long sallow oval grew rounder and less wan; the sombre melancholy vanished like cloud-scud on a day of wind and sun, and the dark eyes lightened to a violet-blue and were filled with sunshine and laughter.   An extraordinarily winsome smile invaded the face . . . pervaded the whole man, I was about to say.

The two friends were about to move away when I noticed the fallen book.   I lifted and restored it, noticing as I did so that it was *The Tragic Comedians.*

"Oh, a thousand thanks . . . how good of you!"   The manner was of France, the accent North-country, the intonation somewhat strident—that of the Lothians or perhaps of Fife.

Who was this puzzling and interesting personality, I now wondered—this stranger like a consumptive organ-grinder, with such charm of manner, perforce or voluntarily so heedless in apparel, and a lover of George Meredith?

This problem was solved for me by the sudden appearance on the scene of my French friend.   After all he had come by this train, but, a traveller in an end carriage, had not seen me on arrival, and, too, had been immersed in that complicated jargon indulged in between foreigners and the British porter which is our Anglo-Franco variety of Pidgeon-English.

We had hardly greeted each other, when he exclaimed, "Ah! . . . so you know him?" indicating, as he spoke, the retreating fellow-traveller in the velveteen jacket and straw hat.

"No? why . . . I thought you would have known . . . why, it is your *homme-de-lettres vraiment charmant,* Robert Louis Stevenson !   I have met him more than once in France, and when he saw me at a station he jumped out and spoke to me

—and at Basingstoke he sent me by a porter this French volume, see, with a kind message that he had read it and desired me not to trouble about its return."

Often, of course, in later years, I recalled that meeting. It was the more strange to encounter Robert Louis Stevenson, and to hear of him thus from a foreigner, at an English railway-station, as only a few days earlier I had received a letter from him, apropos of something on a metrical point which I had written in the *Academy*. How glad I would have been to know to whom it was I handed back the dropped *Tragic Comedians* !

And as the outward man was, so was his genius, so is the country of his imagination. The lands of Stevenson-country know the same extremes: sombre, melancholy, stricken—or radiant, picturesque, seductive; full of life and infinite charm; so great a range between the snow-serenities of Silverado and the lone Beach of Falesa, or between the dreary manse-lands of 'Thrawn Janet' or the desolate sea-highlands of 'The Merry Men' and the bright dance of waters round the Bass and beyond the Pavilion on the Links, or the dreamy peace of 'Will o' the Mill,' or the sunlit glades of Fontainebleau which hid the treasure of Franchard—as, again, between Pew or Huish or other vivid villains of all degrees, from Long John Silver to James More, and the polished Prince Florizel, the Chevalier de Brisetout, the old French colonel in *St. Ives*, the dour David Balfour and the irrepressible Alan Breck, between Dr. Jekyll and Mr. Hyde, between the Stevenson of *Aes Triplex* or *Pulvis et Umbra*, and the Stevenson of *Travels with a Donkey* or *An Inland Voyage*. And through all the countries of Stevenson, as through his genius, as ever with the man himself, the heart-warming, radiant smile is ever near or is suddenly come.

The true Stevenson—because nature and temperament concur in expression with dramatic selection and literary instinct—is continually revealed when he writes of the open.

The most ordinary statements have the leap of the wind and the dance of the sea in them: we are thrilled, as was the hero of *Kidnapped*, at the "first sight of the Firth lying like a blue floor." What intoxication—certainly, at least, for those who know the country—to read of that blithe, windy, East-Scotland coast that Stevenson loved so well, the country so lovingly depicted in 'The Pavilion on the Links, *Catriona*, and elsewhere, that tract of windy bent-grass, with its "bustle of down-popping rabbits and up-flying gulls," where Cassilis watched the *Red Earl* beyond the sea-wood of Graden, where Alan Breck and David Balfour so impatiently awaited the long-delaying boat of the sloop *Thistle*. But those down-popping rabbits and up-flying gulls are too seductive . . . one is mentally transported to the east-wind-bitten sea-sounding shores of the Lothians. The passage must be quoted in full—for here we have the core of the country which Stevenson loved above all else, his own homelands, from Edinburgh and the Pentlands on the north and west to the Lammermuir and the coast of Lothian on the east.

"As we had first made inland" (so the sober David Balfour sets forth in *Catriona*) "so our road came in the "end to be very near due north; the old kirk of Aberlady "for a landmark on the left; on the right, the top of the "Berwick Law; and it was thus we struck the shore "again, not far from Dirleton. From North Berwick east "to Gullane Ness there runs a string of four small islets— "Craigleith, the Lamb, Fidra, and Eyebrough—notable by "their diversity of size and shape. Fidra is the most "particular, being a strange grey islet of two humps, made "the more conspicuous by a piece of ruin; and I mind that "(as we drew closer to it) by some door or window of the "ruins the sea peeped through like a man's eye. Under the

EDINBURGH FROM THE FORTH.
From a drawing by James Cadenhead.]

THE BASS ROCK.
From a drawing by Robert Noble, R.S.A.]

WESTER ANSTRUTHER.
From a soft ground etching by James Cadenhead.]

17, HERIOT ROW, EDINBURGH.

Photo by John Patrick.]

8, HOWARD PLACE, EDINBURGH: The Birthplace of 'R. L. S.'
Photo by John Patrick.]

SWANSTON COTTAGE, In the Pentlands. An early home of R. L. Stevenson.
Photo by John Patrick.]

THE MANSE, Colinton, Midlothian : R. L. Stevenson's early home.
Photo by John Patrick.]

FIDRA, from Dirleton Sands.
From a drawing by Robert Noble, R.S.A.]

"I mind as we drew closer to it, by some door or window of the ruins the sea peeped through like a man's eye."—*Catriona*.

" lee of Fidra there is a good anchorage in westerly winds,
" and there, from a far way off, we could see the *Thistle*
" riding. . . . The shore in face of these islets is altogether
" waste. Here is no dwelling of man, and scarce any passage,
" or at most of vagabond children running at their play.
" Gullane is a small place on the far side of the Ness; the
" folk of Dirleton go to their business in the inland fields,
" and those of North Berwick straight to the sea-fishing
" from their haven, so that few parts of the coast are lonelier.
" But I mind, as we crawled upon our bellies into that
" multiplicity of heights and hollows, keeping a bright eye
" upon all sides, and our hearts hammering at our ribs, there
" was such a shining of the sun and the sea, such a stir of
" the wind in the bent-grass, and such a bustle of down-
" popping rabbits and up-flying gulls, that the desert seemed
" to me like a place that is alive."

Certainly this brings us to the point as to what *is*
Stevenson's country. If we were to follow that wandering pen
of his, it would lead us far afield: through the Scottish lowlands
and the Highland West by Ochil and Pentland to Corstorphine
Height and the Braid Hills, with Edinburgh between them and
the sea; from Arthur's Seat to Berwick Law and from the
moorlands of Pomathorn and La Mancha to Lammermuir,
where it breaks in vast grassy slopes and heath-tangled haughs
to the wild shores between Tantallon and St. Abbs'; from the
lone Solway shores, where the sorrows of Durrisdeer were
enacted, to storm-swept Aros and the foam-edged Earraid of
Mull, and thence by Morven and the Braes of Balquhidder;
and then, southward, through long tracts of England from
Carlisle and winding Eden to Market Bosworth, in a field near
which, it will be remembered, the hero of *St. Ives* and 'the
Major' buried the old French colonel—a fit companion for

Colonel Newcome, if they met, as surely they have done, at the Club of the Immortals. From the Midlands the Great North Road may be struck, whose name haunted Stevenson's imagination like music, so that he dreamed to weave around it one of his best romances; and that in turn will lead to London and the scenic background of so many fantastic episodes, and above all (to the true Stevensonian) to Rupert Street, off Leicester Square, where, it is understood, the ever delightfully urbane Prince Florizel of Bohemia kept a tobacconist's shop. Then would come Burford Bridge, in the heart of Surrey, so wed to a great personal association and to a famous passage in the Essay on Romance. Due south lies the English coast, with all its associations with the boyhood of the hero of *Treasure Island* . . . and its many personal associations with Stevenson himself, who lived awhile at Bournemouth West, in a pleasant house on the pine-lands to which he had given the name of 'Skerryvore,' in remembrance of that greatest achievement of his family 'the lighthouse builders.'

But this covers only a small tract of the literary geography of the Stevenson-lands. Across the near seas are Flanders and the Dutch Netherlands, where David Balfour followed Catriona, and where James More intrigued and idly dreamed to the last: Paris, the background of so many fine episodes, from that of the ' Sire de Maletroit's Door ' and 'A Lodging for the Night ' to the famous scene where Prince Florizel throws the Rajah's Diamond into the Seine : Fontainebleau, with all its happy personal memories of ' R. L. S.' when resident at Barbizon with his cousin 'R. A. M. S.,' * and all its associations with that delightful tale ' The Treasure of Franchard': the lovely

* The late Robert Allen Mowbray Stevenson was commonly known by his initials one of the most lovable of men, an artist, and the most illuminating and suggestive of modern writers on art (his study of Velasquez and Fromentin's *Maîtres d'Autrefois* are, I think, two of the most suggestive and fascinating of modern books on art), he lacked in creative power that energy and charm which in person he had to a degree not less than revealed in R. L. S.

river scenery of *An Inland Voyage*, and the picturesque Cevennes Highlands of *Travels with a Donkey:* and Marseilles and Hyères, each of them 'a paradise' till the Serpent soon or late (and generally, here as elsewhere, soon) entered in guise of a crafty landlord or servant-worry or relaxing climate or fever or other ailment. When I was last in the Hyères neighbourhood I visited the charming villa where Stevenson declared he had at last found the ideal place "to live in, to work in, and to die in"—and understood why, a little later, he alluded to it in terms more vigorous and unconventional than eulogistic! Nevertheless, his Hyères home, and its garden that "thrilled all night with the flutes of silence," had ever a treasured place in his memory.

Then across the wider seas there are the forests of New England, where Ticonderoga wandered, and where the Master of Ballantrae came to his tragic end; the green Adirondacks and the snow-clad heights where the Silverado squatters gained new life and hope; the vast prairies across which the emigrant train wearily toiled; and San Francisco, like a white condor from the Andes at her sea-eyrie by the Golden Horn—the San Francisco whence sailed the Stevensonian schooners of fact and fancy, now bearing 'R. L. S.' to Pacific Isles, now carrying one or other of those adventurers whose very existence on earth was a wellspring of joy to Stevenson's romantic imagination— the San Francisco where he married the lady who as "Fanny Van de Grift Stevenson" was afterwards to share with him the repute won by some of his most fantastic and delightful work. It is, however, pleasanter to turn from California, where, at an earlier period, at Los Angeles and elsewhere, 'R. L. S.' knew so much privation and disheartenment at a time when health, finances, and prospects ran a neck-and-neck race for final collapse, to that wide sunlit ocean where to the imagination Romance for ever sails in a white sloop before a south wind.

The Samoan Islands——here, above all, we may find ourselves at
one of the least unstable of Stevenson's wandering homes! His
only home of late years, indeed, and where the desire of change
and movement ceased to irritate the longing mind acutely, and
where some of his finest work was achieved, and much that was
delightful and fascinating sent out to an ever-widening circle of
eager readers.　Nor, to the lover of Stevenson, can any place
be more sacred than that lonely island in the Pacific, and the
lonely highland forest in the heart of it, at whose summit lies
the mortal part of 'Tusitala,' the teller of tales, the singer of
songs, whose lovely requiem is, in his own words, so unforgettable in their restful music and in the inward cadence of
the heart speaking :——

> Under the wide and starry sky,
> Dig the grave and let me lie;
> Glad did I live and gladly die,
> And I laid me down with a will.
>
> *This be the verse you grave for me ·*
> *Here he lies where he longed to be;*
> *Home is the sailor, home from sea,*
> *And the hunter home from the hill*

　　A friend who saw Stevenson in Samoa told me that once,
on half-jocularly asking him 'what's your secret?' 'R. L. S'
answered: "Oh, it's only that I've always known what I liked
and what I wanted; and that, with the power to convince
yourself and others, is rarer than you think."　And though
that is only a facet of truth, it's an acute flash on life so far as
it extends.　In Samoa as elsewhere he knew what he liked, and
why he liked, whether in life or literature.　Years before, in
An Inland Voyage, he had said the same thing: "To know
what you prefer, instead of humbly saying Amen to what the
world tells you you ought to prefer, is to have kept your soul
alive."

　　But the Stevenson country !　How are we to define that?

We cannot, in this instance, follow the wandering genius of the author whom we all love: a map of 'Treasure Island' we can have, it is true, for who has forgotten that delightful chart which once set so many hearts a-beating? but from the coral-circt isles of the Pacific round the long world of green and grey to the dark Water of Swift, by the wastes of Solway, or to the lone House of Aros by the sea-facing hills of Argyll, to follow the devious track of 'R. L. S.' would be too extensive a trip for us to overtake here. And then, too, there is the Land of Counterpane! How is one to chart that delightful country? We all know that it comes within the literary geography of the imagination, but then that rainbow-set continent itself is as difficult to reach as Atlantis, or the Isle of Avalon, or Hy Brasil, or any other of the Islands of Dreams.

No, obviously we must take the more local sense, and by Stevenson's country mean the country of his birth and up-bringing—" the lands that made him," as he said once. In *his* case, certainly, this does not mean dissociation from his work. The "literary geography of Rudyard Kipling," for instance, would be everywhere save the place where that distinguished writer's forbears dwelt; nor does it matter to any one (be it said without impertinence) that Mr. Kipling lived and wrote at Rottingdean, or wrote and lived in Manhattan. This is neither a compliment nor the reverse: simply a statement of a sentiment many feel . . . a sentiment to which allusion is made in another article in this series, in connection with George Eliot. We are keenly interested in Gad's Hill, in Abbotsford, in Vailima,—in Stevenson's instance, as in Dickens' and Scott's, in every place where he made or attempted to make a home. There are other writers, whose work perhaps we admire as much or more, who, for all we care, might have written their books in a Swiss hotel or a New York boarding-house, or even inside a London 'bus. It is not a thing easily

to be explained, perhaps is not explicable: it is either to be felt,
or isn't.

How would Stevenson himself define his country? In
one of his essays he alludes to youthful seductive avenues to
romance as "Penny plain and twopence coloured." For all
the multi-coloured shift and chance of foreign travel and life in
South-sea climes, I think the 'Twopence coloured' country to
which his imagination and longing would have come for
choice, had to choose one way been necessary, would have been
those beloved home-lands between the links of Gullane and that
old manse by Swanston in the Pentlands. The way would be
by one of those old green drove-roads such as that by which
David Balfour left Essendean after his father's death, when he
set out for distant Cramond, a two-days' long march till he
should come upon the House of Shaws. It would wind
through the Lothians, with many a glimpse of the sea leaning
ashine across the green bar of the landward horizon, or of the
Firth of Forth lying like 'a blue floor.' It would lead by
the Braid Hills to Bristo and the Bruntsfield links—whereby
the hero of *Catriona* fought his fantastic duel with the touchy
Highland officer, Lieutenant Hector Duncansby, who, as he
informed David, was "ferry prave myself, and pold as a lions"
—and so "to the top of a hill," where still the sheep nibble
the sweet grass save when the golfer's artillery drives them to
the furze-garths, to where "all the country will fall away down
to the sea, and, in the midst of the descent, on a long ridge, the
city of Edinburgh smoking like a kiln." The green drove-
road would end, and Edinburgh be entered by way of the
white roads of Liberton or the Braid; and the old picturesque
city be traversed and retraversed this way and that, and of
course, not unmindful of that Howard Place where, at No. 8,
Robert Louis Stevenson was born—to emerge beyond the
Dean Bridge, or where Murrayfield leans over the

Water of Leith and looks towards Corstorphine Hill, whose woods are now metropolitan — at whose familiar landmark, the 'Rest-and-Be-Thankful,' Alan Breck and David Balfour parted when they had all but come upon Silvermills after that long perilous flight of theirs towards and hitherward the Highland line. Then looping Cramond and the House of Shaws, the way would cross over the strath between Corstorphine and Dreghorn, and mount by Colinton and Juniper Green, to embrace that pleasant isolated manse of Swanston, where Stevenson spent so many happy days of boyhood, and to which his thoughts so often lovingly wandered, and, further, the higher Pentland moorland region, to be for ever associated with *Weir of Hermiston*. One can, in a word, outline Stevenson's own country as all the region that on a clear day one may in the heart of Edinburgh descry from the Castle walls. Thence one may look down towards the climbing streets of the old town, with its many closes and wynds, where the young advocate pursued so many avocations to the detriment of his formal vocation; one may think of all Stevenson's personal associations with Edinburgh, and of how St. Ives looked over these very walls, and how, within them, the French prisoners of war 'ate their hearts out': of yonder building, still the Bank of the British Linen Company, within whose doors David Balfour was to find fortune at last, and at whose portal, when the reader comes upon the closing words of *Kidnapped*, the young Laird of Shaws is left standing; of that hidden close yonder, where Catriona Drummond met her fate when she accepted the 'saxpence' that had come "all the way from Balquhidder"; of the gloomy house overagainst the Canongate and the Netherbow where Prestongrange and Simon Fraser spun their webs of intrigue; away down to where the Leith spires glitter against the glittering Forth, whence David and Catriona looked up that morning when Captain Sang brought his brigantine out of the Roads, and saw "Edinburgh and the Pentland Hills glinting above in a kind of smuisty brightness, now and again overcome with blots of cloud," with no more than the chimney-tops of Leith visible because of the *haar*; or over westward to "the village of Dean lying in the hollow of a glen by the waterside," now a grey declivity by a ravine in the very body of the city; or sheer down, where now are pleasant gardens and a continual business of hurried folk and idlers, but once was marish and thick undergrowth of gorse and bramble, to the most splendid street in Europe, changed indeed from the days of *Kidnapped* and *Catriona* and the final upbreak of all the broken families who held by the Stuart dynasty—the *Lang Dykes*, as Princes Street was then called, when it was a broad walk by the water-edge to the north of the grey bristling lizard of the old town; or due westward, past Corstorphine, round which the houses now gather like the clotted foam upon a rising tide, and over Colinton way to Swanston "in the green lap of the Pentland hills," and so to Cauldstaneslap and all the scenery of the history of the Weirs and Rutherfords and Black Elliotts, to where Archie and Kirstie met by night on the moor, and where Lord Hermiston's grim smile seems to be part of the often beautiful but oftener sombre landscape. From distant Berwick Law and the dim blur of the Bass Rock—in certain pages concerning which, both as to the imprisonment there of David and as to how Black Andie entertained him with the awful tale of Tod Lapraik, Stevenson is at the same inimitable height of narrative as with a still broader handling he attained in *Weir of Hermiston*—to the Hawes Inn by the Queen's Ferry, there is hardly a mile of land which is not coloured by the life and romantic atmosphere of him whom we lovingly speak of as 'R. L. S.'

Was he really 'a changeling,' as one of his friends half-seriously averred? No, he was only one of those rare temperaments which gather to themselves the floating drift blowing upon every wind from every quarter ; one of those creative natures which, in their own incalculable seasons and upon their own shifting pastures, reveal again, in a new and fascinating texture and pageant of life, the innumerable flowers and weeds come to them in invisible seed from near and far. But, to many people, Stevenson had something of the elfish character. A bookseller's assistant, who knew him well in the early Edinburgh days, told me that " Mr. Stevenson often gave the impression he wasna quite canny "—not in the sense that he was ' wandering,' but that " he had two ways wi' him, an' you never kenned which was Mr. Stevenson and which was the man who wasna listening, but was, as ye micht say, thinkin' and talkin' wi' some one else." Very likely 'R. L. S.' occasionally gave a fillip to any bewildered fancy of the kind. Some will recall how he himself at one time thought that the unfortunate Scottish poet Ferguson was reincarnate in himself. But others also ' felt strangely ' to him. There is that singular story, told by a friend of the family, Miss Blantyre Simpson, of how the late Sir Percy and Lady Shelley both believed that Shelley had been re-born in Robert Louis Stevenson, and how Lady Shelley went so far as to bear a deep resentment against Mrs. Stevenson as the mother of the child that ought to have been her own !

" Mrs. Stevenson told us, hearing Lady Shelley had called " and was alone, she, glancing at herself in a glass to see there " was no hair awry, went smiling into the room, ready, she " said, to be adored as the mother of the man her visitor and " Sir Percy flattered and praised. But when she introduced " herself, Lady Shelley rose indignantly and turned from her " proffered hand. She accused Mrs. Stevenson of having " robbed her of a son, for she held Louis should have been " sent to her, that he was the poet's grandson; but by some

"perverse trickery, of which she judged Mrs. Stevenson
" guilty, this descendant of Percy Bysshe had come to a house
" in Howard Place, Edinburgh, instead of hers at Boscombe
" Manor."

I do not know if Stevenson ever heard of this story. It
might have touched his mind to some grotesque or tragic
imaginative fancy.

As for his elfin-country, it was not changeling-land; but
that country bordered by the shores of old Romance of which
he traversed so many provinces, and even, as is the wont of
explorers, gave a name to this or that virgin tract, as 'The
Land of Counterpane.'

It would be difficult indeed to say where Stevenson is at
his best. By common consent *Weir of Hermiston* is held his most
masterly achievement, so far as one may discern a finished
masterpiece in a masterly fragment. If I had to name three
pieces of descriptive writing, I think I should say the chapter
on the Bass Rock in *Catriona*, the account of the wild Mull
coast and desolate highlands in *The Merry Men*, and, in another
kind, *A Lodging for the Night*. Probably no living writer—
unless it be Mr. Meredith—has surpassed Stevenson here; as
few, if any, have equalled him in dramatic episode such as the
quarrel of Alan Breck and David Balfour in *Kidnapped* (concerning which Mr. Henry James said once that he knew "few
better examples of the way genius has ever a surprise in its
pocket "), or the immortal duel between Henry Durrisdeer and
the Master of Ballantrae, or the outwardly more commonplace
but not less dramatic and impressive final scene between Archie
Weir and Lord Hermiston. Read these, and then consider how
even a writer of the calibre of Mr. Rudyard Kipling can mis-
judge—as when the author of *Kim* (a book itself commonly
misjudged, I think, and one, surely, that Stevenson would have

ranked among its writer's best) wrote in the unpleasing arrogance of rivalry: "There is a writer called Mr. Robert Louis Stevenson who makes the most delicate inlay-work in black and white, and files out to the fraction of a hair."

It is impossible in a short article to give adequate illustration by quotation. But even a few words may reveal the master's touch. Here is the passage where (in *Catriona*) the Bass is seen at dawn:

> " There began to fall a grayness on the face of the sea;
> " little dabs of pink and red, like coals of slow fire, came in
> " the east; and at the same time the geese awakened, and
> " began crying about the top of the Bass. It is just the one
> " crag of rock, as everybody knows, but great enough to
> " carve a city from. The sea was extremely little, but there
> " went a hollow plowter round the base of it. With the
> " growing of the dawn, I could see it clearer and clearer; the
> " straight crags painted with sea-birds' droppings like a
> " morning frost, the sloping top of it green with grass, the
> " clan of white geese that cried about the sides, and the black
> " broken buildings of the prison sitting close on the sea's
> " edge."

Or, again, take the following from *The Merry Men*:—

> " The night, though we were so little past midsummer,
> " was as dark as January. Intervals of a groping twilight
> " alternated with spells of utter blackness; and it was
> " impossible to trace the reason of these changes in the flying
> " horror of the sky. The wind blew the breath out of a
> " man's nostrils; all heaven seemed to thunder overhead like
> " one huge sail; and when there fell a momentary lull on
> " Aros, we could hear the gusts dismally sweeping in the

" distance.   Over all the lowlands of the Ross the wind must
" have blown as fierce as on the open sea; and God only
" knows the uproar that was raging round the head of Ben
" Kyaw.   Sheets of mingled spray and rain were driven in
" our faces.   All round the isle of Aros the surf, with an
" incessant, hammering thunder, beat upon the reefs and
" beaches.   Now louder in one place, now lower in another,
" like the combinations of orchestral music, the constant mass
" of sound was hardly varied for a moment.   And loud above
" all this hurly-burly I could hear the changeful voices of the
" Roost and the intermittent roaring of The Merry Men."

How virile this is, how vivid and convincing !

That wonderful West described in *The Merry Men* and in
the Highland chapters of *Kidnapped* is seized with extraordinary
insight and sympathetic power by Stevenson, who, though a
Lowlander and Edinburgh-born (and Edinburgh folk, it is said,
are all born with a bit of North Sea ice in their veins and a
touch of the grey east wind in their minds), wrote of the Gaelic
lands with the love and understanding which so often beget
essential intimacy.

Stevenson complained sadly of Thoreau that he had no
waste-lands in his " improved-and-sharpened-to-a-point nature,"
and added that he was " almost shockingly devoid of weaknesses."   None could write so of ' R. L. S.' ; but it is the
weaknesses in which he was so ' shockingly ' conspicuous that,
along with high and rare qualities of mind and nature, as well
as of imagination and art, have endeared to us, and surely will
endear to those who come after us, the most winsome and most
lovable of men of genius.

DICKENS-LAND.

E have each our pet superstition. Some of a morning look for a text of augury, and go about the day's business in comfort, or it may be in tribulation. Others are affected by the apparition of a black cat. There are persons who jealously count the tea-strays in the breakfast-cup; others as sane who rejoice or lament accordingly as the first individual they see is hale, a hunchback, or red-haired. A lady whom I know cannot abide three sparrows at once on the window-sill. With her, I believe, four would not constitute a menace; two would be unworthy of notice; possibly two and a robin might be considered verging on the perilous. The fad of the present confessor is to glance casually into a volume that must be taken up at random before he begins to commit his accumulated wisdom to paper. I believe (for the creatures of whim have vagaries, of course) that the proper thing to do is to glance thus at random into one or other book (selected haphazard) by the author to be written of. But this is not always feasible. As a rule, Pythagoras or Confucius does not lie handy by one's pipe; Lear (Edwin) and the *Bab Ballads* may have been appropriated by the 'Buttons'; and one does not habitually carry the *Encyclopædia Britannica* and the *Library of the World's Best Literature* along with one's bag and tackle to an anglers' inn in Wales or to a Highland hostelry by hill or loch. Besides, the theme may not be an author awaiting the decorator or slater. It may be a subject 'walking its wild lone' (to quote from Mr. Kipling's latest)—such as 'logarithms,' or 'gnosticism,' or the 'binomial theorem.' In such desperate straits the only hope is to seize

the right alphabetical volume of the *Encyclopædia Britannica*, and then follow the example of Mr. Pott, the editor of the *Eatanswill Gazette*, or rather of Mr. Pott's critic, who, that great editor told Mr. Pickwick, compiled his erudite and amazing article on Chinese metaphysics by taking Vol. M of the *Encyclopædia* and reading it through for 'Metaphysics,' and Vol. C and reading it through for 'China' — "and then combined his information, sir."

So, when I began to write this article, I carefully became casual as I approached the Dickens row on my bookshelves. The result was not what I hoped. I had trusted to *David Copperfield* or *Great Expectations*. It was *Bleak House*. I sighed, and opened at the first page which my forefinger thrust out "from the dim destiny of things." And here is what I read (the seeker will find it in the twenty-sixth chapter, in the dialogue between Phil Squod and Trooper George) :—

"And so, Phil," says George of the shooting-gallery, after several turns in silence, "you were dreaming of the country last night ?"

"Yes, guv'ner."

"What was it like ? "

"I hardly know what it was like, guv'ner," said Phil, considering.

"How did you know it was the country ? "

"On account of the grass, I think. And the swans upon it," says Phil, after further consideration.

"What were the swans doing on the grass ? "

"They was a-eating of it, I expect," says Phil. . . .

"The country," says Mr. George, applying his knife and fork : "why, I suppose you never clapped your eyes on the country, Phil ? "

"I see the marshes once," says Phil, contentedly eating his breakfast.

" What marshes ? "

" *The* marshes, commander," returns Phil.

" Where are they ? "

" I don't know where they are," says Phil, " but I see 'em, guv'ner. They was flat. And misty."

The marshes and the country to which Dickens alludes through the mouth of Phil Squod (as earlier in *Bleak House* in the chapter headed " Fog on the Essex Marshes, Fog on the Kentish Heights ")—the scenery, too, of some of Dickens' finest backgrounds, as in *Great Expectations*—are the Cooling Flats beyond Higham and Cliffe, along the reach of Thames some seven miles from Gad's Hill. But, at the moment, I am not thinking of that desolate region ; nor of its heart, Cooling Castle ruins and lonely Cooling churchyard, where poor little Pip was compelled by the villainous Magwitch to promise his return on the morrow with ' a file and wittles,' on the penalty of having his quaking little heart and small liver summarily removed from his trembling little body.

For I am thinking, instead, of the aptness of this page selected at random. It might be paraphrased (and augmented) thus :

READER : " And so you were dreaming of the country of Dickens last night ? "

WRITER : " Yes, guv'ner."

READER : " What was it like ? "

WRITER : " I hardly know what it was like, guv'ner."

READER : " How did you know it was the country ? "

WRITER : " On account of the explicit directions. An' the bits of colour, an' the purple patches on it."

READER : " What were the purple patches doing there ? "

WRITER : " They were just a-enjoying o' themselves, I think."

READER : " The country " [here the Reader waves his

paper-knife admonishingly] . . . " why, I suppose you never clapped your eyes on the country of Dickens ! "

WRITER : " I see the 'This-Way-Private '-way into the heart of it once, guv'ner " [this with a conscious sniff of superiority].

READER : " What *do* you mean, man ? "

WRITER : " The country . . . an' the purple patches, an' the Thames grey, an' the Thames mud, an'—an'—an' the whole o' London, from Wapping Stairs to Wormwood Scrubbs."

READER : " Why, you're mixing up town and country ! I expect you see bits of country a-straddle on London streets ! "

WRITER : " No ; I think I see all London flying country-kites on each of the four winds."

READER : " You mean that in Dickens' country it's mostly London ? "

WRITER : " Pretty much so, commander."

READER : " And what about that Private-Way you spoke of ? "

WRITER : " That lies through Dickens' heart and mind, guv'ner. If you'll go through the one and round the other, you'll soon find your way to Dickens' country. And a beautiful country it is. But it isn't London."

READER : " And what do you mean by that ? "

WRITER : " I mean what I say, commander. For it's a *painted* country, the picture of a country or sketches of bits of a country we see in Dickens-land ; but London's never far off, and Dickens just steps down from it as from a coach, and notes down and sketches free just what he sees. Then he—and we —feel the pull o' London again, an' it's off for Fogtown we are and the Thames shores. He writes like a man who lives in a big town, and enjoys getting out of it for a bit : and he writes like a clever journalist often, with his eye on all the salient features : and he writes sometimes like a fine artist, selecting

REAR OF GAD'S HILL.

Photo by Catharine Weed Ward.]

The Chalet in which the later works were written.

Photo by Catharine Weed Ward.]

BLEAK HOUSE.

1, DEVONSHIRE TERRACE ; Dickens' residence 1840-1850.

Where "Master Humphrey's Clock," "Christmas Carols," and "David Copperfield" were written.

DICKENS' FIRST RESIDENCE.
Here he wrote "Sketches by Boz" and the larger portion of the "Pickwick Papers."

48, DOUGHTY STREET: Dickens' residence 1837-40.
Where he wrote "Oliver Twist" and "Nicholas Nickleby."

DOTHEBOYS HALL.

The Inner Court of the Fleet Prison, with the prisoners playing at rackets.

and ignoring and heightening, and giving the whole (and a lot more) in the fewest lines, and with every word alive and every sentence as well groomed as (let us say) your irreproachable self."

READER : " But there's any amount of fine stuff in Dickens about the country."

WRITER : " Right you are, guv'ner. And especially about the sea and the sea-coast, which isn't exactly country, but still isn't town, any more than a gull on the Serpentine is a land-mew. But you see, commander, if you was to take *all* the country out o' Dickens, why, Dickens would still remain, though we'd miss a lot. It's what's *in* the country *he* cared about. ' Give me London, and let the rest go,' he would have said, if he'd had to make the choice."

READER : " But you might say the same thing of Scott, or Thackeray, or Thomas Hardy ! "

WRITER : " Not a bit of it, commander. Scott and Thackeray always had ' nature ' (the country, you know) in one hand and ' human nature ' in the other ; and wherever they dabbed the one they leavened it with the other, or whenever they worked a bit at the clay they always stuck it up agin the other so that we might see it better and in better proportions. And what Scott did more than Thackeray, Thomas Hardy does more than Scott. Why, there's more ' country ' in almost any chapter of *The Return of the Native* or *Far from the Madding Crowd*, in *The Woodlanders* or *Under the Greenwood Tree*, than in the whole of Dickens."

READER : " Well, I'm tired of this discussion, anyhow."

WRITER : " So am I, guv'ner."

But that, though crudely put, and with striking exceptions ready for arraignment against one, is pretty well ' the way of it.' To map out Dickens' country would be inordinately to map out London ; and for that literary-geographical task a

directory and not a magazine article would be requisite.   If one
could   depict   the   London   scenes   associated   with   Dickens'

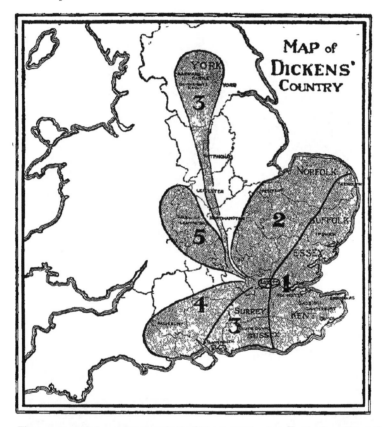

The part marked 1 is pre-eminently the Dickens country, from Yarmouth on the north
to Dover on the south.   Apart from *David Copperfield*, *Pickwick*, *Great Expectations*, etc.,
it comprises Gad's Hill and Broadstairs, for long the novelist's two favourite places of
residence.   Rochester (the Cloisterham, Dullborough, Mudfog, etc., of the novels) may be
called its literary capital.   (Several of the novels, mostly cast in London or other towns, run
into No. 1, as, beside those named, *A Tale of Two Cities*, *Bleak House*, etc.)
    No. 2.   For parts of *Oliver Twist*, *Old Curiosity Shop*, *Barnaby Rudge*, etc
    No. 3.   Mainly for *Nicholas Nickleby* in its two sections, and also in its upper part for
Master Humphrey's Clock.
    No. 4   The country of *Martin Chuzzlewit* away from London.
    No. 5.   The country of *Dombey and Son*.

A favourite spot of Dickens'. The Warwick Inn, near the Old Bailey.

The lodgings of the Six Poor Travellers.

The "Old Curiosity Shop," Lincoln's Inn.

offspring, one would have a Topographical Survey that would vie with the masterpieces of the Ordnance Department. One might start with Captain Sim Tappertit, from Paper Buildings, and go north, west, south and east, finding hardly a street or square or court untrodden once of the clan of Dickens. One may hear much good and ill of Furnival's Inn; but has it any chronicle better than that here (in the first months of his married life) Dickens wrote most of *Pickwick?* Hungerford Stairs may now be forgotten in Charing Cross station. But the name is in the sure keeping of *David Copperfield.* Rumour has it that Lincoln's Inn Fields is no longer what it was; but the pilgrim will not forget No. 58, where Forster lived, and where Dickens read the MS. of *The Chimes* to Carlyle, Maclise and others, and where, too, Mr. Tulkinghorn, of *Bleak House,* had his abode. Much minor poetry has been written at or near Fountain Court, but none so enduring as the unversified episode of Tom Pinch and Ruth. 'The Wooden Midshipman' may be hard to find, but the thirsty explorer in the City may mention Captain Cuttle and perchance be guided to the Minories. In fact, anywhere, from Clerkenwell Green, where the Artful Dodger educated Oliver Twist in the way his right hand should go, to the 'Spaniards' Inn' at Hampstead, where Mr. Pickwick enjoyed tea; from Bow Bells, where to-day another Dombey and Son succeed without a Mr. Carker as manager, to that far suburban west that may almost be said to reach to Stoke Pogis, where not alone lies Gray, but also (in the pious wish of many) Wilkins Micawber, who sighed, on one occasion, to be laid with the rude forefathers of that particular hamlet—anywhere, I repeat, one might wander, with surety of being in Dickens-land, of coming upon some house, court, street, square, or locality associated with the personages of that marvellous tragi-comedy, the 'world' of Charles Dickens.

But in this article, one of a series dealing with

the geography of the imagination, we are to follow 'Boz,' if
not into 'the real country,' at least into the perhaps more
seductive country of Dickens-land, or to those provincial towns
and localities which he commandeered with his pen. I doubt
if mention of Warwick Castle and Kenilworth and Leamington
Priors, with all their associations with Mr. Dombey and the
Hon. Mrs. Skewton, and Withers, the wan page, and Major
Bagstock, with his 'Where's my scoundrel?'—or of the far
north 'King's Head,' at Barnard Castletown, to which Newman
Noggs (when he mysteriously pulled Nicholas Nickleby's leg as
that youth left in the North coach) specially recommended the
forlorn traveller on his way to Dotheboys Hall, for its ale and
other advantages—or even of Portsmouth, with its memories of
the talented Crummles family, Miss Snevellicci, Mr. and Mrs.
Lillyvick, and Nicholas Nickleby's brief theatrical career as Mr.
Johnson—or even of Ipswich and the 'Great White Horse
Hotel,' where Mr. Pickwick had his 'romantic' and embarrassing
adventure with a middle-aged lady in yellow curl-papers—or
even of that inn of inns, the 'Maypole,' at Chigwell, that every
Barnaby-Rudgian loves with an ideal passion, as the Moslem
ecstatic dreams of the 'replete with every comfort' oases of
Paradise—or even . . . But no, there *is* one locality that gives
(as surely as the others mentioned do not give) a quicker thrill
to the Dickens enthusiast than mention of Shadwell and
Wapping and Rotherhithe, of Limehouse Reach and Ratcliff
Highway, of all the gloom-and-comedy dock-land from Southwark Bridge to Millwall : and that, of course, is Yarmouth.
Yarmouth and its neighbourhood. . . . What happy memories
are recalled to the Dickens lover ! Blunderstone, where the
Copperfields lived; Hopton, through which Barkis was wont
to drowse behind the laziest horse in literature; and Gorleston,
or Fritton Decoy, whence (in Barkis' van) David Copperfield
and Dan'l Peggotty and the stout lady who said she was proud

to call herself a 'Yarmouth bloater,' 'viewed the prospect' seaward, and the whole inland circuit from Nelson's Point, the tongue of land where Peggotty and Little Em'ly had their house. Is not the land sacred to the loves of Joram and Miss Omer, the Aucassin and Nicolete of the undertaking business . . . as well as to Little Em'ly and Peggotty and 'Am the good and brave, to say nothing of that gastronomic juggler of a waiter at the 'Angel Inn,' who 'assisted' little Copperfield to 'finish' his dinner?

Yes, in Dickens-land, London has only one possible rival in the imagination. The rest is episodic. Here is 'the other ode' of life.

And as we have nothing to do here with such minor places as America—despite Martin Chuzzlewit's voyage to that country—nor with such out-of-the-way little places as Lausanne, though it was here that so much of *Dombey and Son* was written, and here that, with a longing which was an ache of pain, Dickens so yearned for the London he loved, and wearied for the streets and street-life which, he said himself, were his best inspiration—as, I say, we have nothing to do with chance visitations of any members of the Dickens world to Paris or elsewhere beyond English shores, let us begin at Yarmouth. This is a much simpler plan than to attempt the hundred gates of London, in an effort to travel with Mr. Pickwick, with Nicholas Nickleby, with David Copperfield, with Martin Chuzzlewit, and the many lesser Dickensian wayfarers from the metropolis : a plan suitable for the leisurely procedure of a book, not for the summary disposal of a brief article. I have heard of an enthusiast who yearly repeats the Pickwickian pilgrimage. He drives in a four-wheeler (as did Mr. Pickwick) from Goswell Street ; he has, with the cabby, a Pickwickian argument, on arrival at the 'Golden Cross' Hotel ; and though, as Mr. Pickwick did, he cannot now travel by coach from that hostelry, he starts almost as expeditiously from Charing Cross, whence (very often) local trains emulate the fastest coach. It is his lasting regret that no Mr. Alfred Jingle has as yet rescued him from irate cabby or other perils of street or station. He would give much to hear that rapid interjectionalist warn him to beware of some arch or buttress, at least of uncertain ladder or shaky plank:

"Terrible place — dangerous work — other day — five children—mother—tall lady, eating sandwiches—forgot the arch—crash—knock—children look round—mother's head off —sandwich in her hand—no mouth to put it in—head of a family off—shocking—shocking."

Now, that enthusiast makes an obvious mistake. It is like that of the gentleman who took his second wife along the route of his first honeymoon. Dame Chance abhors the fatuous. Of course, this Pickwickian of to-day never encountered an Alfred Jingle. Perhaps, if he had gone in the opposite direction, and talked politics, or chess, or the Siamese succession, something might have happened. But never along the line of another's merry or romantic fortune !

It is a much better plan to follow the example of Mr. Micawber when he made up his mind to visit Canterbury. What close reader of *David Copperfield* can have forgotten Mrs. Micawber's explanation to David of how Mr. Micawber had been induced to think that there might be an opening for a man of his talent in the Medway coal trade—and how he had decided that, clearly, the first step to be taken was to come and see the Medway. And the inn at Canterbury, where Mrs. Micawber reposed in the odoriferous parlour, under the print of a racehorse, and Mr. Micawber lived with epicurean abandonment when he was not on the look-out for something to turn up (and he expressly spoke, it will be remembered, of " the great probability of something turning

up in a Cathedral town "), had seemed to the Medwayan pilgrims a proper starting-point whence to explore the region
of coal-trade opportunities.

So we may follow Mr. Micawber's example, and say that,
as there's an opening for our talent as *cicerone* to Dickens'
country, we may as well go and look at the country first; and
that something may turn up, in the way of an inspiration of
something to say, at Yarmouth, though that isn't in the country,
but on the sea-shore.

But, after all, when one has reached Bloaterville (as it has
wickedly been suggested to call the ancient burgh), what is
there to see . . . what, that is, of the Dickensian or Copperfieldian Yarmouth?   A great town lies on the Yare, with a
proud suburban villadom on the sea-front; big hotels stare the
little old inns out of countenance.   True, on that sea-front,
about a mile and a half away, near Gorleston Pier, there is a
wooden 'shanty' called Peggotty's Hut.   Unfortunately, the
truth ends there.

No, there is not much to be seen of the Yarmouth of
Dan'l and Little Em'ly, of 'Am and David and the seductive
Steerforth.   Perhaps at dusk one can imagine, at the south
end of the Marine Parade, a black upturned barge or smack,
with little windows and a slim iron funnel doing duty as a
chimney.   If so, the gifted visionary may also hear the deep
tumultuous roar of Dan'l Peggotty singing "When the stormy
winds do blow, do blow, do blow," or Little Em'ly's sweet
laughter, or Steerforth warbling tears from the eyes of his companions.   But now the pilgrim to that spot—then solitary at the
upper reach of a tract of sand and grass between the Wellington
Pier and the South Battery—may much more likely see clusters
of exuberant trippers, or hear the strains of the Jewish harp or
the fell dissonance of the inflated Teuton.   There are many of
the kindred of Miss Mowcher, but that gay and discursive

immortal never visited any inn in Yarmouth save that in the Yarmouth of Dickens' imagination.

Many Barkises may be willing: the breed, to meet in a ramble, is extinct. Yet, behind the town, away by the Lowestoft road, or by Somerleyton Park to Blundeston (it was at Blunderstone Rookery Vicarage, it will be remembered, that Mrs. Copperfield bore her son David) there are still bits of East Anglian country unchanged since the days Barkis guided his carrier's cart (with the horse that could not be driven, but only gradually induced) through green lanes and pastoral byways. And the visitor who has reserved *David Copperfield* to read or re-read at Yarmouth will find certain pleasure in many passages in that enduringly fascinating romance, remarkable alike for their truth in local colour and for their charm in swift and deft impression. And here, too, Dickens showed what he could do as 'a marine artist.' The description of the great storm on the German ocean that brought back the drowned seducer to the home he had ruined, and, with him, his would-be generous and unknowing saviour Ham, is one of the finest things of its kind in literature.

It would be natural to visit the *Barnaby Rudge* country, on the return towards London. The visitor should, for that, go straightway (as he can now do) to Chigwell, and the famous 'Maypole' inn.

On a fine May or June evening—early in the week—one may still have a possible quiet half-hour at the pleasant 'King's Head' of fact, and imagine Mrs. Varden gloating to bewilderment over the superlativeness of that inn of inns, or John Willet ordering that lordly and copious 'something of that sort,' that might have been a roast peacock as well as not, or see for a moment, in the doorway, like a wild flower strayed from the neighbouring forest, pretty Dolly Varden, in her dainty cherry-coloured mantle and little tilted straw hat

F

trimmed with cherry-coloured ribbons ("the wickedest and most provoking headdress ever devised "), or even see, in fancy, Chigwell churchyard, where Barnaby Rudge and his mother rested and ate their scanty meal after their visit to The Warren, while Grip, the raven, having finished *his* dinner, stalked up and down with an appearance of having his hands under his coat-tails and of critically reading the tombstone inscriptions.

After that . . . well, one may go south with *Great Expectations*, and down the Thames reaches, past Cooling Marshes; or through Gravesend, and by Cobham Hall (where the great novelist's writing-chalet, from Gad's Hill, now stands in a pleasant sequestered grove behind this beautiful old home of the Earl of Darnley), to Rochester and the Pickwickian track; or, thence, to the Great South Road, going past the Devil's Punch Bowl on Hindhead Heights, and so to Portsmouth by the long undulations of the Downs—the road traversed by Nicholas Nickleby and Smike on their eventful journey from London to where fate and the Crummles family awaited them.*

This last is a country Dickens knew and loved, though it had not the fascination for him of the dreary Thames marshlands.

"It was a harder day's journey than they had already
"performed, for there were long and weary hills to climb,
"and in journeys, as in life, it is a great deal easier to go
"down hill than up. Onward they kept with steady pur-
"pose, and entered at length upon a wide and spacious tract
"of downs with every variety of little hill and plain to

* When staying at Cobham Hall on one occasion, I came upon an old Jacobean or possibly Elizabethan map of the region from Rochester to Gravesend, and noted that the designation of a stretch of marsh-land not far from Gad's Hill was 'the Pickwick Marsh.' There have been many speculations as to the origin of this famous name, and some have believed it to be an invention. Is it not all but certain that Dickens saw it in this or some other map, and noted the peculiar name for literary use?

" change their verdant surface. Here they shot up almost
" perpendicularly into the sky a height so steep as to be
" hardly accessible to any but the sheep and goats that fed
" upon its sides, and there stood a huge mound of green,
" sloping and tapering off so delicately, and merging so
" gently into the level ground, that you could scarce define
" its limits. Hills swelling above each other, and undulations,
" shapely, uncouth, smooth, and rugged, graceful and
" grotesque, thrown negligently side by side, bounded the
" views in each direction, while frequently, with unexpected
" noise, there uprose from the ground a flight of crows,
" who, cawing and wheeling around the nearer hills, as
" if uncertain of their course, suddenly poised themselves
" upon the wing, and skimmed down the long vista of
" some opening valley with the speed of very light
" itself. . . ."

Or, from London, one may start again at once for the
Martin Chuzzlewit country, with Salisbury as the town to reach ;
or for Leamington and Warwick and Kenilworth, with solemn
Mr. Dombey as companion ; or north to the frontiers of York
and Durham counties, where to-day no Squeers will ask you to
spell 'winder,' and rudely add, on your compliance, " then go
and clean it."

But to get " right away into the real country " (as Richard
Jefferies, for example, would take us) . . . h'm . . . that,
indeed, is difficult. With the ancient dowager, the Hon. Mrs.
Skewton, I may say, " seclusion and contemplation are my
what's-his-name." It may be remembered how, to this, her
eldest daughter snapped that if she meant Paradise she had better
say so. Well, by ' the real country ' I mean Paradise . . . *my*
Paradise, not the background scenery for the comedy of life.
And that I find difficult to discover in Dickens-land.

Let us see, now, how the geography of Dickens' country
pans out. It is not of great extent geographically. In this
respect it is unlike that of Scott, which, apart from embracing
several continental tracts and wide and far regions of the East,
reaches from the Shetland Isles to Dover cliffs; or that of
Stevenson, which occupies so much of the Scottish East and
West, and straggles into England and over to Flanders and down
into France, and then throws long, thin, shining tentacles across
the United States, from the Adirondacks to San Francisco, and
thence across the Pacific to Samoa and the far isles; or that of
Thackeray, which lies beyond London, embracing as it does
divers parts of Europe and far-off Virginia. Dickens-land is,
in a word, rather a huge county than a country. It may be
described as lying between the marches of York and Durham
counties on the north, and Portsmouth and the nose of Kent
on the south; between Salisbury Plain, Warwick and Leamington on the west, and the sea-beaches of Suffolk and the Thames
and Medway estuaries on the east.

A glance at the outline map herewith will bring this
quicker to the reader's realisation. But now just a word on the
neglected literary side of Dickens' life-work.

Perhaps no more striking instance is to hand of the
influence of Dickens, not only in France but in Germany, than
a noteworthy article by M. Téodor de Wyzewa in the
Revue des Deux Mondes, on a remarkable romance by the
German novelist, Gustaf Frenssen.* After a brief summary of
the German romance and of its leading personages, the critic
adds:

     " But, it will be said, why do you thus recommend to us
" personages whom we have long known and loved under
" familiar English names? Your Joern Uhl is really called

* " Joern Uhl " By G. Frenssen. 1901. 31st ed.

"David Copperfield; the simple-natured and heroic Thiess
"Thiessen is, in truth, Dan'l Peggotty. The friend of his
"childhood whom the hero finally marries is not Lisbeth
"Junker, but Agnes Wickfield. Dora is the true name of
"the child-woman. And as to the uncle who sets out to find
"his seduced and abandoned niece, do we not at once recog-
"nise him as Peggotty's brother? All these folk of M.
"Frenssen are already old acquaintances, and it is in fact over
"half a century ago since Dickens moved us with the tale of
"their lives."

Thereafter, having indicated where Gustaf Frenssen's book
is none the less a genuine new book, within its own inspiration
and style, M. de Wyzewa adds:

"Yet none could question the derivation from *David*
"*Copperfield*. The author finds his inspiration in Dickens, as,
"before him, Theodore Storm found it, as the still more
"famous Fritz Reuter found it, as Freytag himself found it,
"to leave unspecified a score of other popular German writers.
"And, in truth, the present opportunity is one wherein to
"testify once more to the extraordinary influence exercised
"throughout the whole of Europe by the author of *David*
"*Copperfield* and *Martin Chuzzlewit*. While the majority of
"his compatriots appear to see in him only an inimitable
"comedian, not only France and Germany but Russia have
"gained abundantly from the central wellspring of his genius.
"When the History of Modern Romance in the second half
"of the Nineteenth Century comes to be written, ' *le nom de
"Dickens devra se trouver en tête de chacun des chapitres.*'"

I would recommend the literary student to read this short
but suggestive article by M. de Wyzewa. The time is

assuredly come when Dickens, as a great novelist of actual life, ought to be more appreciated. Relative neglect or indifference on the part of the small 'reading world' (as distinct from the mainly undiscriminating public) has been succeeded by spasmodic eulogy as futile in kind. I cannot recall any English critic of Dickens who has written more discerningly on the novelist's achievement as a whole than M. de Wyzewa writes in the *étude* to which I have here drawn attention, and from which I am tempted to make this further brief excerpt :

"The work of Dickens is so rich and variegated that
"different races have differently understood and enjoyed. To
"his Russian readers, for example, he is above all the creator
"of Little Nell, the poet of the scorned and the down-
"trodden ; and it is in this respect he has been the master of
"Dostoïevsky and Tolstoï—and it would be a curiously sug-
"gestive study to discover in what way and to what extent
"Dickens' profoundly Christian spirit acted on the opposite
"temperaments of these two writers. For his French
"readers, on the other hand, he is the paramount revealer
"of a realism at once minute in detail and vivid in synthesis
" . . . and, to them, seems to have no notable followers
"among the English novelists of to-day. But it is in
"Germany, perhaps, that his influence has been most potent.
" . . . In the work of Dickens the foremost German
"novelists of to-day appear to have discerned, above all else,
"the veritable types and models of contemporary romance."

Apropos of this foreign appreciation, I wonder if any of my readers has attempted a 'foreign Dickens collection' ? In a fit of aberration I tried it once. It was not (at first) the number of translations that daunted me : many French and a few German I expected. I hailed gladly a Portuguese 'Senhor

Martinho da Londra' in lieu of our friend Chuzzlewit, and welcomed an Italian edition of some of the *Sketches by Boz* under the title "Il Mistero di Orazio Sparkins." But when it came to Polish and Russian I faltered. I had, indeed, already ingloriously withdrawn, when, from 'Kjobenhavn' arrived a 'Pickwick' yclept 'Udtog af Pikvik-Klubbens.' For a moment I rallied, but a mystery in Muscovite finished me. Even long afterward I knew no return of the craze, when a friend sent me from Prague a horrid-looking imprint of 'cweckzcy' consonants, with the (kindly meant) intimation that *Cvrcek u Krbu* was the Czech for "The Cricket on the Hearth."

I have not, I regret to say, yet had time to read *Cvrcek u Krbu*.

SCOTT-LAND.

 WRITE these words in Naples. I mention the fact because of the coincidence that here, in this noisy and malodorous, if sun-loved and resplendent capital of the south, about this time seventy-one years ago Sir Walter Scott began, and then and in the ensuing weeks all but completed, his last romance—the unpublished historical tale entitled *The Siege of Malta*. Here, too, he wrote a shorter tale, *Bizarro*, also unpublished. These were the last efforts of that great genius whose achievements for his own land had been so incalculable, and whose influence throughout Europe we now retrospectively perceive as a continuous energy, not only awakening but compelling. Writers so different in race and genius as Goethe, Tolstoi, and Victor Hugo admitted that the world of literature had known no such torch-bearer of romance since, in poetic drama, the master-magician Shakespeare.

Naples may seem a long way from Scott's country, but in a geographical sense it is the centre of its many scattered lands. If Scotland, if the British Isles, appear to belong to another sphere almost, what of Malta, and Constantinople, and Palestine? what of the remoter East? "The remote East . . . what connection is there between Scott and the far East?" some readers may exclaim. "We remember," some may add, "not only Flanders and Spain because of Quentin Durward and Don Roderick the Goth, as we remember Switzerland and Provence because of Anne of Geierstein, but also Syria and Palestine because of Richard Cœur-de-Lion and *The Talisman*—but what of Constantinople and the remoter East?" Some,

Edinburgh, from Calton Hill.

ABBOTSFORD.

onan's well ").

Ashiestiel, from the Tweed.

THE ETTRICK, from Selkirk.

This small window and door is shown as the Black Dwarf's cottage, Manor Valley.

Edinburgh High Street: Tron Church and Saint Giles'.

Junction of the Manor Water and Tweed ("Black Dwarf").

Ashiestiel and the Tweed.

Tomb of Sir Walter Scott, Dryburgh Abbey.

however, will remember Count Robert of Paris and his adventures in the city of the Sultans; and surely there must be a goodly number who still recall the story of Menie Gray, the 'surgeon's daughter,' and her lovers Richard Middlemas and Adam Hartley, transported from the quiet neighbourhood of Selkirkshire, where Dr. Gideon Gray had his home, to the picturesque and dramatic stage of life in India, the vivid British India of the days when 'the Company' stood for a few hundred scattered Europeans among the millions of sullen and growingly hostile natives.

It is not easy to define 'the Scott country.' If we admit that the lands which it comprises are those which in more or less degree owe somewhat to the magic of his genius, we have to cross not only the Scottish border and the Welsh marches, but to seek remoter regions in Belgium and northern France, by the Rhine and in Switzerland and in sunny Provence, and eastwards again to Bavaria and the Viennese southlands (the imaginary and actual background of the scenes and episodes of *The House of Aspen*), or farther south yet than the Provence of the Rhone, or than that which reaches to the Basque highlands, to where superb Toledo lies in the heart of that Spain which was held in leash by the strong hand of Don Roderick the Goth —Toledo the magnificent, with its towering pinnacled cathedral and lofty square Alcazar, above the curving waters of the Teio, in its vicinage of wide, bare mountains,—

> Rearing their crests amid the cloudless skies.
> And darkly clustering in the pale moonlight,
> Toledo's holy towers and spires arise,
> As from a trembling lake of silver white
> All sleeps in sullen shade, or silver glow,
> All save the heavy swell of Teio's ceaseless flow

And what boy or girl, man or woman, who has once read of Scott's Cœur-de-Lion, or Sir Hugo of *The Betrothed*, or of all the heroic pageant of *The Talisman*, but must recall Engedi by the

Dead Sea, Jean d'Acre and Ascalon, Azotus and Jaffa, and all of that romantic Syria made more romantic still for us by the magician who so moved us of old by Lion Heart and Sir

CHIEF LOCALITIES OF THE SCOTTISH ROMANCES

The Shetland and Orkney Islands "The Pirate." The Country of the Highland Romances
  "Waverley," "Rob Roy," "Legend of Montrose." The Country of the Midlothian
  and Midland Border Romances. The Country of the Eastern Romances, from Perth
  and Loch Leven to the Firth of Tay. The Country of the West, South, and East
  Borders "Guy Mannering," "The Monastery," "Bride of Lammermoor."

Kenneth, the Knight of the Leopard, by the beauty of Lady Edith Plantagenet and by the nobility and chivalry of Saladin ? As we have seen, too, there is Malta of the Knights Templar, then as now the stronghold of the Orient; and Constantinople, the 'Seal of Empire' for long before the days as well as for long after the time when Count Robert of Paris faced life and death within its precincts; and that far remoter region of India where the surgeon's daughter, pretty Menie Gray, had to emerge as best she could from the rival and unrelenting claims of her two lovers, Richard Middlemas and Adam Hartley.

So that, in this wide sense, the Scott country extends from the Hebridean Isles and the coasts of Argyll and the Isle of Man on the west, to the Syria of the tales of the Crusades, and to the Byzantine empire of *Count Robert* and the India of *The Surgeon's Daughter* on the east; and from the Shetland Isles of *The Pirate* on the north, to Aix, the ancient capital of Provence, and to Toledo, the heart of Spain, on the south.

But this would be to delimit frontiers on the vast scale of the geographer occupied with the Roman empire of the past or the British empire of to-day! And yet the difficulty survives. The votes of all youthful lovers of Scott would certainly include the country of Richard and Saladin and Sir Kenneth of the Leopard as lands invaded, conquered, and for ever imaginatively ruled over by Sir Walter. And what foreign admirer would yield the claims of Anne of Geierstein and Quentin Durward?

There is, of course, the obvious alternative of taking as Scott's country solely the lands intimately related to him by natural ties—the region of his birth and upbringing and habitual domicile. That would mean not merely Scotland, but only a small part of Scotland. It would, in a word, be that region wearing Edinburgh as its crown; with its feet laved by the wandering flood of Tweed; with the Lammermuir and the Eildons and the grey seas that wash Fast Castle and St. Abbs, on the east; and, on the west, the brown waters of the

Quair and the Yarrow and the lonely hills overagainst St. Mary's and the Loch of the Lowes.

But that, again, is to limit the designation to the habitat of the man, and to ignore the wider country (that is yet within our own kingdom) wherein he was equally at home, the country of his genius, the country of *Ivanhoe* and *Kenilworth* and *Woodstock*, of *Peveril of the Peak*, of *The Pirate* and *The Lord of the Isles*, of *Guy Mannering* and *Rob Roy* and *The Fair Maid of Perth*, as well as of *Old Mortality* and *The Monastery* and *The Heart of Midlothian*, *St. Ronan's Well* and *Redgauntlet*, and *The Bride of Lammermoor*.

The all but inevitable hyperbole suggests itself, that the country of Sir Walter Scott is the human heart. It is passable rhetoric when a Victor Hugo writes thus of Shakespeare (or himself), but otherwise it is (to quote a delightful phrase I saw recently in the new book of a 'master' who shall be nameless) " one of the facile inadequacies by means of which the torpid delight in evasion." To bring it to the test, one could not well illustrate the country of the human heart—that frontierless and unexploited country which is as compact of reality and mirage to-day as it was yesterday and shall be to-morrow—in an article dealing with the topography of Sir Walter Scott's imaginary and imaginative excursions !

Well, let us begin by following Sir Walter through Scotland. That, at least, is his country more than any other, the country of his birth and people, of his happiness and sorrows, of his devoted love and devoted service—in a word, the country of his life and the country best beloved of him as poet and master of romance.

His was not a day of continuous movement, of constant farings hither and thither, and of frequent travel far afield. Scott, however, was from his boyhood a gad-about from love of the open, of the tale or legend to be heard at hazard, the lurking adventure, the delight of chance meetings. The same spirit that whispered to George Borrow "the wind's on the heath, brother," early whispered to the lad over whose vagrant habits staid old Mr. Scott of Edinburgh used to shake his head in no little sorrow and apprehension, as 'a wandering gangrel.' As boy and youth he lost no opportunity of exploring not only Edinburgh and its picturesque and 'storied' vicinage, or the neighbourhood of Sandy Knowe in lower Tweed-dale, the place of his first memories as a child, but a hundred other localities and "auld biggin's an' the like" in the fascinating region between the waters of Forth and where the Ochils lean to the Pentlands, and the Pentlands fall southward to the streams of Quair and Tweed, and westward wave upward again upon the wilderness of the Lammermuir. To-day, much of this region knows the factory chimney, the shaft of the coal-mine, the noisy frequency of the railway train; but there are still regions even close to Edinburgh where solitude and undefiled beauty may be found, as in the hollows of Pentland, or on the heathery moorland reaches between those strangely foreign-sounding places, Pomathorn and La Mancha. Scott was still a youth when he made the first of his seven annual successive 'raids' into what were then the wilds of Liddesdale. This region, now so familiar and within an hour's reach of the capital, was at the time of Scott's wander-years devoid of a single inn or even wayside public-house, and so remote from 'the world' that his gig, in which in his seventh 'raid,' as Lockhart calls it, he drove part of his route, was regarded with blank amazement, as the first wheeled vehicle that had been seen in these parts. Circumstances, indeed, so well favoured him that in the early manhood and the first years of his happy marriage he was enabled to visit almost every part of Scotland, and even to circumnavigate it— in so far as the word may be loosely used for a series of seafarings along the coasts from Leith on the south-east to Arran and Ailsa

Craig on the south-west.   From the Northumberland moorlands, among which, at Gilsland, he met and wooed Margaret Carpenter (amid scenery he afterwards depicted so well in the opening chapters of his fourth novel, *Rob Roy*), to the far Orkney Isles, whose wild coasts and simple people so much impressed him (though the commemorative novel, *The Pirate*, was not to be written till long afterwards, when it appeared as the fourteenth in his series of romances—written and published when Scott was fifty), he roamed with definite aim, or happily at random, on every possible opportunity.   It was thus he acquired his unrivalled store of legend and ballad and all manner of traditional folk-lore, and thus that he built up that mental treasure of innumerable places, things, and people—afterwards, at any time, imaginatively to be recalled at will—which stood him in such good stead from the days when, as a young man, he gathered the materials for his first important book, the unrivalled *Minstrelsy of the Scottish Border*, till the appearance of the last of the long line of Scottish romances under the signature whose spell had already wandered far beyond the frontiers of Anglo-Saxondom.   One cannot but recall here the remark of his Liddesdale friend and companion, Mr. Shortreed : " He was *makin' himsel'* a' the time, but he didna ken maybe what he was about till years had passed.   At first he thought o' little, I dare say, but the queerness and the fun."

In a sense, the capital of Scott-land proper is Melrose. 'Use and wont' has made it so; the guide-book declares it; and convenience has confirmed the tradition. Ashiestiel and Abbotsford, the two Tweedside homes of the great writer, are easily to be reached thence—the homes where he wrote *The Lay of the Last Minstrel*, *Marmion*, *The Lady of the Lake*, and so many of the still more famous and more enduring romances in prose.   But Melrose is only an arbitrary capital, and one might almost as well decide for Peebles or Selkirk, or even more distant Moffat, each certainly a pleasanter place for temporary residence, if not for merely passing resort, than the dull little town to which the presumed magic of Scott's 'pale moonlight' invitation to view the Abbey still attracts so many disappointed visitors. Edinburgh is the true literary capital of the land of Scott, as of Scotland. If a 'capital of sentiment' must be had, let it be Abbotsford. This has been claimed for Ashiestiel, because here Scott is supposed to have passed the happiest and most fruitful years of his life—a claim not to be sustained from, at any rate, the literary standpoint. True, one enthusiastic chronicler sets forth in reverential awe that, in the little drawing-room at Ashiestiel, "Scott, on a single occasion, entertained three duchesses at once." In the face of so stupendous a claim the objector should retreat benumbed. Nevertheless, one may recall Scott's own brave and heartsome words when, after his crushing financial disasters, on a revisit to Ashiestiel, he recognised the good fortune and happiness of his earlier days, but not to the exclusion of as happy and fortunate days elsewhere. "Here," he wrote in his diary, "I passed some happy years. Did I ever pass unhappy years anywhere? None that I remember. . . ."

And now how best to follow Sir Walter's lead through his own lands? One way would be to take the famous romances seriatim, in order of sequence as they appeared. But this would lead to a tiresome retraversing of familiar ground. Having come, for example, to the extreme south-east with *The Bride of Lammermoor* of 1819, and to the midlands of Tweed (to Kennaquhair, the imaginary centre of that beloved realm of the imagination dominated by the White Lady of Avenel) with *The Monastery* of 1820, one would have to follow a far cry after *The Pirate* of 1821, across Scotland to the Orkney Isles. Then, with the next novel, *St. Ronan's Well*, back at a jump to the beautiful Peeblesshire highlands about Innerleithen and Tweed and Quair waters, already familiar to those who had fared thither with

The Black Dwarf of 1816! Then *Redgauntlet* would take one to the familiar West Border once more, while—ignoring the intervening *The Betrothed*, *The Talisman*, and *Woodstock* as English romances — the ensuing *Surgeon's Daughter* would leave the peripatetic enthusiast with the dilemma of a choice between abiding with Dr. Gideon Gray at Selkirk or following his pretty daughter Menie to far Mysore.

However, for those who would rather, whether in fact or fancy, choose their own way to perambulate Scott's country, let me offer this tabulated schedule.

I. CHIEF POEMS.

Date of Publication	Title	Period	Locality	Scott's Age at Date of Writing
1805	*The Lay of the Last Minstrel.*	Towards end of seventeenth century.	Newark, Yarrowdale, Melrose.	34
1808	*Marmion.*	Aug.-Sep., 1513	Flodden and the Border Lands.	36
1810	*Lady of the Lake.*	c. 1550	The Trossachs.	38-9
1811	*The Vision of Don Roderick.*	Spain under Moorish occupation, and during Peninsular War.	Toledo, etc.	40
1812	*Rokeby.*	1644 (after battle of Marston Moor).	Greta Bridge, Yorkshire	41
1813	*Bridal of Triermain.*	"Arthurian."	Vale of St. John.	42
1814	*Lord of the Isles.*	"Robert Bruce."	Argyll, Arran, Skye, Ayr, Stirling.	43

II THE SCOTTISH ROMANCES

Date of Publication	Title.	Period	Locality	Scott's Age at Date of Writing
1814	*Waverley* (Begun in 1805, and laid aside till 1813.)	Pretender's Attempt in 1745.	Perthshire Highlands, The Lothians, English Border.	34-43
1815	*Guy Mannering.*	1750–1770	Galloway.	44
1816	*The Antiquary*	1798.	Arbroath, etc.	45
1816	*The Black Dwarf.*	1708.	Midland Border.	45
1816	*Old Mortality.*	Covenanters' Rebellion, 1679.	Moffat, St. Mary's Loch, Dumfriesshire.	45
1817	*Rob Roy*	1715.	The Lomond Highlands, Glasgow, etc.	46
1818	*Heart of Midlothian*	1736-51.	Edinburgh also Richmond and the Thames Valley	47
1819	*Bride of Lammermoor*	1700.	East Lothian and Berwick coasts	48
1819	*Legend of Montrose*	Civil War, 1645-6.	West Highlands.	48

THE SCOTTISH ROMANCES—(Continued).

Date of Publication	Title	Period.	Locality	Scott's Age at Date of Writing
1820	*The Monastery.*	Mary Queen of Scots, 1559 (1549–68).	West Border (Vale of Allen)	49
1820	*The Abbot*	Mary Queen of Scots, 1559, 1567-8	Kinross and Loch Leven.	49
1821	*The Pirate*	1700.	Orkney and Shetland Isles.	50
1823	*St. Ronan's Well.*	1800.	Upper Tweed-dale.	52
1824	*Redgauntlet.*	1770.	Annandale, etc.	53
1827	*The Surgeon's Daughter.* *The Two Drovers.* *The Highland Widow.*	End of eighteenth or early in nineteenth century.	South Scotland (and India) and West Highlands.	56
1828	*TheFairMaid of Perth*	1402	Perth and Firth of Tay.	57
1831	*Castle Dangerous.*	1306-7.	Douglas Dale and Lanarkshire.	60

III. THE ENGLISH ROMANCES.

Date of Publication	Title.	Period.	Locality.	Scott's Age at Date of Writing
1819	*Ivanhoe.*	("Richard Cœur-de-Lion"), 1194	Central England and Old Forest region from York to Notts.	48
1821	*Kenilworth*	(Reign of Elizabeth), 1575.	Warwickshire	50
1822	*Fortunes of Nigel.*	(Reign of James I.), 1620.	London.	51
1823	*Peveril of the Peak*	(Reign of Charles II.), 1660-80.	Derbyshire (and Man)	52
1825	*The Betrothed.*	Welsh Wars 1187.	North Wales and Welsh Borders.	54
1826	*Woodstock*	Civil War & Commonwealth, 1652-60.	Woodstock and Blenheim	55

IV. THE FOREIGN ROMANCES.

Date of Publication	Title.	Period	Locality	Scott's Age at Date of Writing.
1823	*Quentin Durward.*	Louis XI. and Charles the Bold, 1470.	Touraine, Flanders, Burgundy.	52
1825	*The Talisman.*	The Crusades, 1193.	Syrian coast and Holy Land	54
1827	*The Surgeon's Daughter* [part of]	Early British occupation of India.	Mysore, &c.	56
1829	*Anne of Geierstein.*	Epoch of Battle of Nancy, 1474-77.	Switzerland, West-phalia, Aix-en-Provence.	58
1831	*Count Robert of Paris.*	The Crusaders at Constantinople, 1096.	Constantinople.	60

G

While this list may be of service to those interested in
Scott's topography, the traveller in Scott's country will also be
able to tell at a glance the period of action of the romance he
may be ' tracking down.'   Again, to the students of literary
natural history, the fact will be significant that Scott's greatest
period—notwithstanding a career of creative energy and ceaseless other activities since earliest manhood—is from his forty-
fifth to his fiftieth year, a time subsequent to what is commonly
considered the finest period of creative energy.   During this
period appeared not only *The Antiquary*, *Old Mortality*, *Rob Roy*,
The Heart of Midlothian, *The Monastery*, *The Abbot*, *The Pirate*,
but in one year (1819), when he was forty-eight, two of his
masterpieces—the finest of his Scottish romances, *The Bride of
Lammermoor*, and the finest of his English romances, *Ivanhoe*—
with, it should be added, the delightful West Highland romance
of *The Legend of Montrose*, written at the same age and also
published in 1819, thrown in !

To attempt a survey of the Scotland of Sir Walter Scott,
one must be up with the eagle at the Kame of Hoy, in the
far isles of Orkney, and down with the seamew in the desolate
sunsets of Ellangowan and the Crooks of Dee, hard by Solway
Moss and the grey shallow waters that divide Scotland from
England.

What a wonderful land that is which has Lerwick for its
capital !   Here we are on what is called the Mainland of
Shetland.   Those savagely picturesque promontories among wild
seas, Sumburgh Head and Fitful Head and St. Ninian's Rock,
how intimate they seem to the visitor long or newly familiar
with *The Pirate* !   Yonder, on Sumburgh crags, stood Jarlshof,
where Mordaunt Mertoun dreamed of his love for Brenda Troil,
who with her stately sister, Minna, lived some twenty miles
away, at Burgh Westa, the home, it will be remembered, of old
Magnus Troil, Udaller of Zetland.   Yonder, south-eastwardly,

lies Harfra, or Stourburgh, where that strange personage, Triptolemus Yellowley, struggled to win the bleak Shetland climate to his own way of thinking in matters agricultural; and,

(1) The country of *The Lord of the Isles*. (2) The country of *The Lady of the Lake*. (3) The country of the Poetic Dramas *The Doom of Devorgoil* (Galloway), *Auchindrane* (Lower Ayrshire seaboard), *MacDuff's Cross* (Fife). (4) The regions also traversed by Scott's poetical genius, whether in original verse or in gathered ballad or folk-song. (5) The country of *Marmion*.

nearer, Fitful Head, sacred to that poor, wild, distracted, and wholly picturesque figure, Norna, 'daughter of the Voluspal,' the Scandinavian Sibyls of life and death and fate. Hidden somewhere among the jagged rocks to the south lies the sea-invaded cavern, the Helyer of Swartaster, where stately Minna Troil used to meet that mysterious lover of hers who had been cast up by the sea. Seaward lies the little isle of Mousa, with on it the so-called Pictish Castle of Mousa, which also, somewhat confusedly, is admitted to be " perhaps the most perfect Teutonic fortress now extant in Europe," the more interesting, at present, as it was the original of Norna's famous witch-tower, placed by Scott on Fitful Head. To-day we may smile at the use of ' refection ' and ' wassail ' and ' revelry ' for the simple luncheon of cold provender with leathern bottle of brandy which the Udaller brought with him when he and his daughters went to consult Norna—with what humiliating results both to the luncheon and the travellers many will remember!—but the visitor who stands in or by Mousa Keep, and has seen Fitful Head, will realise that Norna's pompous words had a certain fitness at their time and place.

But the Scott-pilgrim must go farther yet. The Orkneys beckon. There is the great cathedral of Kirkwall, where Minna Troil had one of her last interviews with Cleveland; and the famous Druidic Standin' Stanes o' Stennis, where the lovers parted for ever; and high Stromness, within sight of which ' the pirate's ' vessel was destroyed. Not even on the wildest shores of Argyll or Donegal are such precipitous rock and tormented seas as are to be viewed off the farther isle of Hoy. And here we come to the Kame of Hoy, between which and the Crooks of Dee in far Galloway lies the Scotland of Sir Walter Scott—in a word, all Scotland. Or one may sail from the Shetlands to the Hebrides, and skirt the west by the Middle Isles, past Iona and ' lone Colonsay ' to beautiful Arran, and so through the *Rob Roy* lands to Glasgow, and thence with *Castle Dangerous* through Lanarkshire, and with *Old Mortality* and *Guy Mannering* to Dumfriesshire and Galloway, and thence,

with one's choice of a dozen beloved romances, along the west
borders and the marches of No Man's Land, or up through
Annandale and Tweeddale, or by Gala Water, or the flood of
Quair, by Selkirk and Peebles and Melrose, and so round by the
Eildons (the blue hills of Scott's heart) and the wastes of
Lammermuir and the sea-swept Lothians, or by Pentland and
Ochil to Edinburgh, and finally to Perth again—the round of
the true ' Waverley route.'

Although Sir Walter invaded England and nowhere met
defeat (indeed, in England, after the immense success of *Ivanhoe*,
none of his romances was received with so much enthusiasm as
The Fortunes of Nigel, the scenery of which is mainly London
and its neighbourhood), he did not, of course, possess it so
absolutely as he held Scotland. Even the Titans have perforce
to observe the law of limitations. But how familiar to many
of us, through the great romancer, the old forest lands of
southern Yorkshire, from Doncaster to Sheffield; all the delightful region between ' the curving Ouse ' and ' the pastoral Don '
from York to the oaks of Sherwood, by Worksop and Mansfield
—for the original vast Sherwood of Robin Hood extended
from Notts on the south to Whitby on the north, whose own
south-eastern woods then ran close to the Second City—and all
the still unspoiled country around Richmond and Fountains
Abbey (to which, it will be remembered, Friar Tuck of
Copmanhurst was attached), with Jorvaulx Abbey and its
memories of Prior Aymer, whose doings in Sherwood Forest
every devotee of *Ivanhoe* must recall. Again, many will recall
that wide region of Derbyshire leading on all sides to the
beautiful highlands of the Peak, with Cheshire, and the Isle of
Man, and so to Castletown by the sea to Rushin Ruins, the
' Tara ' of the Kings of Man. Once more, who having
seen will forget the roads from Cheshire to the Vale of
Llangollen and Caer Dinas Bran into that part of Wales which

was once the principality of Powys, and where the Castle of
Garde Doloureuse perhaps awaits *you* who now read—for none
more fortunate has yet been able to find it, unless Caer Dinas
ruins be indeed none other than the famous mediæval stronghold where the Bahr-Geist made itself (or herself) unpleasant to
'the Betrothed,' and where at last Sir Hugo de Lacy came
back so timely from the wars.   Is not all this region of central
England and Wales sacred to the 'local colouring' of *Ivanhoe*
and *Peveril of the Peak* and *The Betrothed*?   Then, of course,
there is Warwickshire (a rich county, indeed, in literary history,
with all its associations with Shakespeare, Walter Scott, and
George Eliot), whose heart is Kenilworth, so easily to be reached
now from Leamington or Warwick or Coventry, which so happily
gave its name to the romance which Scott had originally
entitled *Cumnor Hall*.   Then come the shires of Oxford and
Gloucester, also so familiar to readers of *Kenilworth*, as well as of
Woodstock.   Finally, Lord Nigel Olifaunt leads us to London.
Here, however, we cannot feel that Dickens and Thackeray
need fear their famous rival.   The country of London was
never a country to Scott, as it was a country of infinite variety
to the author of *Vanity Fair*, and as it was the half real and half
fantastic country of Cockaigne to the author of the many-
volumed Saga of Boz.   Scott naturally was alive to the fascination of Fleet Street, with its innumerable memories before and
after the disappearance of 'Alsatia,' and never walked Chancery
Lane without remembering that there Abraham Cowley was
born, and that there good Izaak Walton kept a shop and
dreamed the happy dreams of the *Compleat Angler*.   He
paid 'fascinated visits' to Fetter Lane, where the revolu-
tionary leather-seller, Praise-God Barebones, worried his
neighbours' peace and harassed their already harassed souls;
and to those sad 'bournes of pilgrimage' near Shoe Lane
where Sir Richard Lovelace, "that beautiful cavalier and

gracious poet," and Thomas Chatterton ('le martyre suprême' as a famous French poet somewhat inconsequently calls the poor lad of genius), died in want and misery; and to Salisbury Square, on the south side of Fleet Street, where Richardson wrote

SCOTT IN ENGLAND

Pamela. But these were visits of literary curiosity, such as you or I or any may make. Most of Scott's London is west of Temple Bar, but probably there are few who have cared to follow Julian Peveril to the site of the old Savoy and elsewhere by Waterloo Bridge and Charing Cross, though perhaps in crossing St. James's Park some have recalled that here Fenella Peveril (of one famous novel) led Julian to the presence of Charles II., and that here Lord Nigel (of the other famous romance) drew his sword on Lord Dalgarno, and then fled for his life across Westminster to Alsatia by the Fleet. There are allusions, of course, to localities in London, in other of Scott's romances (*The Heart of Midlothian* and *Kenilworth*, for example), but, except for the doings of Nigel Olifaunt and his 'man,' Richard Moniplies, and of Julian and Fenella Peveril, Scott's London is rather a phantom city. Lovers of Greenwich Park, however, will care to recollect the account of the meeting there of Lord Nigel and King James.

Here we cannot pursue ' Scott's country ' farther. In truth, the frontiers should be at the borders, for all the charm of *Ivanhoe* and *Kenilworth* and *Woodstock*, *The Betrothed*, and *Peveril of the Peak*. These invasions were conquests in a foreign land, and in a sense are no more to be accounted Scott's country than Syria is his country because of *The Talisman*, or Touraine and Flanders, Switzerland and Provence, are to be accounted provinces of his realm because of *Quentin Durward* and *Anne of Geierstein*, or Constantinople is to stand with Edinburgh because of *Count Robert of Paris*. Otherwise, how are we to deny Hades as ' the country ' of Virgil and Dante and Milton? or, to come to our own time, how are we to exclude the Moon from the geography of Mr. Wells' 'country,' or the Eternal City from that of Mr. Hall Caine! And has not Mr. Wilson Barrett written of Babylon, or Jerusalem, or some other oriental place with notable daughters, without our association of him and the Orient for evermore? Yet one would hardly think of Rome as Mr. Hall Caine's country, or as Zola's either, though that master gave us (within narrow limits) a real Rome; nor of the Moon in connection with Mr. Wells, quite in the same way as, for example, we associate Wessex and Mr. Thomas Hardy; and though Virgil wrote of Hades, 'his country' was the bee-pastures of central Italy, and its centre not the painful scene of the continual exercise of Tantalus and other unfortunates, but the white villa by Naples shore, or the quiet home in the lovely hill-country of Campania.

No, the 'country' of a great writer, the country of a Walter Scott or a George Eliot, is that where life first unfolded, and where its roots are, and which the heart enshrines. And that country, in the instance of Scott, is the little northern land of mountain and flood, from the Kame of Hoy in the North Sea to the Crooks of Dee beyond Solway Water.

THE COUNTRY OF GEORGE ELIOT.

NE day last spring, when I was travelling in Touraine, a literary gentleman from Rennes (as I discovered later) entered the compartment of which I was the sole occupant. A few casual words led to the offer on my part of one or two new issues of Parisian literary magazines which had reached me at breakfast; and that accepted offer led in turn to a chat about certain books and writers with which and whom more than one of the magazine articles were vehemently concerned.

After a time my companion politely turned the conversation to the subject of contemporary English poetry, of which he showed a refreshingly complacent ignorance, apart from his acquaintance with Shelley and Mr. Swinburne through the free if sympathetic renderings of M. Rabbe and M. Mourey. Of ' living ' poets he thought ' Keat ' was the nearest in approach to the excellence of Verlaine: but " there was also beauty . . . yes, the unmistakable touch in M. Wilde and in the fine Patérson, whose death so young was a scandal to the gross materialism of the London *bourgeoisie*." Whether Patérson preceded or succeeded ' Keat ' I do not know: his name and fame, with his unmerited sufferings and shameful Britannic neglect, are alike unknown to me. I have an idea that my friend had heard of Chatterton, whose name by a mysterious Gallic alchemy had known a resurrection in France as Patérson. I am sorry to confess, however, that I had not the moral courage to admit, then and there, that I was a degree lower even than the average Britannic *bourgeois*, in so far as I knew nothing either of the name or fate of a bard worthy to be ranked with ' Keat.'

Naturally, therefore, when my Rennes friend alluded to his admiration for the 'Georges Sand of England,' and how ' George Eliot ' had also something of the quality of Balzac, I feared that a Parisian sparrow had but uttered a name on the housetops of Rennes. But no, my friend spoke of *Adam Bède* and *Mid-le-Marche*, of *Félix 'Oltt* and *Le Moulin du Floss*, of *Seelas Marnèr* and *Romóla*, as if intimate with each of these masterpieces. He did really know something of the romances of the ' Grand Magicien Sir Scott,' and had read several tales of Dickens in their French translation, and a version of Thackeray's *Vanity Fair :* and this (with his having wept over a prose rendering of ' In Memoriam '), along with his more erudite acquaintance with ' Keat ' and Patérson, had apparently been his justification (alas! unsuccessful) in a recent application for a Foreign Literature lectureship at Rennes University.

With some of his views I agreed, from others I disagreed. Then I discovered that all these matured results of meditation had been culled from M. Brunetière's interesting study of the famous English novelist, and that the only Rennesesque addition was in the appellation of "the Georges Sand of England," a crudity for which M. Brunetière would not have thanked his Breton colleague. Finally, I asked my companion who were his favourite personages in these fine romances of ' Madame Eliot,' and to my astonishment he specified Mrs. Poyser, la Tullivère (Maggie), and . . . George Henry Lewes!

Then, to finish my bewilderment, he gave me two Poyserisms in English—one of which was (and is) as mysterious and untraceable as the premature masterpiece and early death of Patérson; while the second I at last disengaged from the maze of a weird originality of pronunciation, having by a flash of insight or exacerbated memory discovered ' Craig ' (the gardener at Donnithorne Chase, in *Adam Bede*) from

'Lecraygue'—and so arrived at "he's welly like a cock as thinks the sun's rose o' purpose to hear him crow."

This witticism, in an Anglo-Franco dialect, was evidently a source of pure happiness to my friend. 'Ah, the English humour!' he exclaimed, chuckling.

All this comes back to me when I take up my pen to write on the country of George Eliot. And much else . . . from Charles Reade's dictum that *Adam Bede* is "the finest thing since Shakespeare," to Mr. Parkinson's, who says it "pulsates from opening to finish." For (the confession *must* be made) even the Rennes enthusiast as to *Mid-le-Marche* and *Félix 'Oltt* would in point of enthusiasm be worthier to write this article. We have all our limitations; and with genuine regret (for I find myself in an embarrassing isolation from the collective opinion of the wise and good) I have to admit my inability to become enthusiastic over the actual country of George Eliot in so far as I know it apart from its literary glamour and associations. Nor, apart from the dairy-passages and a few delightful pages in the earlier novels, am I 'transported,' as one critic has it, by the George Eliot country of the imagination. Of course, this is not an absolute statement. I have read (and can now read) with keen pleasure much of the descriptive parts of *Adam Bede* and *The Mill on the Floss*, as, in another respect, I could at any time re-read with pleasure most of *Silas Marner*, and the whole of *Mr. Gilfil's Love Story*. There are pages in *Middlemarch* which must surely appeal to every mind and every heart. But I can't honestly say much more; and, as Mark Twain suggests, it's better if one is a fool to say so and be done with it, than to leave the remark to others to make. Nothing would tempt me to read *Daniel Deronda* again, and, like a thundercloud above the vistas of my past, looms the memory of the weary travail through *Romola!* As for *Theophrastus Such* . . . well, if repeated perusal of it were introduced as a punishment in a revised penal code, crime among the cultured would certainly decrease.

After all, the point of divergence is not one to interest most people. Abstract points in the eternal controversy as to what is and what is not art are like the diet of John the Baptist in the wilderness—delectable, till introduced to the domestic table. "Remove your locust, your wild and sugary honey, and yourself, to the wilderness," is the reception to be expected !

Fortunately, critic and readers, and all who care in any degree for the genius, the humour, the pathos, and the charm of George Eliot, can get over into her country by one bridge at which is no gate where ' Art ' levies toll. For the rest, I am ready to admit, as Mrs. Poyser remarked of one of her antipathies, that I " ought to be hatched over again and hatched different." As for taking the part of that wilfully perverse creature, the critic with a theory, or his kind, I am of the persuasion of Mr. Gedge, the landlord of the ' Royal Oak ' in George Eliot's most popular tale, " Ay, sir, I've said it often, and I'll say it again, they're a poor lot i' this parish—a poor lot, sir ; big and little,"—and Mr. Gedge, it will be remembered, hardened in his opinion with the change and chance of the unsteady planets, for when, in a dim hope of finding humanity worthy of his regard, he moved from Shepperton to the ' Saracen's Head ' in a neighbouring market town, he ceased not in iterating " A poor lot, sir, big and little ; and them as comes for a go o' gin are no better than them as comes for a pint o' twopenny—a poor lot."

There are some authors in connection with whom we are more interested to know where they dreamed and thought and wrote than to learn the geography of their imaginative inhabitings and excursions. It is not so with Balzac or Zola, for example. To know where the author of the *Comédie*

Humaine plied his unwearying pen, or where the architect of
the House of Rougon Maquart sedulously cemented, day by
day, an allotted section of his patient edifice, is a matter of
almost no sentimental interest. It is otherwise in the instances
of, say, Charlotte Brontë, Sir Walter Scott, George Eliot. One
might find it rather difficult to demonstrate the point posi-
tively, or to explain the why and wherefore; but probably
most of my readers will concur with me in the conclusion.

In the instance of George Eliot the personal interest is
exceptionally dominant. Possibly this is because her personality, her strenuous life in the things of the mind and the
spirit, the lamp of a continual excellence, win us more to the
homes wherein she herself dreamed and thought and worked
than to those of her imaginary personages. Perhaps, again,
it is because she suffered—'travailed in the spirit' as an old
writer has it—throughout her life, and that every domicile
has its memories of things endured in the spirit and weighed
with sadness in the mind. Taking it in its whole course, her
life was a happy one, in so far as it is possible for us to make
a general estimate of what constitutes happiness; but her mind
continually played the austere puritan to the very feminine
nature, her intellect habitually stood by, throwing shadows
across her naturally blithe and ardent temperament.

Mr. Cross has given us a pleasant sketch of the cottage
home in Warwickshire, Griff House, on the Arbury estate,
near the village of Chilvers Coton and the town of Nuneaton,
where Mary Ann Evans, the daughter of a Staffordshire man
who had begun the working years of life as a carpenter and
risen to be the land-agent of a wealthy Warwickshire county
family, lived till she was twenty-one. She was not, however,
as sometimes stated, born here: but at South Farm, Arbury,
close by—though Mr. Evans moved to Griff House while his
little girl was still a baby. Here, in this quiet and rural district

of the somewhat grimy coal region of Warwickshire, amid
scenes and scenery which indelibly impressed themselves upon
her mind, to be afterwards reproduced with a vivid and loving
fidelity, Miss Evans grew to womanhood. Life, however, had
become somewhat circumscribed and lacking in mental stimulus,
and it was with pleasure she went with her father in the spring
of 1841—shortly after she had come of age—to a semi-rural
house in Foleshill Road, outside Coventry. The event was of
signal moment in her life, for it was now she formed a
delightful acquaintanceship with Mr. and Mrs. Charles Bray
of Rosehill, and Mrs. Bray's sister, Miss Sara Hennell—
an acquaintanceship which was not only the chief charm
and stimulus of her early years of womanhood, but
deepened into a friendship of the utmost value and happiness, which lasted nearly forty years. Rosehill house and
garden may still be seen in the outskirts of Coventry: the
'other house,' as she calls it, that from 1841 to 1849 was her
'earthly paradise.' It was here, apparently, that Mary Ann
became 'Marian'; and here that the eager intellectual life
first quickened in production, and that of a kind remarkable
for a young woman in the England of the 'forties—a translation
of Strauss's *Leben Jesu*, a task followed by English renderings
of philosophico-religious writings by Spinoza and Feuerbach.
It was a happy and fruitful time that came to a vital change
with the death of Mr. Evans in 1849. Though the Foleshill
Road home was broken up, and Marian Evans went abroad to
break the spell of sorrow and prolonged association, she returned
to the neighbourhood of Coventry and to her beloved Warwickshire lanes and canals and flat, damp lands, and stayed with her
friends the Brays till, at the age of thirty-two, she made her
first definite change in life, and removed to London. The
occasion was the assistant-editorship of the *Westminster Review*,
but it was the beginning of the long and brilliant career in

literature whereby the obscure Warwickshire Marian Evans
became the world-famous 'George Eliot.' It will be easy for
Londoners who wish to see the early London home of this
celebrated novelist, to do so; for it is no farther away than
Richmond.   Here, in rooms at No. 8, Park Street (close to
the beautiful Park 'George Eliot' so often frequented and so
much loved, reminiscent to her as it was of Arbury Park, and
of parts of the wooded districts of Warwickshire), were written,
during the years 1855-8, not only *The Sad Fortunes of the Rev.
Amos Barton, Mr. Gilfil's Love Story*, and *Janet's Repentance*—
collectively republished as *Scenes of Clerical Life*—but also the
most enduring in popularity of all the great writer's books, *Adam
Bede*.

In 1859 George Henry Lewes and George Eliot (for
Marian Evans was now not only 'George Eliot,' but also had
wedded her life to that of the brilliant and versatile man of
letters to whom personally she owed so much, but also through
whose influence her art was so often to know the blight of
an essentially uncreative and unimaginative mind) moved to
Wandsworth, where, at a house called Holly Lodge, in
Wimbledon Park Road, they lived from February, 1858, till
March, 1860, and where perhaps the most beautiful of all
George Eliot's books was written, *The Mill on the Floss*.   The
next change was to the well-known home at The Priory, North
Bank, St. John's Wood, where from November, 1863, till after
the death of G. H. Lewes and till shortly before her marriage
early in 1880 with Mr. J. W. Cross, George Eliot had her
London residence.   Here she wrote some of her most discussed
books—*Felix Holt, Middlemarch*, and that brave and fine effort
in dramatic poetry of one who was neither a dramatist nor a
poet, *The Spanish Gypsy*.

Far and away the best portrait of the famous novelist in
her prime is that made in 1865 by Sir Frederick Burton, now

The South Farm, Arbury, George Eliot's birthplace.

MARKET DAY, NUNEATON. (Nuneaton is the "Milby" of "Janet's Repentance.")

GEORGE ELIOT'S OLD SCHOOL, NUNEATON.

GRIFF HOUSE, George Eliot's home from 1820 to 1841.

INTERIOR OF GEORGE ELIOT'S SCHOOL AT NUNEATON.

THE VICARAGE STUDY, NUNEATON.

This room is probably the old drawing-room of the vicarage which figures in two of the stories comprised in *Scenes of Clerical Life*. It was here that Amos Barton's affairs were discussed, while in later time the same room witnessed little Mrs. Crewe's attempts to entertain the Bishop.

GRIFF HOLLOWS, supposed to be the "Red Deeps" of "The Mill on the Floss."

in the National Portrait Gallery; and friends who knew her well during her last years at The Priory have assured me that the likeness was as admirable then as when it was made. From 1876 till the year of her death George Eliot had also a delightful summer home near Godalming, in Surrey—The Heights, Witley; and here she passed some of her happiest days in late life, though even here not without a longing for the less interesting or beautiful, but more intimate, scenery of 'her own country,' Warwickshire, North Stafford, and the southlands of Derby. It was neither in her own land, nor at The Heights, nor The Priory that, on December 22nd, 1880, the great writer died, but at No. 4, Cheyne Walk, Chelsea, a few doors from where Rossetti still dreamed and wrote and painted, a few minutes' walk from where Carlyle still worked and brooded.

The country of George Eliot should, in a sense, be called the Four Counties. Of these, Warwickshire and North Stafford-shire bulk the largest, in the map of our Imaginative Geography. Derbyshire leans against them from the north; to the east are the winds and floods of Lincolnshire. Conveniently this country may be said to extend from Gainsborough—that old town on the Trent so familiar to readers of *The Mill on the Floss* as St. Oggs—to Coventry and Nuneaton. In all her years spent in or near London (with her brief residings abroad), George Eliot was never in mind and spirit long away from this country of her early life, love, and imaginative and sympathetic intimacy. She lived a dual mental life: intellectually with the remote and austere minds of the past; reminiscently and recreatively with the people, episodes, and scenery of her beloved 'Shepperton' (Chilvers Coton) and 'Hayslope' (Ellaston), her ever affection-ately regarded 'Snowfield' (Wirksworth), 'Milby' (Nuneaton), and 'St. Oggs' (Gainsborough)—for the most part now dull and uninteresting tracts and localities of the shires of Stafford and Warwick and Lincoln, transferred henceforth by her genius

H

to the more vivid and fascinating 'Midlands map' of the Atlas of the Countries of the Imagination. It is rarely we come upon any revelation of 'Mrs. Lewes' or 'Mrs. Cross' in the domestic capacity of lady of the household—as when she writes to her friend Mrs. Congreve, shortly after settlement at The Priory in St. John's Wood, that she is occupied with no imaginative work, but is renewing "a mind made up of old carpets fitted in new places, and new carpets suffering from accidents; chairs, tables, and pieces, muslin curtains, and down-draughts in cold places"—and this although, "before we began to move, I was swimming in Comte and Euripides and Latin Christianity."

Whatever may have been the drift of opinion in the middle epoch of the nineteenth century, it is probably the all but general opinion to-day that the George Eliot of literature is the George Eliot who is 'swimming' in memories of the people and episodes and places known so intimately in her early life and ever recalled so vividly, and not the George Eliot who 'swam' with "Comte and Euripides and Latin Christianity," or the abstract thinkers and philosophies for which the phrase may stand as a collective analogue.

Frankly, of what worth are all the stately but unvivified pages of *Romola*, or the long and wearying digressions in *Daniel Deronda*, or the meandering and inconclusive speculations of *Theophrastus Such*, in comparison with the rich human interest and loving and exquisite familiarity of books of a *lived* actuality such as *Adam Bede* and *Silas Marner* and *The Mill on the Floss*? Do we not recall the dairies of Donnithorne Hall Farm (and their presiding genius, Mrs. Poyser—in the roll-call of George Eliot's personages as outstanding a figure as Mr. Micawber or Sam Weller in the roll-call of Dickens's personages, as Baillie Nicol Jarvie in that of Scott's, or Becky Sharp in that of Thackeray's, or Handy Andy in that of Lover's) with far keener pleasure, alike in imaginative realisation and in the sense of perfected and satisfying art, than even the keenest pages of what in its day was considered the masterly philosophic thought of *Middlemarch*, the perturbing sociological questionings in *Felix Holt*, or the dignified intellectual display of erudition in *Daniel Deronda* and *Romola?* Nor do I think that this change in standpoint is due solely to that contemporary intellectual deterioration in ideals and mental powers of which we hear so much. In some measure, at least, I take it, it is due to an ever developing sense of the true scope and true beauty and true limitations of literature, not as a pastime adaptable to every range of feebleness and capacity, but as an art, an art requiring as scrupulous observance on the part of the jealous reader as on that of the ambitious writer. Let us remember our friend Mr. Gedge, the landlord, and not get into the habit of dismissing our contemporaries as " a poor lot, sir, big and little— a poor lot!"

If one were to take a census as to the literary capital of ' George Eliot's Country,' it would probably result in the election either of Chilvers Coton, near Nuneaton (the ' Shepperton ' of the early stories, and the novelist's home till she was of age), or, and the more likely, of Ellaston, the ' Hayslope ' of *Adam Bede*. Many years ago the present writer edited a popular periodical for young readers; and on one occasion, in the literary page, the question was editorially proclaimed: " Who are the two most famous persons in George Eliot's novels, and what are the two best known localities?" The answers were (for competitions of the kind) exceptionally personal, and by far the greater number declared, on the first count, for Mrs. Poyser and Maggie Tulliver (the latter run close by poor Hetty, by Dinah Morris, and by Adam Bede); and, on the second, for Donnithorne Hall Farm (Hayslope), and ' Red Deeps,' where Maggie Tulliver used to meet her lover Philip Wakem (though this choice was perhaps due in considerable part to a recent article in the same periodical on the Griff Hollow of fact and fiction, *à propos* of Maggie's pathetic story).

And probably this verdict would be returned from any like consensus to-day. It is difficult to imagine any heroine in George Eliot's novels and tales usurping the place of Maggie Tulliver : it is impossible to think of Mrs. Poyser being dethroned from her pre-eminence.

One great charm of George Eliot's Country is that it is real country, loved and understood for itself as well as being the background of the humours and sorrows and joys of human life, loved for its own intimate charm as well as for its real and imaginary dramatic associations. There is nothing of more winsome charm in George Eliot's writings than her description of this very real and intimate country of her love and knowledge. True, these are remembered more as one remembers last spring in Devon, or summer in Surrey, or autumn in Wales or the Highlands : as the sum of many lovely and delightful things, days, and hours. There are few descriptive passages for memory to isolate and recall, for George Eliot had little preoccupation with words for the sake of their own beauty—an artistic lack more obvious, naturally, in her verse than in her prose.* But (perhaps in *The Mill on the Floss* especially) it would be easy to find many winsome collocations, delightful in themselves apart

---

* Since this article was written I have seen the late Sir Leslie Stephen's recently published admirable monograph on George Eliot, and cannot refrain from a corroborative quotation on this point of the artistic sense of the value of words. Sir Leslie Stephen had too finely trained a taste to accept the high claim so often made for George Eliot as a poet. She lacked, he says, "that exquisite sense for the value of words which may transmute even common thought into poetry. Even her prose, indeed, though often admirable, sometimes becomes heavy, and gives the impression that, instead of finding the right word, she is accumulating more or less complicated approximations." [In case of any confusion of issues, it may be added that no critic has ever more finely and sanely done justice to and interpreted all that made the genius, "all the mental, moral, and spiritual energy that went to make up the wonderful spirit whom we know as George Eliot."]

from the interest or charm of context. Turn to *The Mill*, and chance perhaps upon—

"The rush of the water, and the booming of the mill,
"bring a dreamy deafness, which seems to heighten the
"peacefulness of the scene. They are like a great curtain of
"sound, shutting one out from the world beyond."

Or upon—

"Maggie could sit in a grassy hollow under the shadow
"of a branching ash, stooping aslant from the steep above
"her, and listen to the hum of insects, like tiniest bells on the
"garment of Silence, or see the sunlight piercing the distant
"boughs, as if to chase and drive home the truant heavenly
"blue of the wild hyacinths."

But in all the George Eliot Country of fact there is no locality so fascinating as that immortalised (in *Adam Bede*) as Hayslope and its neighbourhood. The seeker will easily find it, under its actual name of Ellaston, whether in a map or if he be afoot or acycle in the Midlands on a George Eliot pilgrimage, by looking for the curving stream of the Dove where it divides Loamshire and Stonyshire (as the novelist calls Staffordshire and Derbyshire), near Norbury railway station. Our one quotation from *Adam Bede* (whence one could delve so many beautiful passages and pages) must be of this Hayslope vicinage.

". . . From his station near the Green he had before
"him in one view nearly all the other typical features of this
"pleasant land. High up against the horizon were the huge
"conical hills, like giant mounds intended to fortify this
"region of corn and grass against the keen and hungry winds
"of the north; not distant enough to be clothed in purple

" mystery, but with sombre greenish sides visibly specked with
" sheep, whose motion was only revealed by memory, not
" detected by sight; wooed from day to day by the changing
" hours, but responding by no change in themselves—left for
" ever grim and sullen after the flush of morning, the winged
" gleams of the April noonday, the parting crimson glory of
" the ripening summer sun.   And directly below him the eye
" rested on a more advanced line of hanging woods, divided
" by bright patches of pasture or furrowed crops, and not yet
" deepened into the uniform leafy curtains of high summer,
" but still showing the warm tints of the young oak and the
" tender green of the ash or lime.   Then came the valley,
" where the woods grew thicker, as if they had rolled down
" and hurried together from the patches left smooth on the
" slope, that they might take the better care of the tall
" mansion which lifted its parapets and sent its faint blue
" summer smoke among them."

Here we have not only typical English scenery of the North
Midlands—with heights and uplands, wood and valley, the oak
or beech surrounded manor - house . . . and beyond it the
hamlet of Hayslope and the grey square tower of the old church
—but are in the heart of the country of George Eliot. If, to-day,
much of the pastoral quiet of Hayslope, much of the green loveliness of the regions now so intimately associated with Adam
Bede and poor Hetty and Mrs. Poyser, with Amos Barton and
Silas Marner, with Mr. Gilfil and Maggie Tulliver, exist only
in the pages of a great writer, and seem dull and commonplace,
fretted by the smoke of mines and the passage of coal-trains
and the encroachment of the plague of bricks and stucco, the
fault does not lie with George Eliot. We have the land as it
is: she limned for us the country as it was.

THACKERAY-LAND.

THE lover of Thackeray will at once exclaim, and with some justice, "The literary geography of 'Thackeray' . . . impossible!" "George Eliot was easy for you," such a one may add,—"you had only to omit the Florence of *Romola* and restrict yourself to three counties : the Brontë country will be easy, for except in *Villette* you will not need to cross the Channel, nor even to linger long in London : Dickens himself was easy, for the ground covered by Nicholas Nickleby or David Copperfield or Martin Chuzzlewit in their beyond-London wanderings is almost as familiar as the home-circuit of Mr. Pickwick, or as the metropolitan background of *Bleak House* or *Little Dorrit*—while as for what occurs across the water, the *Tale of Two Cities* is soon overtaken. Even Walter Scott and Stevenson, for all their pen-wanderings as far overseas as Syria and Samoa, could by skilful loops be lassoed to your service. But how are you to limn the literary geography of Thackeray, unless you at once relinquish any attempt to go beyond Bath and Exeter, or even to stray from London . . . unless, at farthest, to those marine suburbs of Vanity Fair, Brighton and Boulogne ? "

True, so far, on both counts. The polar centre of Thackeray-land is that Guest-room in the Reform Club in Pall Mall where the famous portrait by Lawrence still cheers and dignifies the lunching novelist of to-day, still benignly consoles the harassed scribe whose monotonously recurrent nocturne is in three movements—to the Reform Club dinner, thence through the cigar-lit valley of dyspepsia, then to the leader-writer's room.

The Thackerayan home-county is London . . . that

London bounded by Holland Park on the west, by St. Paul's
on the east, by Pimlico on the south : the London whose heart
is Pall Mall, whose chief arteries are Piccadilly and St. James's
Street, Regent Street, and all that mysterious entity ' the West
End '—from Jermyn Street to the ' beyond Gadira ' of those
Metropolitan Pillars of Hercules, Tyburn Gate and Knights-
bridge.   Above all, Thackeray's London consists of Belgravia
and Mayfair, with Piccadilly as Vanity Fair Avenue.   If ever
any great writer was a Londoner, it was Thackeray.   Not Dr.
Johnson returning to the Mitre Tavern after those Hebridean
experiences . . . wherefrom, after too much rain, and too
much brose, and too much Boswell, he coined or set his seal
upon the opprobrious term ' Scotch ' to the after-satisfaction of
all South-Britons and the resentment of all Scots '—nor Charles
Lamb warming to the nocturnal glow of the Strand after one
of his visits to the Lakeland of his great friends, with whose
genius he sympathised, but not with their taste in exile—nor
Dickens, when at Broadstairs the sea and keen air lost their
spell, and he would have bartered both with joy for the dirt
and noise of Fleet Street—none of these was more truly a
Londoner than William Makepeace Thackeray, born in Calcutta,
a student at Weimar, a newspaper correspondent and happy
married man in Paris, a great novelist-in-the-making at a
château in Picardy.   We cannot imagine Thackeray country-
wed, as was Marian Evans or Charlotte Brontè, or a countryman
like Walter Scott, a Transatlantic or Samoan exile like
Stevenson, a country-dweller like Mr. Thomas Hardy, a Surrey
recluse like Mr. George Meredith.   One is apt to think of
Charles Dickens as pre-eminently the Londoner among modern
writers.   But Dickens (as he said once), for all that he was as
dependent on London as an orphan-suckling on its milk-bottle,
lived a great part of his mature life in maritime or inland Kent.
True, when he was writing *Dombey and Son* at Lausanne he

yearned for London, not only with the nostalgia born of life-long affection and associations, but with all the longing of the creative artist for the living sources of the imagination. It was, however, the near approach, the intimate touch, that Dickens needed . not to work and sleep and wake in an urban home, nor to lunch regularly at the Reform, nor to dine often at the Garrick, nor enjoy or undergo the social round. But though Thackeray spent some early years in Paris, and travelled east and west, he was ever happiest in London; in absence ever longed to return; never wished to live beyond the frontiers of St. James's Street on the east, of Kensington on the west. That he (or his pen-self) affixed the cartoon of *Punch* to the great Pyramid . . "at nineteen minutes past seven, by the clock of the great minaret at Cairo," if we may take him literally . . is by no means insignificant. In another sense, Thackeray, when abroad, was continually affixing a cartoon of British superiority, or British badinage, or British indifference, on persons and things and episodes to him distasteful or uncongenial. Even in his maturity, in his most famous work, this tendency was continually indulged, and sometimes offensively, as, for example, in the remarks on foreign 'Society' at Rome, in the episode of the final meeting of ' Mme. de Rawdon ' and Lord Steyne. It is this that more than any other reason makes so much of his early writings, more particularly his travel-papers, so wearisome now, often, alas! so banal. There is no great writer of our time who has committed so much that is commonplace in thought and observation, and commonplace and often jejune in style. Thackeray's name has become a fetish, and if one whisper a contrarious opinion it is to be snubbed with contumely. But the Thackeray of *Vanity Fair*, of *The Newcomes*, of *Esmond* is one person, the Thackeray of a vast amount of indifferent 'pot-boiling' is another. If the present writer had not a deep admiration for the author of the three great works named, he would be more chary of such expression of opinion as to so much else of Thackeray's work. A complete indifference could hardly mean other than a serious deficiency in oneself. But to say that one must accept as excellent in kind what one really finds commonplace and outworn, and often perverse and in the worst bourgeois taste, simply because of a great reputation, is to range oneself with those fanatics who (in their infatuation for a name, and not for the achievement *per se*) would have us accept *Count Robert of Paris* as masterly because it bears one of the greatest of names as author, or would have us accept *Titus Andronicus* as great literature because it is (or is by many supposed to be) by Shakespeare, or would have us accept as treasurable all the dross and *débris* to be found along the starry path of Robert Burns.

Doubtless many a reader will be moved to like reflections if he turn to these much-praised travel-sketches of the great author, whose fame by some singular irony seems to grow in proportion as the literary temper and taste of a later day slowly but steadily recede from all in his work related to the occasional and accidental, the accent of the hour, the bygone and the crude.

But the topographical Thackerayan will insist now on those two other delightful ' Sketch-Books,' which also appeared " under the travelling title of Mr. Titmarsh," to quote from the author's dedication of the later of the two to Charles Lever: *The Paris Sketch Book* and *The Irish Sketch Book*.

Probably hundreds of Thackeray-admirers, unable to re-peruse with pleasure the long so much belauded, but surely wearisomely overdone and now less regarded *Book of Snobs*, can turn again with pleasure to these high-spirited and amusing records of days and hours, of persons and things: in Ireland, from the Giant's Causeway to Cork, and from Dublin to Galway; in Paris, from Heaven-knows-what-all, from Carica-

tures and Melodramas, to George Sand and the New Apoca-
lypse.   Nevertheless, it would be absurd to say that in these
we have to seek the geography of Thackeray-land.   He took
his holiday thus once in a way; but his own land, the true
country of Thackeray, lies elsewhere—in so far as a novelist
whose country is human nature can be restricted at all by the
literary geographer.   No, let there be peace among the lovers
of that immortal work—not even is this land to seek in *The
Kickleburys on the Rhine*, for all the Becky-Sharp-like little ways
of "Miss Fanni, la belle Kickleburi," as the enamoured
Adolphe spoke of 'Miss K.' to the philosophic Alphonse; for
all that is told of the maturing in wisdom of Lady Kicklebury,
. . . who, it will be remembered, was finally brought to admit
decisively, if incoherently, "that Shakespeare was very right in
stating how much sharper than a thankless tooth it is to have a
serpent child"; for all that is set forth concerning Mr. Titmarsh
(the *real* M. Angelo!), Captain Hicks, the mild Mr. Milliken,
and "his soul's angel and his adored blessing" Lavinia and her
chronic effort to be calm, and all other companions of pilgrimage in that celebrated Tour Abroad.   And yet . . . who
would willingly relinquish such a vignette of natural beauty as
that of Deutz and the Drachenfels . . . a fragment radiant
with that true Thackerayan light—recognisable ever, whether
playing on things or places or persons—which we all love?

"[When I woke up it was Cologne, and it was not
"sunrise yet.]   Deutz lay opposite, and over Deutz the
"dusky sky was reddened.   The hills were veiled in the mist
"and the grey.   The grey river flowed underneath us; the
"steamers were roosting along the quays, a light keeping
"watch in the cabins here and there, and its reflections
"quivering in the water.   As I look, the skyline towards the
"east grows redder and redder.   A long troop of grey horse-

"men winds down the river road, and passes over the bridge
"of boats. You might take them for ghosts, those grey
"horsemen, so shadowy do they look; but you hear the
"trample of their hoofs as they pass over the planks. Every
"minute the dawn twinkles up into the twilight; and over
"Deutz the heaven blushes brighter. The quays begin to
"fill with men; the carts begin to creak and rattle, and wake
"the sleeping echoes. Ding, ding, ding, the steamers' bells
"begin to ring: the people on board to stir and wake: the
"lights may be extinguished, and take their turn of sleep:
"the active boats shake themselves and push out into the
"river: the great bridge opens, and gives them passage: the
"church bells of the city begin to clink: the cavalry trumpets
"blow from the opposite bank: the sailor is at the wheel, the
"porter at his burden, the soldier at his musket, and the
"priest at his prayers. . . .

    "And lo! in a flash of crimson splendour, with blazing
"scarlet clouds running before his chariot, and heralding his
"majestic approach, God's sun rises upon the world, and all
"nature wakens and brightens."

In this passage from an early work we have the real
Thackeray. It is in all ways characteristic, and would appear
still more convincingly so if quoted to its close: for it was
Thackeray's liking to conclude even the lightest of his longer
writings with a passage of personal emotion, of a sudden tidal
eloquence, informed at the close with a note of deep religious
feeling. But the actual lines quoted are interesting in that they
reveal the author's favourite method in description . . . his
aptitude for the salient feature, his instinct for the accumulation
of images and facts in short intimately-related sentences, and
oftenest with the use of the colon. It is interesting, too, as we
have in this early developed method and manner of Thackeray

ın description a prelude to the method and manner of a still greater master of prose; for Mr. George Meredith . . . the George Meredith of *The Ordeal of Richard Feverel*, of *Beauchamp's Career*, of *Sandra Belloni* and *Vittoria* and *Diana of the Crossways* . . . was in his youth an eager student of Thackeray, and unquestionably was influenced by him more than by any contemporary author except possibly Thomas Love Peacock.

Not, however, that the reader of Thackeray will easily find many like passages, except in the Travel-Sketches—French, Irish, 'Cornhill to Cairo,' to the later 'Little Sketches' from Richmond to Ghent, Brussels, and Waterloo. There is no other great novelist who indulges so seldom in descriptive detail, who so rarely limns his personages or relates their experiences against the background of nature, whether of scenic effect or of the great elemental forces. Thackeray's method is in this respect the extreme contrast to that of the greatest of his contemporaries, Victor Hugo. It is as inconceivable that he could have written any book even dimly approaching *Les Travailleurs de la Mer*, as it is inconceivable that Victor Hugo could have written such vast meandering tales as *Pendennis* or *The Virginians* in the minor key throughout, without a touch of melodrama, without the perpetual background of the natural world and all the elemental forces. Not that we need seek a foreign writer with whom to point the contrast. Thackeray had two great contemporaries at home whose genius recognised and demonstrated the immense imaginative value of 'background.' Who that remembers some of the most impressive pages in *Great Expectations* or *David Copperfield*, or recalls all the mature achievement of the author of *Shirley* and *Jane Eyre* and *Villette* . . . or, it may be added, that book of cloud and wind, of storm-swept moors and storm-tossed hearts, *Wuthering Heights*—can fail to regret that Thackeray had not, with his compeers Charles Dickens and Charlotte Bronté, that larger vision and deeper intellectual and artistic sentiment which has since been so distinguishing a feature of every great achievement in contemporary imaginative fiction . . . in France from Chateaubriand or Victor Hugo to the author of *Les Pêcheurs d'Islande*, in Russia from Turgeniév and Tolstoï to Maxim Gorki, in our own country from Walter Scott to Mr. Thomas Hardy? It is, in all probability, this lack in Thackeray that more than all else accounts for what a recent critic alludes to as "the growing contemporary revolt against his vague discursiveness on the one hand, and his general newspaperiness of method on the other " . . . that is, the method of the journalist who considers the relation of facts and circumstance and conversation to be all in all—or at best to need no more than circumstantial comment.

A really intimate knowledge of his writings, however, would enable one, if not to refute, at any rate greatly to modify, any inference that Thackeray lacked the power to create in "the two worlds that are yet one world." That he can describe in beauty no reader of his earlier writings need be reminded; that, and more and more as he grew older, he became (actually or apparently) artistically indifferent to all save action and motive and the general externals of human life, it would not be easy to disprove. In the writings of his final period, with the exception of a few passages in *The Virginians*— and, considering the inordinate length of that book, how few these passages are!—it is extraordinary how little stress is laid on or how little note is taken of natural environment or background. Let the reader turn to the three final novels, *Lovel the Widower*, *The Adventures of Philip*, and the unfinished *Denis Duval*, and he will probably concur in this opinion.

In *Philip* I remember that the charming wife of the hero on their honeymoon in Paris wrote that she and Philip walked home under " a hundred million blazing stars "—and I honestly doubt if in the whole novel there is anything of the kind more detailed! True, I have not looked at the novel in question for some years, till a rapid glance a little while ago in order to verify my quotation; nevertheless, I still abide by my doubt. In this respect it is interesting to contrast three ' last works '—each left unfinished—by acknowledged great writers: *Denis Duval, Edwin Drood*, and *Weir of Hermiston*. In *Denis Duval* we are never acutely aware of external nature and the elemental forces of nature; in *Edwin Drood* the reader feels the influence of both at the outset; in Stevenson's superb fragment we are ever aware of the great loneliness of the Pentland solitudes, of the coming of rain and storm and serene peace, of the magic of moonlight, of the subtle fascination of familar and yet ever unfamiliar vistas, of the indescribable presence and secret influence of the hill-wind—and all this without for a moment hindering the movement of the drama, without once diverting the reader's rapt attention. No one would be so uncritical as to compare on any other ground two books so different in method, intention, and achievement as *Denis Duval* and *Weir of Hermiston*, except that they are thus linked in the accident of fragmentary finality.

In any endeavour, then, to define the literary geography of Thackeray-land it would be necessary to relinquish the idea of a chart of all the divers parts, places, and remote regions between Palestine in the East and Virginia in the West touched upon by Thackeray's facile pen. From Jerusalem to the Rhine, from Athens to Galway Bay, from Brussels to Baltimore, is too extensive for any topographer to attempt. The Thackerayan lover and student will find his time cut out for him, if he wish to make a chart of all his author's wanderings with the names of every place mentioned in the vast wilderness of his writings! From 1840 to 1860 . . . in these twenty

years from Thackeray's thirtieth year to his fiftieth, from the
days of the immortal Yellowplush and the first appearance of a
Titmarsh and the tale of the Great Hoggarty Diamond, to the
close of the great period that culminated in *The Newcomes* and
the advent of the final period that began with *The Virginians*—
in the work of this score of years the would-be geographer will
find ample material for a sufficiently bewildering place-puzzle,
from the "London, E.C." of the early and repellent *Catherine* to
the little town of Chur in the Grisons in the essay "On a Lazy
Idle Boy," ultimately included in the author's latest completed
work, the *Roundabout Papers*.

But as this is one of the latest—possibly *the* latest—of
Thackeray's few latter-day topographical passages, it must be
quoted for the delectation of the present literary-geographers:

"I had occasion to spend a week in the autumn in
"the little old town of Coire or Chur, in the Grisons,
"where lies buried that very ancient British king, saint,
"and martyr, Lucius, who founded the Church of St.
"Peter on Cornhill. . . . The pretty little city stands, so to
"speak, at the end of the world—of the world of to-day, the
"world of rapid motion, and rushing railways, and the com-
"merce and intercourse of men. From the northern gate,
"the iron road stretches away to Zurich, to Basle, to Paris,
"to home. From the old southern barriers, before which a
"little river rushes, and around which stretch the crumbling
"battlements of the ancient town, the road bears the slow
"diligence or lagging vetturino by the shallow Rhine,
"through the awful gorges of the Via Mala, and presently
"over the Splügen to the shores of Como. . . . I have
"seldom seen a place more quaint, pretty, calm, and pastoral
"than this remote little Chur. What need have the
"inhabitants for walls and ramparts, except to build summer-

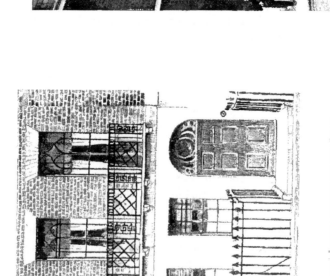

Thackeray's home from 1846 to 1853, at 13 (now 16), Young Street, Kensington, where "Vanity Fair," "Pendennis," and "Esmond" were written.

Thackeray's residence at No. 13, Great Coram Street Brunswick Square, from 1837 to 1840.

After a drawing by Edgar Wilson.

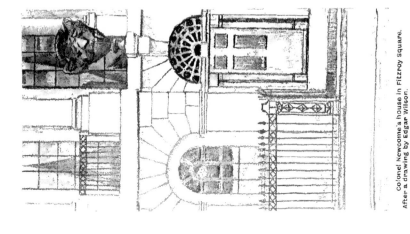

Colonel Newcome's house in Fitzroy Square.
After a drawing by Edgar Wilson.

Thackeray's house in Onslow Square, where he lived from 1853 to 1862.

"FOUNDER'S TOMB" in the Charterhouse

The writing-table and chair used by Thackeray at Young Street, Onslow Square, and Palace Green.

The house at No. 2, Palace Green, Kensington, in which Thackeray died.

" houses, to trail vines, and hang clothes to dry on them ?
" No enemies approach the great mouldering gates: only at
" morn and even the cows come lowing past them, the
" village maidens chatter merrily round the fountains, and
" babble like the ever voluble stream that flows under the
" old walls . . . a quiet, quaint, pleasant, pretty, old
" town ! " *

How characteristic that touch early in this quotation
. . . " to Zurich, etc., *to home* " ! That is Thackeray speaking
as to a circle of intimates. We can almost imagine him saying
Hear, hear! to the mocking adieux of a man whom he would
have detested as mercilessly as he would have ' scotched ' the
fantastic vogue of which he was the representative . . . to the
" soon we shall see once more the tender grey of the Piccadilly
pavement; and the subtle music of Old Bond Street will fall
furtively upon our ears," of the ' tragical buffoon ' disguised for
us as Esmé Amarinth in the most brilliant satirical comedy
given us since the vast drama of *Vanity Fair* . . . *The Green
Carnation.*

It is no use to think of following Mr. Titmarsh and the
Kickleburys to the Rhine, or of tracking Joseph Sedley and
Dobbin to Paris, or of ' being in at ' that famous episode of
Miss Rebecca and the Pumpernickel students—still less to
pursue that indomitable searcher after the Flesh-pots in her
latter-day migrations throughout Europe, from Tours to
Töplitz, from St. Petersburg to Boulogne. Of course, if a
Thackerayan reader find himself in Brussels he may, with a
phantom Henry Esmond, seek the convent-grave of the Sœur

---

* This, the first of the *Roundabout Papers*, was originally the editorial prologue
to the new *Cornhill*—the *Cornhill* with Thackeray at the helm. Was there ever a more
delightful set-off to a new magazine than this charming, sunny, and humorously
winsome essay, with all its ingenious allusions to other novelists ?

I

Marie Madeleine, once the gay and fashionable Lady Castlewood, and poor Esmond's unhappy mother—or, with a
phantom Amelia Sedley, will hold his breath while the darkness of an imaginary night of Waterloo follows the dull echo of
the guns, and thousands of other praying or sobbing women
await the dread coming of after-battle tidings.   If a visitor to
Boulogne-sur-Mer, could he possibly omit a stroll to the
Château de Brequerecque, where in 1854 Thackeray lived for
a time, thinking out and touch by touch creating the most
lovable of all his characters, Colonel Thomas Newcome?   In
Paris, of course, such an one could not possibly be without
thought of the Hôtel de la Terrasse, where Becky Sharp lived
awhile; without a reminiscence of Terré's Tavern in the Rue
Neuve des Petits Champs, immortalised in the Ballad of Bouil-
labaisse.   If perchance, again, such an one be a passing visitor
to remoter Strasburg—not a likely place, one would think, for
Thackerayan associations!—would he not instinctively seek for
some prototype of heroic Mary Ancel, or watch a phantom
Pierre Ancel riding wearily from the western gate, or feel
inclined secretly to identify in some harmless passer-by the
treacherous Schneider, that provincial understudy for the great
parts of Robespierre and Marat in the terrible Melodrama of
the Revolution?   In Strasburg of to-day, however, even such
an one would look in vain for any possible counterpart to that
other gentleman whom the good Pierre first saw in Schneider's
room (Schneider, ex-abbé, ex-monk, ex-professor, quondam
editor of the Songs of Anacreon, once Royal Chaplain and one
of the Illuminati at the capital of Würtemberg—become at last
a bloodhound to the bloodstained Directorate of France)—the
gentleman with a red night-cap ornamented with " a *tricolor*
cockade as large as a pancake," with a huge pigtail, seated at
a greasy wine-stained table, moved to frequent exclamatory grief
and bibulous tears by the book he is reading, *The Sorrows of*

Werther, and ever and again ejaculating ' O this poor Charlotte!'
or, ' Ah, Brigand ' . . . the sentimental gentleman whom
Pierre Ancel thought to be a tender-hearted lamb for all his
wolf's clothing, but whom Schneider, on his abrupt entrance,
thrusts from the room with the significant remark, " You
drunken talking fool . . . fourteen people are cooling their
heels yonder, waiting until you have finished your beer and
your sentiment—

> " That fellow," continued Schneider, turning to me, " is
> " our public executioner : a capital hand too if he would but
> " keep decent time : but the brute is always drunk, and
> " blubbering over *The Sorrows of Werther*."

These, and a score—a hundred—other instances, might be
adduced ; but then a series of maps, not a précis of a London
Thackeray-Directory, would be needed.   Even in our own
country the localities to be sought would be far apart . . . as
Clevedon Court, in Somersetshire, the beautiful original of the
' Castlewood ' of *Esmond* ; as Larkbeare House, near Ottery St.
Mary in Devon, the early home of Thackeray's mother, and
where he spent his holidays as a boy—a neighbourhood remem-
bered by him later when he was writing *Pendennis*, where Ottery
St. Mary, Sidmouth, and Exeter are alluded to as 'Clavering St.
Mary,' ' Baymouth,' and ' Chatteris '; as the scattered Irish and
English county backgrounds in *The Memoirs of Barry Lyndon*,
Vanity Fair, *The Newcomes*, *Pendennis*, *Adventures of Philip*, *Lovel
the Widower*, etc., etc., . . . from Tunbridge Wells to Taunton,
from Brighton to Bath.   It would indeed be rash to assert of
almost any fairly well known place that, if not 'brought in,' it is
at least unmentioned in Thackeray's writings. How few readers,
for example, would have thought of Strasburg in connection
with any Thackerayan romance, long or short? And only the

I 2

other day, in an article about Thackeray's wide range, its writer stated in effect that Florence was perhaps the only English-frequented town, and Rome the only capital, with which Thackeray had no literary dealings in his fiction—evidently oblivious, for one thing, of a certain famous heroine who in Florence kept house for awhile with the unattached Madame de Cruchecassée, or, at a later date, as Madame de Rawdon, met at the Polonia ball in Rome, and for the last time, the great Lord Steyne.   Then, again, to take a still more detailed instance, what of the thirty-fifth chapter of *The Newcomes*?

Brighton, of course, is a place apart: a detached suburb, rather, for is it not Thackeray's 'London-by-the-Sea'? For the ardent Thackerayan to visit Brighton without a single reminiscence would be as out of the question as to lunch in the Strangers' Room at the Reform Club and not look at Lawrence's famous portrait of the great man, or dine at the Garrick and have no heed of Durham's massive 'bust' or of Sir John Gilbert's charming posthumous portrait.   Nowhere more than at Brighton was Thackeray ' possessed ' by his imaginary personages —though, as he is reported to have said on one occasion, " in London they become almost too actual! "   It was from Brighton that (in 1849, when he was thirty-eight, and had suddenly become nationally famous by the publication in book-form of *Vanity Fair*) he wrote to his friend Mrs. Brookfield, " Being entirely occupied with my two new friends, Mrs. Pendennis and her son Arthur Pendennis, I got up very early again this morning.   He is a very good-natured, generous young fellow, and I begin to like him considerably."   It was to the same friend that he wrote on another occasion from Paris : ". . . I have been to the Hôtel de la Terrasse, where Becky used to live, and shall pass by Captain Osborne's lodgings.   I believe perfectly in all these people, and feel quite an interest in the inn in which they lived."

In London itself I suppose Thackeray enthusiasts were formerly wont to seek more than any other place (for now Godalming claims what was once the glory of Smithfield) the Charterhouse—the Grey Friars of *The Newcomes*, and for ever now associated with the beloved memory of incomparable Colonel Newcome. Others, perhaps, sought first those "dark alleys, archways, courts and backstairs" of the Middle Temple, so beloved by Thackeray; and in particular Brick Court, and the stairs leading to the chambers once occupied by Goldsmith . . . visiting these no doubt for Thackeray's sake rather than for other associations, though remembering his " I have been many a time in the chambers in the Temple which were his (Goldsmith's), and passed up the staircase, which Johnson and Burke and Reynolds trod to see their friend, their poet, their kind Goldsmith—the stair on which the poor women sat weeping bitterly when they heard that the greatest and most generous of all men was dead within the black oak door." For the many who prefer a 'favourite-character association' than one more strictly personal, there is ample material indeed. Even the all but omniscient lifelong 'cabby' might be puzzled to make his way to all the addresses that could be given him. Even he might go astray in Suburbia if his 'fare' directed him to drive from Russell Square (where the ever-to-be-remembered Sedleys of *Vanity Fair* once lived) to that familiar-sounding and yet postally unknown address whither they migrated . . . St. Adelaide's Villas, Anna Maria Road, W.—" where the houses look like baby-houses; where the people, looking out of the first-floor windows, must infallibly, as you think, sit with their feet in the parlours; where the shrubs in the little gardens in front bloom with a perennial display of little children's pinafores, little red socks, caps, etc. (polyandria polygynia);

whence you hear the sound of jingling spinets and women singing; whither of evenings you see City clerks padding wearily. . . ."

Among the numberless houses, rooms, chambers, etc., connected with the personages of *Vanity Fair, The Newcomes, Pendennis, The Adventures of Philip*, and so many other writings down to 'Our Street' and 'Mrs. Perkins' Ball,' each Thackerayan reader must select for himself. He may wander as far west as the Brompton boarding-house where Miss Bunion ate her daily breakfast chop, and spent the rest of the day in the composition of 'The Deadly Nightshade' or other of its passionate successors; or may wander into the City and in a counting-house and as a worthy drysalter behold Poseidon Hicks —in his impassioned but highly respectable youth the author of *The Death-Shriek* and *The Bastard of Lara*, and later of *Idiosyncrasy: in Forty Books, Marat: an Epic*, and *The Megatheria* (" that magnificent contribution to our Pre-adamite literature "), and other delicate trifles—a mere Mr. Hicks like one of ourselves, immersed in the commonplace task of checking figures or posting up his ledger. Or he may keep to Central London, and in Fitzroy Square look up at the house occupied by Colonel Newcome, its black door " cheerfully ornamented in the style of the end of the last century with a funereal urn in the centre above the entry, with garlands and the skulls of rams at each corner "; or may pass through Mayfair and take a glance at Gaunt House, with all its memories of ' the wicked markiss,' *en route* to visit trim Major Pendennis breakfasting at his club, occupied as usual with a pile of letters from lords and ladies galore, and scowled at as usual by the envious and unfashionable Glowry. But if something less imposing than a morning club-visit to Major Pendennis, or more reputable than a stroll to the sponging-house in Cursitor Street where Rawdon Crawley ' learned life' after the festivities at Gaunt House, be desired, is there not adjacent Curzon Street, where the same gentleman and the immortal Becky "demonstrated to the world the useful and interesting art of living on nothing a year" . . . that 'narrow but respectable mansion' where Mrs. Rawdon Crawley, who was not given to superfluous admirations, and in whom familiarity ever bred contempt, for the first time had a brief aberration of admiration for her husband, when he suddenly abandoned himself to the bodily chastisement of the Right Honourable the Marquis of Steyne, Lord of the Powder Closet, etc., etc., etc., the event that the (for once) impulsive Becky considered had 'ruined' her life.

The quest, as already hinted, might better befit the Wandering Jew, with unlimited time at his disposal! To follow in every detail the vicissitudes of Becky alone would enable the enthusiast to qualify as a prince of European couriers. Where did not Mrs. Rawdon Crawley . . . whether so called, or Mrs. Rawdon, or Madame de Rawdon, or Madame Raudon, or Madame Rebecque, etc., etc. . . . not set her wandering foot —from far St. Petersburg and remote Töplitz to neighbouring Boulogne, where, with good Mrs. Newbright, it will be remembered that 'Mrs. Becky' worked flannel petticoats for the Quashyboos and cotton night-caps for the Cocoanut Indians, and generally made heroic efforts to seem a spotless dove.

Since Becky's wanderings would alone suffice to defeat the literary geographer, perhaps the wisest thing for the enthusiast in Thackeray-land is to content himself with visiting those places in his beloved London the great novelist himself most loved, and the homes where he lived. The Charterhouse, or wonderful memories, is gone; but the Middle Temple remains, the 'Garrick' and the 'Reform' are as they were. One cannot 'begin at the beginning' as children ask of a familiar story, in either sense; for our hero was born at far-away Calcutta, and as to his earliest manhood, with its unfortunate marriage—that belongs to Paris.*   But one may start with his first London home, No. 18, Albion Street, Hyde Park, where he came soon after his marriage (on the sudden collapse of *The Constitutional*) —to his mother's house, in fact—and began regular literary work as a contributor to *Fraser's*, and where his eldest daughter, so well known to all lovers of literature as Mrs. Richmond Ritchie, was born.

Thackeray's first ' own home' in London was at 13, Great Coram Street, Brunswick Square, where he resided from 1837 to 1840 (*æt*. 26-29), and wrote *The Paris Sketch-Book* and other early efforts, and where was born his second daughter, who became the wife of the late Sir Leslie Stephen.   Of greater literary interest is 13 (now 16), Young Street, Kensington, where Thackeray lived from 1846 to 1853, and wrote the greater part of *Vanity Fair*, *Pendennis*, and *Henry Esmond*.   A very famous seven years of his life were those when his home was at 36 Onslow Square, South Kensington—" a pleasant, bowery sort of home, looking out upon elm-trees," as Mrs. Richmond Ritchie records.   It was here that the new and, for his own sake, too famous Editor of the *Cornhill Magazine* became the target for many arrows of supplication, which *ought* to have been shot off against the editorial citadel at Messrs. Smith, Elder's ; and it was here he wrote the closing chapters of *The Newcomes*, the famous *Lectures on the Four Georges*, *The Virginians*, part of *The Adventures of Philip*, and some of the *Roundabout Papers*.   " His study," says his daughter, " was over the drawing-room, and looked out upon the elm-trees."   Finally, there is the more imposing last home, No. 2, Palace Gardens, Kensington, which he had built for him in 1861 in accordance with his own designs and growing

---

* The apartments in the Rue Neuve St Augustin, where Thackeray took Miss Shawe after their marriage at the British Embassy in August, 1836, may still be seen, and much as they were when the young "English correspondent" of *The Constitutional* here took up home-life and (as he thought) journalism as a profession

needs; and here, on the day before Christmas of 1863, he died
—a man still young in years, as we now compute the average
span, but aged by sorrow, prolonged strain, and the ceaseless,
nervous expenditure of an over‑busy life. At his death
Thackeray stood out so great, at his best one can hardly yet say
how great, a genius of laughter and tears, that few will deny
the aptness of the tribute of one of the homage-bearing poets
of a Sister Nation :—

> And so *Hic Jacet*—that is all
> That can be writ or said or sung
>   Of him who held in such a thrall,
> With his melodious gift of pen and tongue,
> Both nations—old and young.
>
> Honour's a hasty word to speak,
> But now I say it solemnly and slow
>   To the one Englishman most like that Greek
> Who wrote *The Clouds* two thousand years ago.

THE BRONTË COUNTRY.

T HE real Brontë country is to be sought in two regions: in and just beyond the West Riding of Yorkshire, in those windy uplands and wide reaches of sombre moor which lie away from Haworth, away from the highways 'where excursion-drag and motor-car corrupt: and . . . in the Brontë books. Broadly speaking, the *Jane Eyre* country is all round Kirkby Lonsdale: the *Shirley* country is south of Bradford, and may be said to be bounded by Gomersall, Birstal, Brighouse, Mirfield, Heckmondwike, and back to Gomersall; while the *Wuthering Heights* country can only be indicated by the region around Haworth. 'The Withens,' of which a drawing by Mr. Greiffenhagen appears in the text, is on the hill-top above Haworth, and is supposed to represent the situation of Wuthering Heights. The house itself, as detailed in Emily Brontë's famous romance, is a composite picture; the interior having been suggested by Ponden Hall, near Haworth, and the exterior by High Sunderland, Law Hill, near Halifax. This, at least, is the opinion of those best acquainted with the topography of the subject.

A friend, who has never been north of the great shoulder of Sir William in Upper Derbyshire, and who read this summer for the first time, at a remote moorland farm, *Wuthering Heights* and *Shirley*, told me that he knew the Brontë country as thoroughly as any one not a native—"and a native in love with it, at that"—could do. "For," he added, "a north-country moorland-track is the same wherever the whaup calls, the kestrel hovers, and the heather-bee hums, and it matters little whether 'tis in Peakland, or the West Riding, or where Carlyle first drew breath, or up by the Eildons or beyond Ochil." And, to no small extent, that is true, I think. Certainly one can understand *Jane Eyre* and *Shirley* and *Wuthering Heights* without even a glimpse of Haworth Parsonage or Cowan Bridge School or any other of the much-visited buildings or sites or localities: certainly, for some at least, these books will seem far more near and intimate when dissociated from these and all the paraphernalia of tradition, when read or pondered with only wide dun or purple moorlands around, with cloud and wind, the lapwing, the floating kestrel, and the wild bee for company.

Neither familiarity nor love blunted Charlotte Brontë's own perspicacity in this respect, where, if allowable to any, surely some exaggeration might be pardoned in her. She herself wrote of this home-tract of Haworth, " Mills and scattered cottages chase romance from these valleys; it is only higher up, deep in among the ridges of the moors, that Imagination can find rest for the sole of her foot, and even if she find it there, she must be a solitude-loving raven— no gentle dove."

Nevertheless, Haworth is still the goal of a number of wayfaring enthusiasts, drawn thither by a genuine love of or keen interest in the Brontë novels and their authors. Some quarter of a century ago, Sir Wemyss Reid, in his sympathetic monograph on Charlotte Brontë,* wrote as follows:

" No other land furnished so many eager and enthu-
"siastic visitors to the Brontë shrine as the United States,
"and the number of Americans who found their way to
" Haworth during the ten years immediately following the
" death of the author of *Jane Eyre* would, if properly

---

* It is from this volume, published by Messrs. Macmillan, that some of our illustrations are taken.

" recorded, astonish the world.   The bleak and lonely house
" by the side of the moors, with its dismal little garden
" stretching down to the churchyard, where the village dead
" of many a generation rest, and its dreary outlook upon the
" old tower rising from its bank of nettles, the squalid houses
" of the hamlet, and the bare moorlands beyond, received
" almost as many visitors from the other side of the Atlantic
" during those years as Abbotsford or Stratford-on-Avon."

To-day the stream of visitors is greater than ever.   Since
the opening of the Brontë Museum in May, 1895, over
twenty-five thousand persons have paid for admission, and of
course this number is far from representing the total of those
who have made pilgrimage to Haworth.   Even the American
element, though not what it was, is still largely represented.
As, in reply to a comment, an old weaver caustically remarked,
" Aye, we Haw'rth folk doan't spake Yorkshire waäy ony moar:
'tis awl gooid Lunnon an' 'Amurican' naah, thèy saäy."
Whether the cause is in greater railway facilities, in better
roads and accommodation for bicyclists, or in the enhancement
of public interest through the many Brontè essays, reminiscences, and other writings which have appeared of late, or in
all three equally, multiplied by that great factor, a convenient
and interesting goal for a fresh-air spin or week-end holiday,
need not be disputed.
By the way, let the unwary visitor not be allured by the
many glowing descriptions of the moorland weather and moorland beauty at all seasons of the year and at all times.   The
West Riding moorland and most of the moorlands of Derbyshire are sombre beyond any other regions of the kind in
England; in stormy and cold weather they may be impressive,
but in the prevailing dull greyness and ever recurring rains they
have neither the spell of 'lovely solitude' nor 'a grave beauty

all their own,' but often are simply wide dreary stretches of waste
land, without the wildness and glow and beauty of Exmoor, or of
the highlands of Wales and Cumberland, or of the great moors
of Scotland, or even of the heath-covered rolling heights about
Danby, between the York plain and Whitby above the sea.
There are hours in spring, and many days in summer, and
sometimes weeks in early autumn, when they are to be seen in
beauty and enjoyed with deep delight by all who love solitude
and great spaces and the breath and freedom of the desert. But
ordinarily the country here is sombre and depressing, and all the
more so (as in so many parts of Derbyshire) from the frequent
signs of discarded or failing human industries, shafts of deserted
mines, stacks of forsaken mills, smokeless cottages, and rude
unkempt villages on their downward way to become still ruder
and more unkempt hamlets. As to the spring climate, about
which biographers who have not been at Haworth at that
season are apt to become dithyrambic, here is one from many
incidental allusions in Charlotte Bronte's delightful letters to
Miss Ellen Nussey. It is in a letter from Haworth in the late
spring of the year in which she was engaged upon *Jane Eyre*.
" I wish to know whether about Whitsuntide would suit you
for coming to Haworth. We often have fine weather just then.
At least I remember last year it was very beautiful at that
season. Winter seems to have returned with severity on us at
present, consequently we are all in the full enjoyment of a cold.
Much blowing of noses is heard, and much making of gruel
goes on in the house." About the middle of May she writes
again, " I pray for fine weather, that we may be able to get out
while you stay." There we have the weather-burthen of many
letters: the 'just then' that so rarely comes off, the 'at least I
remember' that qualifies too flattering retrospection. In a word,
if one were to spend nine months of the year at Haworth,
one would soon come to understand the gloom and depression

which often weighed so heavily on Charlotte and Emily Brontë, loving daughters of the moorlands though they were.

But of course they of all people knew and loved the remoter regions of the West Riding as none who have written of the sisters can do. It is their love of the lonely moorlands, the understanding of their fascination, of their spell upon the imagination, which has given the most enduring beauty to certain pages of *Shirley* and *Jane Eyre* and *Wuthering Heights*. If one remembers Charlotte's famous ' Necropolis ' passage (that has so much of the monumental solemnity and slow impressive cadence of the De Quincey of the *Suspiria*), in *The Professor*, one will recollect how the writer took with her this phantom of Death, this image of Melancholia, out into the lonely solitudes. " . . . She lay with me, she ate with me, she walked out with me, showing me nooks in woods, hollows in hills, where we could sit together, and where she could drop her drear veil over me, and so hide sky and sun, grass and green tree." If one remembers this, and a hundred kindred passages in Charlotte's books and vivid letters, one also will recall other passages in these and in her sister Emily's wonderful pages, as full of charm and loveliness seen and recreated as in this from *Wuthering Heights*:—

" He said the pleasantest manner of spending a hot July
" day was lying from morning till evening on a bank of heath
" in the middle of the moors, with the bees humming
" dreamily about among the bloom, and the larks singing
" high up overhead, and the blue sky and bright sun shining
" steadily and cloudlessly. That was his most perfect idea of
" heaven's happiness. Mine was rocking in a rustling green
" tree, with a west wind blowing, and bright white clouds
" flitting rapidly above ; and not only larks but throstles and
" blackbirds and linnets and cuckoos pouring out music on
every side, and the moors seen at a distance broken into

"cool dusky dells; but close by great swells of long grass
"undulating in waves to the breeze; and woods and sounding
"water; and the whole world awake and wild with joy. He
"wanted all to lie in an ecstasy of peace. I wanted all to
"sparkle and dance in a glorious jubilee. I said his heaven
"would be only half alive; and he said mine would be
"drunk. I said I should fall asleep in his; and he said he
"could not breathe in mine.

Or, again, this passage by Charlotte, wherein (as Lowood)
she alludes to Cowan Bridge, where she was at school, when a
terrible outbreak of typhus "transformed the seminary into a
hospital " :—

"Pleasure in the prospect of noble summits, girdling a
"great hill-hollow, rich in verdure and shadow; in a bright
"beck full of dark stones and sparkling eddies. . . . A bright,
"serene May it was: days of blue sky, placid sunshine, and
"soft western or southern gales filled up its duration. And
"now vegetation matured with vigour; Lowood shook loose
"its tresses; it became all green, all flowery; its great elm,
"ash and oak skeletons were restored to majestic life;
"unnumbered varieties of moss filled its hollows; and it made
"a strange ground-sunshine out of the wealth of its wild
"primrose-plants. . . . Have I not described a pleasant site
"for a dwelling, when I speak of it as bosomed in hill and
"wood, and rising from the verge of a stream? Assuredly,
"pleasant enough; but whether healthy or not is another
"question. The forest-dell where Lowood lay was the cradle
"of fog and fog-bred pestilence, which, quickening with the
"quickening spring, crept into the Orphan Asylum, breathed
"typhus through its crowded school-room and dormitory, and
"ere May arrived, transformed the seminary into a hospital."

Into all of Patrick Brontë's children something of the moorland character seems to have entered. Their note of wildness is in all, their note of stern silence, their aloofness. There is no "dying" tragedy in literature to surpass the slow indomitable decline of Emily Brontë, fearless, silent, almost unnaturally implacable to the end. Even the gentle Anne shared this indomitableness so characteristic of the whole family. Crude in knowledge of life and crude in art as is *The Tenant of Wildfell Hall*, it was a heroic moral effort on the part of a sensitive and shrinking nature to depict what was, to that delicate self, in the last degree painful and indeed repulsive. It is said that some of frail physique will endure the mental and bodily torture of surgical operation far better than the more robust, and it has always seemed to me that Anne Brontë, in this pitiful and, it must be added, intolerably weary and superfluous fictitious rendering of the sordid tragedy of Branwell Brontë's life, showed the same dauntless courage as made Branwell die standing, as made Emily refuse all comfort or aid when day by day Death plucked at the tearing strings of her life, as enabled Charlotte to endure in noble patience when, at Emily's death following Branwell's, and at Anne's following Emily's, and at her own failing health and broken hopes, and, above all, bitter suffering through her father's savage derision and driving away of the one lover to whom her own heart turned, that too familiar "horror of great darkness fell upon me."

The proud aloofness, the almost arrogant independence, so characteristic of the moorlanders, was seen to the full in the Brontë family, and stands revealed in their published writings and letters. A single instance of an ordinary kind will suffice. Here is one, from Charlotte's correspondence in the spring of 1850, shortly after her return from London subsequent to the publication of *Shirley* :—

The Old Parish Church Tower.

After a drawing by M. Greiffenhagen.]

Haworth.

After a drawing by M. Greiffenhagen.]

Church steps and street, Haworth.
After a drawing by M. Greiffenhagen.]

WITHENS, the original of Wuthering Heights.
After a drawing by M. Greiffenhagen.]

Haworth to-day. Evening mist rising from the valley.

After a drawing by M. Greiffenhagen.

"I believe I should have written to you before, but I
"don't know what heaviness of spirit has beset me of
"late, made my faculties dull, made rest weariness, and
"occupation burdensome. Now and then the silence of
"the house, the solitude of the room, has pressed on me
"with a weight I found it difficult to bear, and recollection
"has not failed to be as alert, poignant, obtrusive, as other
"feelings were languid. I attribute this state of things
"partly to the weather. . . . I have ere this been warned
"of approaching disturbance in the atmosphere by a sense
"of bodily weakness, and deep, heavy mental sadness, which
"some would call presentiment. Presentiment indeed it is,
"but not at all supernatural. . . . I have had no letters
"from London for a long time, and am very much ashamed
"of myself to find, now that that stimulus is withdrawn,
"how dependent upon it I had become. I cannot help
"feeling something of the excitement of expectation till post-
"hour comes, and when day after day it brings nothing I
"get low. This is a stupid, disgraceful, unmeaning state
"of things. I feel bitterly enraged at my own dependence
"and folly. However, I shall contend against the idiocy.
" . . . I had rather a foolish letter from Miss —— the other
"day. Some things in it nettled me, especially an unneces-
"sarily earnest assurance that in spite of all I had gone and
"done in the writing line I still retained a place in her esteem.
"My answer took strong and high ground at once. I said
"I had been troubled by no doubts on the subject, that I
"neither did myself nor her the injustice to suppose there
"was anything in what I had written to incur the just
"forfeiture of esteem. I was aware, I intimated, that some
"persons thought proper to take exceptions at *Jane Eyre*,
"and that for their own sakes I was sorry, as I invariably
"found them individuals in whom the animal largely pre-

K

"dominated over the intellectual, persons by nature coarse,
"by inclination sensual, whatever they might be by education
"and principle."

Nor was Charlotte ever to be won by presumption or
flattery. In that lonely Haworth parsonage, where in their
childhood she and Emily and Anne, and Branwell too in his
own irregular way, as again in youth and maturity, had written
so much and so significantly achieved, she ever preferred her
obscurity and isolation. Had she been able, with due regard to
herself and others, to maintain an absolute isolation from
'Currer Bell' and that mysterious individual's writings, I do
not doubt she would have so decided. To many, perhaps to
most people, this has ever seemed, and seems, a foolish and
illogical attitude. There are, nevertheless, a few writers who
share with Charlotte Brontë the deep desire to be left alone in
their private life, and to be known and judged solely by their
writings, irrespective of 'the personal equation,' of sex, or
circumstance. "Of late," she writes on one occasion, "I have
had many letters to answer; and some very bothering ones from
people who want opinions about their books, who seek
acquaintance, and who flatter to get it; people who utterly
mistake all about me. They are most difficult to answer, put
off, and appease, without offending; for such characters are
excessively touchy, and when affronted turn malignant. Their
books are too often deplorable." There were fewer books—
deplorable and other—and fewer autograph-scribes and would-
be interviewers, in the Haworth days: did Charlotte Brontë
write to-day she would probably, being Charlotte Brontë, take
still 'higher and stronger ground.'

What a wonderful family, this Brontë clan! One wonders
—so potent was the strain transmitted to each of Patrick
Brontë's children—if the two elder sisters, Maria and Elizabeth,

had lived to womanhood, what they too would have achieved. Certainly the elder, at any rate, showed herself in her short life 'a true Brontë'—'a true Prunty' might have been the more exact phrase, if Dr. J. A. Erskine Stuart, the latest and most thorough enquirer into the subject, had not all but conclusively shown that the Rev. Patrick Brontë and his family had never been known as 'Prunty' in County Down. Imagine for a moment if the Shakespeare family had been as united in genius as that of the Brontës, imagine the torch-flame at the close of the sixteenth century! But neither Shakespeare's sister, Joan Hart, nor his daughter, Susanna Hall, nor Judith (who became Mistress Thomas Quiney in her thirty-first year, a month before her father's death), can for a moment wear the steady light of Charlotte Brontë or the tragic flare of Emily or the mild glow of Anne. As for Hamnet, Shakespeare's son, he died long before he could emulate either the youthful vices or other wandering fires which, later, were the death-lights of Branwell.

But to the Brontë country. Where is really the literary geography we associate with this name? It is not only around Haworth, of course, though that bleak place is its heart, because of all lived and suffered and done there, of so many ambitions and hopes come to naught there, of so much there achieved, of all the passion and energy of five strenuous lives confined to this bare, unattractive house, restricted to these horizon-meeting moors. Roughly, it may be said to extend from Thornton, four miles to the west of Bradford, to Scarborough on the eastern sea. At the one, Branwell Brontë and three of his sisters were born; at the other, and at Filey, Charlotte knew some of the darkest (and yet for literature some of the most memorable) hours of her life—days, too, of consolation and peace, days wherein *Villette* matured; and here, too, Emily came when nearing death, and here Anne died, and rests.

Thornton is certainly worth a visit for any who would trace

and imaginatively re-live the experiences of the Brontë sisters. It is easily reached by tram from Bradford, of which it is indeed practically a part—in fact, Thornton and Haworth can now both be visited easily in the space of a day, from and back to Haworth: though, almost needless to say, that is not the way to make the pilgrimage, nor any other of the kind.

Charlotte and Emily were too young, when their father and his family of six moved from Thornton parsonage across the upland region between it and Haworth, to leave us any literary association of direct experience in connection with this thriving little town—in the Rev. Patrick's day a mere hamlet of some fifty scattered cottages. It is not of much interest to look at a house where a noted person was born, unless thinking and significant experience began there, or events of import occurred. Pilgrims do go to visit the Old Bell Chapel (or what is left of it); but why, it is a little difficult to understand. There's an inscription :—" This chapel was beautified, 1818. P. Brontë, incumbent." This might more appropriately have been adapted for an inscription at Haworth: "This house is beautified because of the genius of Charlotte and Emily Brontë."

In other respects times have not changed much. The old vehement note of religious bigotry is still emphatic in these regions of the West Riding. Not that bigotry is worse there than elsewhere. The Cornish Plymouth-Brother, the Welsh Methodist, the Highland Free-Churchman might even consider the Haworth variety lax. But in the Rev. Patrick Brontë's day it was rigorous indeed. Dr. J. A. Erskine Stuart tells an anecdote sufficiently illustrative. One Sunday morning Mr. Brontë was descried at his bedroom window apparently in the dire act of shaving. A spiritual volcano shook Thornton. The incumbent was approached, and upbraided. The amazing thing is that a man of so violent and often uncontrollable temper did not by word or action show his contemptuous indignation: there could be no more convincing comment on the bitter religiosity of the period than the fact that he earnestly explained to a member of his congregation: "I never shaved in all my life, or was ever shaved by any one else. I have so little beard that a little clipping every three months is all that is necessary." Ah, that was in 1820: such things do not happen now. Perhaps. A few years ago a Glasgow minister was seriously reproved by his elders because, in order to reach his church in time to conduct the service, he (having suddenly been summoned to the side of a dying parishioner, and so having left himself no time to walk to the church) took a cab. This summer a friend of the writer was in Ross, and told him that in a particular parish three members of the Free Kirk congregation were 'refused the tokens' (*i.e.*, prohibited from public participation in the Communion) for no other reason than that, during a holiday abroad, "they had stayed too long in Paris!"

The best way to see the Brontë country, the country of *Jane Eyre* and *Shirley* and *Wuthering Heights*, is to view it afoot, and to start from Thornton, either direct or by a detour to visit Cowan Bridge, a charming neighbourhood, though associated with no little suffering on the part of the Brontë girls, and especially Charlotte. Mrs. Gaskell's description is due either to the disillusioning effect of a visit in dull or wet weather at the wrong season, or to prejudice derived from passages in Charlotte's writings, letters, or conversation.

Perhaps the thing best worth remembering in Charlotte's childhood is the anecdote (by at least one biographer 'located' at Thornton) to be found in the third chapter of Sir Wemyss Reid's delightful and sympathetic memoir, where, and with obvious exactitude, he says the Brontë family were already a Haworth.

"There is a touching story of Charlotte at six years old,

" which gives us some notion of the ideal life led by the
" forlorn little girl at this time, when, her two elder sisters
" having been sent to school, she found herself living at
" home, the eldest of the motherless brood. She had read
" *The Pilgrim's Progress*, and had been fascinated, young as
" she was, by that wondrous allegory. Everything in it was
" to her true and real: her little heart had gone forth with
" Christian on his pilgrimage to the Golden City, her bright
" young mind had been fired by the Bedford tinker's descrip-
" tion of the glories of the Celestial Place; and she made up
" her mind that she too would escape from the City of
" Destruction, and gain the haven towards which the weary
" spirits of every age have turned with eager longing. But
" where was this glittering city, with its streets of gold, its
" gates of pearl, its walls of precious stones, its streams of life
" and throne of light? Poor little girl! The only place
" which seemed to her to answer Bunyan's description of
" the celestial town was one which she had heard the ser-
" vants discussing with enthusiasm in the kitchen, and its
" name was Bradford! So to Bradford little Charlotte
" Brontë, escaping from that Haworth Parsonage which she
" believed to be a doomed spot, set off one day in 1822.
" Ingenious persons may speculate if they please upon the
" sore disappointment which awaited her when, like older
" people, reaching the place which she had imagined to be
" Heaven, she found that it was only Bradford. But she
" never even reached her imaginary Golden City. When
" her tender feet had carried her a mile along the road, she
" came to a spot where overhanging trees made the high-
" way dark and gloomy; she imagined that she had come to
" the Valley of the Shadow of Death, and, fearing to go
" forward, was presently discovered by her nurse cowering
" by the roadside."

The country between Thornton and Denholme, a slow ascent of about two miles, is dreary at all times save on a radiant day of spring, when every ditch is a glory, and the birds sing as though truly birds of Paradise. From waste-land Denholme to low-lying Potovens farm, and thence across a lonely and fascinating expanse of true moorland, the wayfarer (following the track of the Brontë family on their laborious migration, in 1820, from their first Yorkshire home across Thornton Heights) will pass Old Allen, Flappit Spring, and Braemoor, and will

THE BRONTË COUNTRY

come at last upon Worth Valley, from which, by a steep street, Haworth climbs and lies like an exhausted lizard along the summit. As the comparison has struck several observers, it is no fanciful image.

Cowan Bridge, it may be added, is not on the Bradford high road. It lies near Kirkby Lonsdale, on the Leeds and Kendal road; and can most easily be reached by the cyclist *viâ* Keighley or Skipton. Thence on to Giggleswick and Ingleton, below the vast and bare rise of Ingleborough, till the banks of the little Leck are reached and Cowan Bridge is seen at the entrance to the pleasant valley of the Lune. Later, Charlotte went to Roe Head School, on the Leeds and Huddersfield road, and here we are in the heart of the Brontë country, and pre-eminently of the country of *Shirley*.

If one had to choose any single tract at once for its own beauty and charm and its literary association, it might be that delightful reach of upland from Cowan Bridge to Tunstall, with its fine old battlemented church, where both Charlotte and Emily often worshipped, and its lonely ruin of Thurland. Though not true moorland, it is a lovely country—a windy, grassy, tree-enlivened region such as the author of *Wuthering Heights* had her joy in.

But it is not the Haworth region, or the wider regions of *Jane Eyre* and *Shirley*, that is exclusively the Brontë country. It is there the two most famous of a truly remarkable family lived from childhood and wrote their books and spent the greater part of their days. But the greater had a genius which won other dominions.

No lover of *Villette* would think of excluding London from the country of Charlotte Brontë. In a sense she made London uniquely her own on that night when Lucy Snowe for the first time slept in the great city—alone, friendless, aimless, unknowing even in what neighbourhood she was. " I wet the pillow, my arms, and my hair, with rushing tears. A dark interval of most bitter thought followed this burst [. . . till at last I became sufficiently tranquil. . . .] I had just extinguished my candle and lain down, when a deep, low, mighty tone swung through the night. At first I knew it not; but it was uttered twelve times, and at the twelfth colossal hum and trembling knell, I said; 'I lie in the shadow of St. Paul's.' "

The secret spell of London is there, more than in any

elaborate phrasing of emotion and effect. How admirable, too, the reticence and the veracity of the brief account of her first impressions on that wet February night when, after a fifty mile run, the North coach left her at the old inn by Ludgate Hill! " My reader, I know, is one who would not thank me for an elaborate reproduction of poetic first impressions; and it is well, inasmuch as I had neither time nor mood to cherish such; arriving as I did late, on a dark, raw, and rainy evening, in a Babylon and a wilderness, of which the vastness and the strangeness tried to the utmost any powers of clear thought and steady self-possession with which, in the absence of more brilliant faculties, Nature might have gifted me.

" When I left the coach, the strange speech of the cabmen and others waiting round seemed to me odd as a foreign tongue. . . . How difficult, how oppressive, how puzzling seemed my flight! In London for the first time; at an inn for the first time; tired with travelling; confused with darkness; palsied with cold; unfurnished with either experience or advice to tell me how to act, and yet . . . to act obliged."

After that, the deep colossal boom of the great cathedral's bell, and " I lie in the shadow of St. Paul's," come as with the sound of solemn benediction.

That first night of London, Charlotte Brontë, as Lucy Snowe, has made her own. With the same powerful reserve she etches for us impressions of the first morning. " The next day was the first of March, and when I awoke, rose, and opened my curtain, I saw the risen sun struggling through fog. Above my head, above the housetops, co-elevate almost with the clouds, I saw a solemn, orbed mass, dark blue and dim— THE DOME. While I looked, my inner self moved; my spirit shook its always-fettered wings half loose; I had a sudden feeling as if I, who never yet truly lived, were at last about to taste life.   In that morning my soul grew as fast as Jonah's gourd."

In truth, this first experience of London is that of an innumerable company of brave and fine youths and girls who, in hope or despair, come up alone to this Metropolis of Hopes and Despairs.   It is not that of Lucy Snowe only, child of genius, but of her obscure brothers and sisters of actual life. Of these, many have come with literary aspirations, with young hearts astir with the foam of enthusiasm for names and places sacred by cherished associations.   What young dreamer of literary fame has not thrilled when, knowingly or unknowingly, he has for the first time found himself suddenly in Paternoster Row?   But let Lucy Snowe stand for all of us: her London-at-first-sight is that of the obscure many.

"Having breakfasted, out I went.   Elation and pleasure "were in my heart: to walk alone in London seemed of "itself an adventure.   Presently I found myself in Pater- "noster Row—classic ground this.   I entered a bookseller's "shop, kept by one Jones; I bought a little book—a piece "of extravagance I could ill afford. . . . Mr. Jones, a dried- "in man of business, stood behind his desk : he seemed one "of the greatest, and I one of the happiest of beings.

"Prodigious was the amount of life I lived that morn- "ing.   Finding myself before St. Paul's, I went in; I "mounted to the dome; I saw thence London, with its "river, and its bridges, and its churches; I saw antique "Westminster, and the green Temple gardens, with sun "upon them, and a glad blue sky of early spring above, and "between them and it, not too dense, a cloud of haze.

"Descending, I went wandering whither chance might "lead, in a still ecstasy of freedom and enjoyment; and I "got—I know not how—I got into the heart of city life.

"I saw and felt London at last: I got into the Strand; I went
"up Cornhill; I mixed with the life passing along; I dared
"the perils of crossings. To do this, and to do it utterly
"alone, gave me, perhaps an irrational, but a real pleasure.
"Since those days I have seen the West End, the parks, the
"fine squares; but I love the city far better. The city seems
"so much more in earnest: its business, its rush, its roar, are
"such serious things, sights, and sounds. The city is getting
"its living—the West End but enjoying its pleasure. At
"the West End you may be amused, but in the city you are
"deeply excited."

Both in its vividness and in its crudeness that stands for a
multitude.

As for that wonderful tiny etching of the Thames by
night, which stands out in this famous 'London' chapter of
Villette, it is as unforgettable as anything in *Bleak House* or
Great Expectations; as 'brazen and imperishable' as that
horrible stewardess on board the *Vivid*, who made poor Lucy's
first night on the river so miserable. And what a touch of the
real Charlotte Brontë—of the whole fearless, indomitable Brontë
clan, from the upright and intolerant and sometimes all but
intolerable incumbent of Haworth, to the broken Branwell,
unworthy brother of the dauntless Charlotte and the heroic
Emily, who, despite all his sins and weakness, had yet
strength to defy nature and die standing—in the last words of
this passage :—

"Down the sable flood we glided; I thought of the
"Styx, and of Charon rowing some solitary soul to the Land
"of Shades. Amidst the strange scene, with a chilly wind
"blowing in my face and midnight clouds dropping rain
"above my head; with two rude rowers for companions,

" whose insane oaths still tortured my ear, I asked myself if I
" was wretched or terrified. I was neither."

Then is not Brussels for ever associated with *Villette*. . . .
surely the greatest and most enduring of all the Brontë books ?

My own last sojourn in the Brontë country was on a day
of autumnal beauty, a day so serene amid so great a richness of
earth-born purple and suspended rose and azure, that it almost
reached unrest because of its radiant but poignant peace. It
was at lonely Tunstall, under the shadow of the time-blackened
walls of Thurland, and I was thinking, not of the elder and
greater sister, but of that stormier, less controlled, less mature
spirit who, from what all students of life would call an
impossible basis, and with architecture and ornament justly
condemnable as unreal or trivial, reared in *Wuthering Heights*
one of the great edifices in the realms of the imagination. But,
as I rose to leave, and gave one farewell glance at the glowing
solitudes beyond, the words that suddenly came upon me in a
vivid remembrance were of the more powerful and steadfast
genius of the author of *Villette*—*Villette*, whose very name
sounded so remote, here in this silent Westmorland upland.
But they fitted the hour, the place, and the mood.

AYLWIN-LAND: WALES AND EAST ANGLIA.

TO have two regions named in the terms of romantic geography, and each to bear the like name and to owe the same origin, is, unquestionably, a rare distinction for any author. In that map of the Literary Geography of Great Britain which the present writer outlined a year or so ago for his own amusement, before this series was begun—and has hitherto refrained from sharing with an eager world on account of his radical inability to draw either a straight line or a proper curve, or even to arrange the counties and place the towns in recognisable proportion and exactitude—there is a tract of East Anglia as well as a tract of North Wales which bears the legend *Aylwin-land*. The designation is not an arbitrary one of the literary geographer. The traveller in East Anglia learns speedily from local paper or guide-book that he is in a tract of coastland strangely ignored by the Ordnance-surveyor, but known to all cultivated people (such as you and I and the local chronicler) as 'Aylwin-land': and as 'Aylwin-land' a still wider region of North Wales, with Snowdon as its centre, is now acclaimed by the district-heralds to all visitors to the Principality.

Quite frankly, I had accepted much of this with 'a saline Punch,' as a French friend of mine once translated 'a pinch of salt.' Wales is conservative, and Wales is very Welsh, and the Welsh do not appreciate the English usurper; and I thought that an imaginative Aylwin-intoxicated Cymric Child, humbly but honourably employed at one of Messrs. Smiths' station bookstalls, had given himself over to a contagious frenzy. To hear on all sides that Wales had not only taken an Englishman's novel to its heart, but accepted it as truly interpretative and representative, and everywhere owned it, borrowed it, talked about it, referred to it, and magnificently advertised it, seemed . . . well, unusual. However, when last autumn I found myself in Wales for a few weeks, I was not long in discovering that at least in the instance of the railway bookstalls and the bookshops in towns and 'resorts,' Mr. Watts-Dunton's famous romance was to be seen on sale everywhere. "Just so—it was *to be seen* on sale everywhere," remarked significantly the late Mr. Whistler once, on a similar statement as to a friend's book ; but the evidence was satisfactory that no Whistlerian 'just so' applied in this case. Then there's the outside evidence. That a Welsh paper, circulating among Welsh people, should state, "There is scarcely a home in Wales where a well-thumbed copy of *Aylwin* is not to be found," is remarkable enough. But has not the *Quarterly Review* itself committed the statement that "*Aylwin* is the representative Welsh novel"? has not the *World* likened the Aylwinian booming of North Wales to the booming of the Highlands-and-the-Islands by the *Princess of Thule* ? has not the *Saturday Review* ceased from troubling a contemporary, and given *Aylwin* a Cymric lift-up while bestowing a low-down Welsh kick to " all the professional educationalists of Wales " ? Are not these and many other things written in the chronicles of our unambiguous Press and in the tablets of Raymond Blathwayt ?

" Facs are jist facs : ye ma' ca' them pairtridges if ye like, but they're jist facs, an' nae mair and nae less." And with Simon MacClucket we may agree at once to accept the three incontrovertibles :—

(1) That *Aylwin* is the representative romance of East Anglia, and that along the East Anglian coast north of Lowestoft is ' Aylwin-land.'

(2) That *Aylwin* is the representative romance of North

Wales, and that Snowdon is the centre of (Welsh) 'Aylwin-land.'

(3) That *Aylwin* is the representative romance of the East Anglian Gypsies, wherever they are, and is (in the sixpenny edition) largely indulged in by self-respecting Romany *chals* and *chis*, and is accepted by them as (so to say) 'their official organ.'

(Further)

The Registrar's baptismal statistics show a significant decrease in the popularity of Gladys, Marie, Esmé, etc., etc., and a concurrent increase in the popularity of Sinfi, Rhona, Winnie, and even Videy. As to Rhona, indeed, there will soon not be a semi-detached villa replete with every home comfort without its Rhona. 'Cyril,' 'Hal,' and even 'Panuel' too, have a good show: and rumour has it that 'Dukkeripen' has been snatched by a Welsh pioneer unable to read English, but whether for a male or a female Welshlet I know not.

I wonder if any other first romance has ever had so swift and so great a success. We all know the enormous vogue of *David Copperfield*, of *Vanity Fair*, of *Endymion*, of *Middlemarch*, though neither Dickens nor Thackeray nor Disraeli nor George Eliot came suddenly before the reading public with one or other of these books. Mr. Thomas Hardy had written much and long before the immense vogue of *Far from the Madding Crowd*; the late William Black served a thorough apprenticeship before, as Edmund Yates had it, he danced the Highland Fling from Paternoster Row to Piccadilly; and even *Lorna Doone* took time to ripen in public taste. Perhaps the nearest comparison is with *John Inglesant*. But even here the likenesses in destiny are superficial. Mr. Shorthouse's famous book had known no premonitory wagging of tongues: when it did leave the author's hands it evinced an apparently incurable tendency to emulate the home returning 'strayed' cat; and even when at last published, success came tardily, reluctantly almost, and the author found himself famous when much of the savour of fame was gone.   Needless to point to the difference between the present supreme rank of *The Ordeal of Richard Feverel* and its first reception and slow growth in general esteem.   Now that I think of it, *Trilby* is the only contemporary instance I can remember of the immediate and vast success of a first romance by a new writer.

However, we are not concerned here with the origins and literary history of Mr. Watts-Dunton's famous romance, but solely with its literary geography.

In a sense *The Coming of Love* may be merged meanwhile in its prose compeer.   Both books are faithful mirrors of the same spirit, the same individuality, the same experiences, the same outlook on the things of life and eternity.   The Rhona Boswell of the one is the Rhona of the other : *dukkeripens* and *chals* and *chis* are unstintedly common to both.

In calculating the literary geography of any author one has to bear in mind the author's own natal place and early environment.   The colours seen in childhood are those with which in maturity whatever is enduring is depicted.   It is sometimes stated that literature, that poetry in particular, can and even should be independent of any knowledge on the reader's part of what influences shaped and what inward and extraneous things coloured the threads out of which the web is woven. " We have the web: that is enough," is, in effect, the plea. Perhaps ' Kubla Khan ' or ' The Ancient Mariner ' is cited, with the incontrovertible comment that Coleridge never was in a Himalayan gorge or never saw a live albatross, either on an unsailed sea or any other.   Here, it is argued, is proof that the landscape and seascape of the imagination need have as little to do with actual knowledge or early familiarity as have the coasts of Elizabethan Bohemia with the frontiers of the Bohemia of

KELMSCOTT MANOR.   The Thames side home of William Morris and of Rossetti, and the "Hurstcote
Manor" of Aylwin.
From a water-colour.]

LLYN LLYDAW, the Welsh lake, where Winifred was supposed to be drowned.
Valentine and Co.]

Entrance to the Pass of Llanberis.

The East Anglian Coast near Aylwin's birthplace.
From an original water-colour drawing.]

RHONA BOSWELL. St. Ives Bridge on the Ouse.
From an original oil painting.]

A landslip on the Norfolk coast.

Rossetti's Drawing-Room described in Aylwin.
After a water-colour drawing.]

FAIRY GLEN, BETTWS-Y-COED.
Valentine and Co.]

Franz-Josef. The argument, however, is not to the point—any more than the fact that Blake, who was never at sea, once miraculously etched the desolation of tempestuous ocean.

It will, I think, be found demonstratable that in by far the greater number of instances the early environment of a writer is what counts most in his mature expression of nature as a background to the play of human emotions and passions and life lived. The inward shaping force remembers better than the controlled function which we call memory. Perhaps, for example, when Mr. Swinburne was writing his 'Sea-Garden' and kindred lyrics, or the sea-choruses of 'Tristram of Lyonesse,' or 'By the North Sea,' or 'In the Bay,' or his ballads of Tynewater, he had no thought to strike the note of locality, which is accidental, but was more concerned to give us that greater utterance where locality is as unimportant, as indesiderate as in Blake's 'Ocean' or Coleridge's 'Ancient Mariner.' But when we know how so much of the poet's boyhood was spent by the then lonely, land-slipping shores of the Isle of Wight, by the Cornish headlands, by the grey tempestuous seas off the north-east coast, in the moorlands and wide solitudes of his ancestral Northumbrian home, we can discern not merely their reflex in the poems named, but recognise one fundamental reason of the distinctive excellence of these particular poems . . . that accent of intimate familiarity which lifts them in him to our own more intimate regard, for the instinct of the reader knows the difference between what is merely depicted, however beautifully, and what is *thought in* to the very fibre of the thing created. It is to *thinking in* to the inmost fibre of what consciously and unconsciously Tennyson remembered of his Lincolnshire homeland that the most subtle and convincing natural image of 'In Memoriam' is due. Ruskin's childhood and boyhood and early manhood was a kind of processional festival through highland and lakeland beauty, in

L

Cumberland, in Scotland, in Switzerland, in Italy; and from first to last in his work there is a processional festival of beauty wherein mountain and vale, Alp and hill-loch and sealike lake, cloud and wind and wave, continually transact their phantom life. It is almost jejune to cite the instance of Sir Walter Scott: from *Waverley* to the 'Twa Drovers,' from the lay of Thomas of Ercildoune to 'The Lay of the Last Minstrel' . . . in one and all of those poems and romances of Scotland, we discern anew the intimate features of that Scotland where as child and boy and man the great captain of romance gathered both wittingly and unwittingly his inexhaustible store of pristine reminiscence.

And, certainly, Mr. Watts-Dunton was fortunate in his early environment, his early impressions, and his restricted wanderings. For him, as boy and youth, nature meant East Anglia, the sombre German Ocean, cloud-towered Fen-land, and the romantic beauty of North Wales. A fortune indeed for any imaginative youngster to have, as background for actual life and as scenic background to the life of dreams, that wonderful Fen-country which has all the aërial scope and majesty of Holland with a unique austerity of beauty all its own: that turbulent grey North Sea, which has in its habitual aspect so much of eternal menace, but whose beauty can also be so radiant: that lovely and romantic mountain-land of Wales, where Snowdon, the ancient mountain of the Druids, rises in isolated grandeur. How deeply he was influenced, how fully he absorbed the inexhaustible beauty, how profoundly he was moved by this early familiarity with Nature in some of her most compelling aspects, is abundantly evident in *The Coming of Love* and in *Aylwin*.

The author's own country is, of course, East Anglia. Here he was born; here his early life was spent; here one of the chief events in his life occurred, afterwards to be of such potent

influence in his life—his intimacy with the better class of
gypsies, the Gryengoes or horse-dealers (till recently a pros-
perous and reputable body of this migratory people, but now
for the most part shifted to America), and in particular with
the two types of Romany womanhood he has made so unforgettable in Rhona Boswell and Sinfi Lovell; and here, in later
years, he wandered often with George Borrow, prince of literary
gypsydom.

In a letter which Mr. Watts-Dunton wrote some time ago
to the *Lowestoft Standard* . . . concerning some correspondence
in that paper concerning the crypt below Pakefield Church
(introduced with so much effect in *Aylwin*, but at which some
critics demurred in the mistaken supposition that no East Anglian
church, all in that region of England being in the Perpendicular
style, had a crypt) . . . is an interesting personal statement,
which may aptly be quoted here. Having settled with the
crypt-objectors, he adds: "With regard to the identifica-
tion of the 'Raxton Hall' of the story, I had, at the time
when *Aylwin* was written, many years ago, a reason for wishing
it to remain unidentified. My one idea was to retain what I
may call the peculiar 'atmosphere' and the mysterious spectral
charm of the East Anglian coast, which stands up and confronts
the ravaging and insatiable sea. Hence I gave so much and no
more of the actual local description of the various points of the
coast as might enable me to secure that atmosphere and that
charm. That I have been successful in this regard is pretty
clear, judging from the enthusiastic letters from East Anglians
that have been reaching me since *Aylwin* first appeared. This
is very gratifying to me, for I love the coast; it is associated
with my first sight of the sea, my first swim in the sea, and my
first meeting with Borrow, as described in my obituary notice
of him in *The Athenæum*. And when I saw in the newspapers
last year the word 'Aylwin-land' applied to the locality in

L 2

which *Aylwin* is' laid, I felt a glow of pride which not all the kind words of the critics have been able to give me."

Except in one masterly romance, Mr. Baring-Gould's *Mehalah*, and in certain chapters of *David Copperfield*, maritime East Anglia had not met with anything like adequate recognition on the part of the romancists. It is a land of infinite charm, if that charm has little of the picturesque, as the picturesque is commonly understood, and still less of the grand, as the grand in nature is commonly understood. Of course ʽThe Broadsʼ are well-known and loved, as are certain tracts of the Fen-country; and from Skegness to the Wash there are towns and ʽresortsʼ so numerous and so populous that long reaches of solitude might appear as unlikely as on the curve of Kent from Herne Bay to Margate. But it is amazing what immense tracts of solitude are to be found both inland and on the seaboard of East Anglia. It is, to many people, not less amazing what a spell ʽthe dark landsʼ of the Lincolnshire fens, the Norfolk marshlands, the sea-lands of Suffolk, have for some.

One great charm for those who love waste places and solitude is the sense of something tragical in nature. That element is conspicuous in the powerful appeal of the wilder or more desolate regions of maritime East Anglia. When, with nothing visible but a vast level of seemingly unstable land, a land sombre in aspect and intricately interwoven with dark, still, sinuous canals and blind water-alleys and spreading uncertain fens, with perhaps not a house or a human being in sight, and overhead the immense and almost oppressive dome of the sky . . . generally so grey or so cloud-strewn in the continual conflict of the winds, but sometimes of a prolonged and imposing serenity, and often, especially in autumn and winter, filled with the most marvellous emblazonry of radiant flame . . . the spirit may not be moved to blitheness, and may well be affected to melancholy; but it is also habitually uplifted to those unpassing things of which great solitary spaces and still loneliness and all the sombre phantasmagoria of land and sky are symbolic. But, apart from this, it is impossible for an imaginative mind to confront such aspects, in such a region, without a more or less painful recognition of the brevity and insignificance of the material world. Everything beneath and around one seems shifting, uncertain, unstable, phantasmal: a wavering image, to adapt Goethe's phrase. Everything beyond and above seems ominous, imminent, inevitable. For below this emotional impression is the knowledge that a tremendous duel has long been fought here, is still being fought, and that almost certainly the land is fighting against implacable and stronger forces. Sea and land, these are the titanic protagonists in the gigantic natural drama that is being enacted all along the northlands from Finistère to Jutland, and nowhere more swiftly and surely than on the coasts of Holland, Denmark, and East Anglia.

We hear often of the continual land-slipping along our eastern and southern coasts, and oftener of that along Norfolk and Suffolk, and of the persistent encroachments of the sea. Few of us are moved to any anxiety, for to the inlander the peril is neither imminent nor obvious, and the ordinary mind is slow to apprehend what is not immediately obvious, or to be moved by what is not imminent. But even the general apathy is now being aroused. This is due in part to the deepening anxiety and emphatic warnings of many physical geographers and other authoritative observers, but still more to the rapid and many evidences afforded during the last year or two . . . years of frequent storm and flood, with the water-loosened lands yet further disencumbered from their natural bonds and safeguards, with high and devastating tides and continually encroaching seas. When that remarkable and enthralling little book, Mr. Beckles Willson's *Story of Lost England* was published a year or

two ago, many hasty critics assumed that its data were
perturbing only to a few dwellers on our extreme coasts; and
stress was laid rather on the appalling devastations of ancient
history than on the not less implacable duel that has been
enacted ever since, and is now nearer to rather than more
remote from tragical issues.   It is deeply regrettable that there
are no Parliamentary statistics concerning the present state of
erosion : that there is no scientific and systematic observation of
the coasts most affected.   Even the concentrated item of knowledge that, within the modern period, we have lost by submersion
many hundreds of square miles of territory and no fewer than
thirty-four towns and villages, did not induce a Parliamentary
inquiry.   The authentic statement, with its menacing implication, was almost everywhere received with the idea that it was
all in the past tense.*   But even the most casually remembered
records of 1903 and the first months of 1904 show how futile
is such unreasoning optimism.   This very morning I read, in
the five-days'-old papers that have just reached me where I
write, of the alarming havoc wrought by floods, gales, and tidal
seas, at the end of February and the beginning of March ; of
torn beaches and snatched lands and submerged shores along
our southern and eastern coasts, of the collapse, so long
threatened, of Dunwich Cliff, and of incalculable and in many
cases irremediable damage, where not total loss, along the whole
of maritime East Anglia.†

In the Fens, in the Broads, on the vast sombre East Anglian
marshes and meadowlands, an imaginative mind cannot but often
become aware of this tragical duel.   Nowhere in England is
it so near and present a reality.   Dunwich, Sidestrand, many

---

* So many readers will know Sheringham that it may be of interest to quote a
single item of the long and convincing tale of evidence adduced by Mr Beckles
Willson, namely, that in 1829 a frigate could float (in 20 feet of water) where, only
forty-eight years before, stood a cliff 50 feet high, with houses upon it !
† Since this article appeared, another and disastrous landslip has occurred at
Cromer.

another picturesque spot is doomed ; and, inland, many a pastoral track to-day will in a not distant morrow feel the salt tide sweeping irresistibly across it.

Much of the tragical fascination, as well as of the charm, of the very real beauty of both inland and maritime Norfolk, is naturally to be found in *Aylwin*. The author himself has more than once witnessed one of those landslips which are the dread of the region, and readers of his famous romance may recall the description of the collapse of the cliff-front beyond the old church's ruins. (The passage occurs, it should be borne in mind, in a scene of great dramatic intensity and profound emotion.)

"My meditations were interrupted by a sound, and
"then by a sensation such as I cannot describe. Whence
"came that shriek? It was like a shriek coming from a
"distance—loud there, faint here, and yet it seemed to come
"from me! It was as though I were witnessing some
"dreadful sight, unutterable and intolerable. . . . At my
"feet spread the great churchyard, with its hundreds of
"little green hillocks and white gravestones, sprinkled here
"and there with square, box-like tombs. All quietly asleep
"in the moonlight! Here and there an aged headstone
"seemed to nod to its neighbour, as though muttering in
"its dreams. The old church, bathed in the radiance,
"seemed larger than it had ever done in daylight, and
"incomparably more grand and lovely. . . . On the left
"were the tall poplar trees, rustling and whispering among
"themselves. Still, there might be at the *back* of the church
"mischief working. I walked round thither. The ghostly
"shadows on the long grass might have been shadows
"thrown by the ruins of Tadmor, so quietly did they lie
"and dream. A weight was uplifted from my soul. A

" balm of sweet peace fell upon my heart. The noises I
" had heard had been imaginary, conjured up by love and
" fear; or they might have been an echo of distant thunder.
" The windows of the church, no doubt, looked ghastly, as
" I peered in to see whether Wynne's lantern was moving
" about. But all was still. I lingered in the churchyard
" close by the spot where I had first seen the child Winifred
" and heard the Welsh song. . . . I went to look at the sea
" from the cliff. Here, however, there was something
" sensational at last. The spot where years ago I had sat
" when Winifred's song had struck upon my ear and awoke
" me to a new life—*was gone !* ' This, then, was the noise
" I heard,' I said; ' the rumbling was the falling of the
" earth; the shriek was the tearing down of trees.' Another
" slice, a slice weighing thousands of tons, had slipped since
" the afternoon from the churchyard on to the sands below.
" ' Perhaps the tread of the townspeople who came to
" witness the funeral may have given the last shake to the
" soil,' I said. I stood and looked over the newly-made
" gap at the great hungry water. Considering the little
" wind, the swell on the North Sea was tremendous. Far
" away there had been a storm somewhere. The moon
" was laying a band of living light across the vast bosom
" of the sea, like a girdle."

Again, all readers of *Aylwin* will remember that beautiful
opening scene where the boy who is to be the hero of the
romance is discovered sitting on the grassy cliff-edge by the
sea: and how at once the author strikes that note of correspondence on which the present writer has just dwelt.

" . . . sitting there as still as an image of a boy in
" stone, at the forbidden spot where the wooden fence pro-
" claimed the crumbling hollow crust to be specially

"dangerous—sitting and looking across the sheer deep gulf
"below. . . . The very gulls, wheeling as close to him as they
"dared, seemed to be frightened at the little boy's peril.
"Straight ahead he was gazing, however—gazing so intently
"that his eyes must have been seeing very much or else very
"little of that limitless world of light and coloured shade.
" . . . Moreover, there was a certain something in his eyes
"that was not gypsy-like—a something which is not uncom-
"monly seen in the eyes of boys born along that coast,
"whether those eyes be black or blue or grey; a something
"which cannot be described, but which seems like a reflex
"of the daring gaze of that great land-conquering and daring
"sea."

And it was through a landslip that Henry Aylwin became
crippled for his later boyhood and youth.

"My punishment came at last. The coast, which is
"yielding gradually to the sea, is famous for sudden and
"gigantic landslips. These landslips are sometimes followed,
"at the return of the tide, by a further fall, called a 'settle-
"ment.' The word 'settlement' explains itself, perhaps.
"No matter how smooth the sea, the return of the tide
"seems on that coast to have a strange magnetic power
"upon the land, and the *débris* of a landslip will sometimes,
"though not always, respond to it by again falling and
"settling into new and permanent shapes."

*_**

Mr. Watts-Dunton has recently communicated to more
than one interviewer the answer to the doubtless often asked
question as to when he first formed his acquaintance with the
gypsies: but to Mr. Blathwayt he was perhaps more explicit.
From these, and his introduction to Borrow's *Lavengro* in the

'Minerva' series, his obituary articles in *The Athenæum* on George Borrow and Francis Hindes Groome, and his prefaces to later editions of *Aylwin*, we know that the acquaintance began before 'the Gypsy' became 'seductive copy,' before the author of *Aylwin* had thought of the literary aspect at all. One wonders what would have happened if some vivid romance had forestalled *Aylwin* during the many years it lay in a retirement as obscure, if not as wholly forgotten, as that in which *Waverley* lay for so long. Would the author have still published the cherished work of his maturity, or—as I have an impression, possibly a wrong impression, that I have read in some interview or personal article—would he have refrained from entering into the lists with any competitor ? It is known to a few that another equally authentic romance of gypsy life was written about the time that *Aylwin* was published, but has never seen the light of print; for, though distinct in style, locality, and indeed whole conception and treatment, it could not have appeared subsequent to Mr. Watts-Dunton's romance without the injustice of allegations that it was following suit in what seemed a promising vogue. Well, fortunately no such misadventure happened for Mr. Watts-Dunton, and so he came unchallenged into his kingdom, a kingdom where his eminence is all the more marked because of pioneers such as George Borrow, Francis Hindes Groome, and Godfrey Leland.

> " ' I shall never forget ' (says Mr. Watts-Dunton, in his
> " interview-reminiscences) ' my earliest recollections of the
> " gypsies. My father used sometimes to drive in a dog-cart
> " to see friends of his through about twelve miles of Fen
> " country, and he used to take me with him. Let me say
> " that the Fen country is much more striking than is
> " generally supposed. Instead of leafy quick hedgerows, as
> " in the midlands, or walls, as in the north country, the fields

"are divided by dykes: not a tree is to be seen in some parts
"for miles and miles. This gives an importance to skies
"such as is observed nowhere else, except on the open sea.'"

Mr. Watts-Dunton's local partiality must be allowed for
here, of course: the same effects with kindred conditions are to
be seen, and sometimes even more impressively, in Holland,
in Denmark, throughout Flanders, in much of Picardy, in the
vast Yorkshire flats, along the immense level solitudes of
Solway, in the bare dreary Cornish moorlands, on Exmoor, and
elsewhere.

"In the Fen country the level, monotonous greenery of
"the crops in summer, and, in autumn and winter, the vast
"expanse of black earth, make the dome of the sky, by
"contrast, so bright and glorious that in cloudless weather it
"gleams and suggests a roof of rainbows; and in cloudy
"weather it seems almost the only living sight in the
"universe, and becomes thus more magical still. And as to
"sunsets, I do not know any, either by land or sea, to be
"compared with the sunsets to be seen in the Fen country.
"The humidity of the atmosphere has, no doubt, a good deal
"to do with it. The sun frequently sets in a pageantry of
"gauzy vapour of every colour, quite indescribable. . . .
"The first evening, then, that I took one of these
"drives, while I was watching the wreaths of blue curling
"smoke from countless heaps of twitch-grass, set burning by
"the farm labourers, and which stretched right up to the
"sky-line, my father pulled up the dog-cart, and pointed to
"a ruddy fire, glowing, flickering, and smoking in an angle
"where a green grassy drove-way met the dark-looking high
"road some yards ahead. And then I saw some tents, and
"then a number of dusky figures, some squatting near the

"fire, some moving about. 'The gypsies!' I said, in the
" greatest state of exultation, which soon fled, however, when
" I heard a shrill whistle, and saw a lot of these dusky people
" running and leaping like wild things towards the dog-cart.
" 'Will they kill us, father?' I said. 'Kill us? No,' he
" said, laughing; 'they are friends of mine. They've only
" come to lead the mare past the fire and keep her from
" shying at it.' They came flocking up. So far from the
" mare starting, as she would have done at such an invasion
" by English people, she seemed to know and welcome the
" gypsies by instinct, and seemed to enjoy their stroking her
" nose with their tawny but well-shaped fingers and caressing
" her neck. Among them was one of the prettiest little
" gypsy girls I ever saw. When the gypsies conducted us
" past their camp I was fascinated by the charm of the
" picture. Outside the tents in front of the fire, over which
" a kettle was suspended from an upright iron bar, which I
" afterwards knew as the kettle-prop, was spread a large
" dazzling white tablecloth covered with white crockery,
" among which glittered a goodly number of silver spoons. I
" afterwards learnt that to possess good linen, good crockery,
" and real silver spoons was as ' passionate a desire of the
" Romany *chi* as of the most ambitious farmer's wife in the
" Fen country.' It was from this little incident that my
" intimacy with the gypsies dated. I associated much with
" them in after life, and I have had more experience among
" them than I have yet had an opportunity of recording in
" print. Though they hail from India originally, and though
" their language is broken Sanscrit, yet they have none of the
" religions of the East. They are intensely conscientious as
" regards one another. They believe in the Romany ' sap,'
" that is, the snake which bites, or, as we should call it,
" 'conscience.' Perhaps the most interesting thing about

"the real gypsy is the way in which he speaks Romany all
"over the world. It is, of course, greatly modified by the
"country in which he lives—Spain, Wales, Hungary,
"Roumania, Roumelia; but it is all broken Sanscrit. They
"are a very gifted people, very highly musical. They live a
"life that is utterly apart, a life with its own habits, its own
"customs, its own signs."

***

"I need not describe the journey to North Wales," says
Henry Aylwin at the beginning of the third part of the
romance which bears his name: and we must be content to
leave that much-tried but occasionally somewhat exasperating
'hero' in the parlour of the Royal Oak at Bettws-y-Coed. It is
a temptation, indeed, to follow him on the second morrow of
his arrival in Wales—despite "the rain and clouds and mist in
a region of marshy and boggy hillocks"—to that wayside inn
where we first hear of Winifred Wynne's mysterious 'Dukkeripen' . . . which is not (as *Punch* explained) a species of
waterfowl, but the dread fatality of a curse. For here it is that
we first encounter Sinfi Lovell; and than that first encounter
with the real if not the nominal heroine of *Aylwin*, or than the
vivid description of old Lovell's beautiful *chavi*, I know nothing
in its kind more fascinating. It says much for the unforgettable
novelty and power of this chapter that it remains unaffected by
the still more beautiful, dramatic, and infinitely pathetic chapter
which follows—that which describes the hero's coming upon
poor distraught Winnie in the lonely cottage on the hillside.

From this point onward the book is full of the mountain
beauty of Wales. A score of lovely names come back upon
one, besides the great name of Snowdon: Mynydd Pencoed,
Llyn Llydaw (where Winifred was supposed to be drowned),
Llyn Ogwen, Llanbeblig, and the Swallow Falls and the Fairy
Glen, Llyn Idwal, sombre Llanberis, and so forth.

"My passion for North Wales," Mr. Watts-Dunton
told a friend, "is of a very early date.   It was twenty years
"before the publication of *Aylwin* that I first dwelt upon its
"unique charms, and gave a portrait of Sinfi Lovell in *The*
"*Athenæum*.   Although I am familiar with the Alps and
"other mountain ranges, no mountain scenery has for me
"the peculiar witchery of Snowdon.   In the manuscript of
"*Aylwin* there was much more writing about Snowdon than
"appears in the printed volume.   Snowdon, the home of
"the Druids, is indeed the mysterious dominant centre of
"the book.   But the story was much too long for market
"purposes.   Its length appalled me, and I was impelled to
"cut out some thousands of words of description and sym-
"bolical suggestions.   This has always grieved me, and it
"grieves me much more now that I know that Welsh
"people, who would have enjoyed those passages, have taken
"the book to their hearts. . . . It is a source of pride to
"me to know that, as a Welsh newspaper has said, 'There
"is scarcely a home in Wales where a well-thumbed copy
"of *Aylwin* is not to be found.'"

In a book so full of the sentiment of the Welsh highlands,
it is not easy to select an adequately representative descriptive
passage.   Perhaps none could be better than the beautiful finale
of the closing Llanberis chapter . . . a time by which every
reader will be inclined to sympathise with, if not to endorse,
the author's avowal . . . "other mountainous countries in
Europe are beautiful . . . but for associations romantic and
poetic there is surely no land in the world equal to North
Wales" :—

"The sun was now on the point of sinking, and his
"radiance, falling on the cloud-pageantry of the zenith, fired

"the flakes and vapoury films floating and trailing above,
"turning them at first into a ruby-coloured mass, and then
"into an ocean of rosy fire. A horizontal bar of cloud,
"which, until the radiance of the sunset fell upon it, had
"been dull and dark and grey, as though a long slip from
"the slate quarries had been laid across the west, became
"for a moment a deep lavender colour, and then purple, and
"then red-gold. But what Winnie was pointing at was a
"dazzling shaft of quivering fire where the sun had now sunk
"behind the horizon. Shooting up from the cliffs where the
"sun had disappeared, this shaft intersected the bar of clouds
"and seemed to make an irregular cross of deep rose."

* *

But before we leave ' Aylwin-land,' east and west, a word
should be said for a little outlying Thames-side parish. Every
one familiar with the life of William Morris and Dante Gabriel
Rossetti knows of Kelmscott Manor, the delightful ' old-world '
riverside home on the upper reaches of the Thames, where
so much of the verse of both poets was written, and of
which the present writer has something to say in a later
article in this series—that on the Literary Geography of the
Thames. Here, too, certain chapters of *Aylwin*, certain poems
of *The Coming of Love* volume, were written. It is to Kelmscott Manor, too, disguised as Hurstcote Manor (one recalls
Rossetti's lyric, "Betwixt Holmscote and Hurstcote, the river-
reaches wind") that the heroine of *Aylwin* comes when at last
in her right mind again—and, needless almost to point out at
this late date, the painter D'Arcy who there befriends her, and
Sinfi also, is no other than Rossetti.

It is with regret that every reader must say good-bye to
these three women, who are half of this world and half of the
imagination—Winifred, Sinfi, and Rhona. Even Videy Lovell,
indeed, for all her naughty ways, is too rare and delightful a

vision in contemporary fiction to let go from our ken without regret. To those who have been in intimate touch with average gypsy-life she is, to say the least of it, as vividly real as either of her sisters, few as are the lines which are spared to her.

Certainly their literary sponsor's first meeting with a Romany encampment is a matter of no little moment.

It is in the fifth section of the first part of *Aylwin* that we first come upon that wonderful glimpse of (in literature) an all but wholly new gypsy life—for though George Borrow preceded the author of *Aylwin*, and is still first of all who have re-created gypsy life for us, he has not revealed to us just what Sinfi Lovell and Rhona Boswell reveal. It is true that neither of these can ever oust the perhaps more commonplace but intensely real and human Isopel Berners. It is obvious, too, that Sinfi Lovell, though 'real' both in the imaginative and the actual sense, is not (despite the enamoured claims of the author and even other gypsologists) a *type—i.e.*, is not distinctively typical, of the gypsy girl . . . otherwise that wandering people would long ago have snared the hearts of all the poets of the world, have compelled all songs and all music to their service, and created a new order of ideals. It is nothing against the verisimilitude of her portraiture, against the fictional and directly personal statements of her limner or the corroborative evidence that is now available, to aver that Sinfi is no more a representative gypsy woman than a representative Welsh or English or any other racial type. Wherever or among whatsoever people she lived she would be that outstanding and abstract beauty—'the eternal phantom, Helen'—which may have the external accident of period or of locality or of race, but is really independent of those, being far above the ordinary upper reaches of her own 'type.' We believe in her, not only as Sinfi Lovell, but as a real gypsy girl; but we know that 'Sinfis' must be as rare among the gypsy people as her like would be among any other people. Helen of

Troy was a Greek woman, but was not 'Greek women';
Cleopatra was an Egyptian, but was not 'Egyptian women';
and certainly Sinfi Lovell, though a gypsy woman, is not 'gypsy
women.' But it is Mr. Watts-Dunton's distinction to have
given us two new women in that roll of what Blake calls 'the
wooers of dreams,' that roll of beautiful women from Homer's to
Shakespeare's, from Scott's to George Meredith's. As for Rhona
Boswell, she is one of the freshest and brightest inspirations of
modern writing : 'the silver bells' of her laughter will long be
heard both in poetic and prose literature, and in the vast and
varied geography of literature itself there will always be a little
woodland niche called 'Gypsy Dell.'

M

THE COUNTRY OF CARLYLE.

T is no small fortune for a writer to have as his birthland a region of beautiful names, of old and romantic associations. The poetry of these enters the blood. Youth may not note, and manhood or womanhood may ignore, but in maturer years the very mention of an obscure hamlet, a running water, a field by the burnside, will flood the memory with light as wonderful as moonshine. Think of how Chaucer, Spenser, Milton, Wordsworth, Burns, Scott, have filled their verse with the quiet music of old places, old names. What charm in those pages of Stevenson, when, from some mountain solitude in Colorado or from the isles of Samoa, he recalls the manse at Swanston, or the grey-green links opposite Fidra or the Bass, or the green hollows of Pentland! To the Devonian and the Cornishman what pleasure to come upon the fragrant old-world names in the romances of Charles Kingsley and Blackmore and Baring Gould! Tennyson declared once, when passing through an ancient hamlet in West Sussex, "What good luck to be born in this county of quaint and lovely names! Where else would one find a peasant called Oswald Paris or Stephen Songthrush ? and would any one but a Sussex yokel call the swallow a 'squeaker' and the cuckoo a 'yaffer,' and 'transmogrify' the wild arum into 'lamb-in-the-pulpit'?" And I recall a like remark made to me many years ago by Matthew Arnold, from whom I first heard of that lovely Buckinghamshire region now made easy of reach by the railway extension from Rickmansworth . . . that valley of the Chess where he loved to angle, and where he composed so much in prose and verse: "What a happy fortune to be a

native of a region like this, with such delightful names as
Chenies and Latimer and Chesham Bois and Chalfont St. Giles.
. . . Norman roses in old Saxon homesteads!"

However, even a Northerner may not always be able to
appreciate the beauty of certain names familiar north of the
Tweed: Camlachie, the Gorbals, Drumsheugh, they are not
euphonious. So, for their own sake, we must not expect
Southron sympathy for the names of the two most famous
places in the Carlyle country. Ecclefechan and Craigenputtock
do not make a delicate music. The lyric poet would regard
either with disgust. But for Thomas Carlyle there were no
word-bells to ring a more home-sweet chime. He could dis-
pense with these, however, when recalling the names of other
native localities made musical to the ears and the memories of
his countrymen: Kirkconnell Lea, wedded to deathless ballad-
music; Solway Moss, with its echo of tramping hoofs and lost
battle-cries; Annan Water, and the dark Moor of Lochar, and
solitary Cummertrees, lonely lands of *The Red Gauntlet*; silent
Caerlaverock, that once was Caerlaverock of the Bugles; the
dim Water of Urr; Drumlanrig Woods; Durisdeer among the
hills; the heaths of Sanquhar; the Keir Hills, where the first
cuckoo is heard; the dark narrow water of Sark, bordered with
yellow flag and tangled peat-moss, that once ran red with the
blood of English thousands. Then there are Nithsdale and Esk-
dale, and Strathannan, in whose heart the Bruce was born and
Burns died; Repentance Hill, with its grey peel, where once
the Lord Herries, Warden of the West March, stained his soul
with the blood of hapless men, so that to this day the ballad-
singer croons of how

He sat him on Repentance Hicht
An' glower'd upon the sea,

Tynedale Fell, overlooking the mountain-lands of Cumberland
and Galloway; Glenesslin, where once the forbidden hymns of

M 2

the Covenant rose on Sabbath morns; Cluden Water, where
the harps of Faery have been heard; and Irongrey Kirkyard,
where Helen Walker, immortal as Jeanie Deans, sleeps in peace.
A score or more names of like beauty and import will come to
the mind of the North-countryman of the Marches, from
Gretna Green to where shadowy Loch Urr sends her dark
waters past Craigenputtock Hill (that long prow-shaped Crag
of the Hawks where Carlyle and Emerson spent hours one
summer day discussing the immortality of the soul); then
southward beyond Glaisters, where 'Teufelsdröckh' for long
took his solitary 'gloaming-shots,' as, in a letter to his mother,
he calls his twilight walks; and at last to that grey water of
Solway whose tidal flow farther east will wash Glencaple Quay
—that small haven whence seventy years ago the packet-boat
was wont to sail with south-faring passengers for the port of
Liverpool, and that one August morning in 1831 carried
Thomas Carlyle out of Scotland to seek fortune with the
manuscript of *Sartor Resartus*.

The country of Carlyle is an actual country. We do not
seek it under the guidance of his imagination, either in the
Sartor Resartus of a fictitious Germany, or in the turbulent
Paris or the wild and distorted France of *The French Revolution*.
It is certainly not to be found in the *History of Frederick the
Great*, or in that of *Oliver Cromwell*. The Carlyle country is
the native land, the native regions, where the great writer spent
his boyhood and youth and so much of his early manhood;
where he returned whenever he could; whither his remembrance and longing continually went; the lands of his love, his
people, his strength, his heart.

There is, of course, one obvious exception—London. The
hackneyed phrase 'the Sage of Chelsea' reveals the extent to
which, in the general mind, Carlyle has become supremely
identified with one locality, and that in a city he did not love,

and where his least happy if his most famous years were lived. As 'the Sage of Chelsea' he will doubtless long be remembered; "like old china," as he remarked once, "however cracked and timeworn, that is preserved because of the shibboleth of its name." Doubtless he would have much preferred to be known as the Sage of Annandale. Perhaps, if he could, he would very gladly have prevented any such nomenclature at all. He did not love labels, though an adept at affixing them.

I recollect an amusing story told by the late Dr. George Bird (that delightful raconteur, whose vivid memory embraced half a century of intimate acquaintance with many of the most distinguished men and women of the Victorian era), though it was not, I fancy, at first hand, and for all I know to the contrary may have already appeared, though I have not met with it. One day Carlyle was walking with a friend near the Marble Arch end of Hyde Park ("black-felt coat, whitey-grey trousers, wide whitey-grey felt hat, old-fashioned stock, a thick walking-stick, hair more grizzly than usual, beard still more so, face furrowed, a heavy frown"), and had stopped to listen to a stump orator addressing an indolent and indifferent crowd on the question of the franchise. Suddenly a rough-hewn worthy detached himself from a group, and, without word of greeting or other preamble, addressed himself to Carlyle in a broad Annandale accent.

"Whit, now, ye'll be Tam Carlyle frae Ecclefechan?"

The great man nodded, his eyes twinkling.

"An' they ca' ye the Sage o' Chelsea?"

"They do, puir buddies!" (this in the same vernacularism).

"Weel," said the man scornfully, "I've heard o' the wurrd applyit in connection wi' a burrd I'll no name, but never afore this wi' a self-respecting *mon!*"

Carlyle laughed heartily, but remarked afterwards to his

companion that his compatriot's crude satire " had the gist o' guid common-sense in 't,"—" for who am I," he added, " or who is any man, to be held above all his fellows as the *Sage*, and worse, as *the* Sage ? "

But though it would be impossible to ignore Chelsea in connection with the ' literary geography ' of Carlyle's life, we will all agree doubtless as to his ' country ' being restricted to what he himself, in pride and love, would have called his own land.   That land, of course, lies between the Water of Sark on the east—the boundary between Cumberland and the Scottish border—and the Water of Urr on the west, where Galloway lies against the farther highlands of Dumfries.   It includes Dumfries town and Annan, where the boy ' first learned the humanities' ; Mainhill Farm, where his parents lived, and that was so long a home to him; the farms of Hoddam and Scotsbrig; Templand, where he and Jane Welsh were wedded; Craigenput- tock, where his happiest years were spent; and, ' capital ' of the Carlyle country, Ecclefechan, where he was born, and where at last he was brought again to rest in peace with his own people.

It has been a moot point with many correspondents and commentators, in connection with this series of Literary Geography, whether regions where a famous author has spent time and which he has commemorated in his writings should be ranked as his ' country.'   Some have thought that a writer's ' country ' should be the lands or regions brought under the sway of his imagination, as Provence and Palestine in the instance of the author of *Quentin Durward* and *The Talisman*, as Samoa or Silverado or Fontainebleau in the instance of Stevenson. Others have held that the ' country ' should be the actual country of birth and upbringing and residence.   Others have gone further, and argued that wherever a great writer has sojourned and where he has thought out or actually composed romance or poem or other rare achievement, there is his land, or at least one of his outlying provinces. It might be pleasant to say that because Carlyle spent a time with Sir George Sinclair at Thurso Castle, and from the shores of Caithness dreamed across the North Sea towards Iceland of the Vikings, therefore Caithness has become part of his 'country.' Even so un-Carlylean a place as Mentone might be thus claimed for him. But, obviously the plea is fallacious. Can, for example, the Isle of Wight be considered as within Turgeniev's 'country,' because there the great Russian sojourned awhile and wrote one of his most famous romances? Can Kensington Gardens be considered an appanage of Chateaubriand-land, because the great Frenchman composed *Réné* in the pleasant shadow of these Bayswater glades? Or is Wimbledon (is it Wimbledon?) a section of the vast territories of the Rougon-Macquart clan because M. Zola dwelt there awhile in exile with Mr. Vizetelly, and on an epic scale pondered a *London?* Imagine Voltaire's ironical smile if informed that the Voltaire country included certain parishes of Surrey and Middlesex; or Heine's caustic comment if told that the hardly-by-him-beloved British capital was a section of Heine-land?

Perhaps the happiest compromise is in the instance of a writer like George Eliot, whose own country and whose most enduring country of the imagination are practically identical.

In the instance of Carlyle there need not be much perplexity. His wanderings from Dumfriesshire in the north or from Chelsea in the south were few and unimportant. Little of his work was done abroad; though the *Reminiscences* were begun at Mentone in 1867, whither Carlyle went in December with Professor Tyndall. More notable were the German wayfarings, when Carlyle was on the quest of Frederick's battlefields. He travelled in Flanders, in Holland, in Ireland: brief visits, and in his literature, unimportant. In East Anglia, of course, one would not forget his raid into Cromwell-land.

Cromwell was begun in 1842, and in a letter to Thomas Erskine of Linlathen the author spoke of his "three days' riding excursion into Oliver Cromwell's country: where I smoked a cigar on his broken horse-block in the old city of Ely, under the stars, beside the graves of St. Mary's church-yard; and almost wept to stand upon the flagstones, under the setting sun, where he ordered the refractory parson—'Leave off your fooling, and *come out*, Sir!'"

Between the Solway coast and that of far Caithness, there are few parts of Scotland, save the remoter Western Highlands and Isles, which at one time or another he had not visited. In Kirkcaldy, on the Fife coast, he lived a couple of years, school-mastering, when but a youth himself. Not much was done here in actual achievement; but much reading and study were accomplished; and in his long walks with Irving, afterwards to become so famous, Carlyle learned much that he could not have found in books. Here, again, he stayed awhile in 1874 with his friend Provost Swan. I have seen an unpublished photograph of him at this time, taken in the garden of friends who lived near North Queensferry; and certainly, to judge by appearances, witty and winsome Jeanie Welsh 'had her handful,' as they say in Fife. As her husband remarked to Mr. Symington, when complaining once of the exaggerations of the photographer, "I'm revealed as an old, rascally, ruffian, obfuscated goose."

Kirkcaldy is hardly a place to suggest poetry, but there are few passages in Carlyle more haunting than that memory of 'the lang toon' in the *Reminiscences*: "the beach of Kirkcaldy, in summer twilights, a mile of the smoothest sand, with one long wave coming on, gently, steadily, and breaking in gradual explosion, accurately gradual, into harmless melodious *white*, at your hand, all the way (the *break* of it) rushing along like a mane of foam, beautifully sounding and advancing, ran

Craigenputtock.

CARLYLE'S BIRTHPLACE: Ecclefechan.
The upper window on the right belongs to the room in which Carlyle was born

ECCLEFECHAN.

The top room—used as Carlyle's work-room.

SCOTSBRIG: Ecclefechan.

Carlyle's House—Chelsea.

from south to north. . . . We roved in the woods, too, some-times, till all was dark.''

Again, and not least of his temporary homes away from his own 'country,' was Kinnaird House, in a glen near Dunkeld. Here, while a resident tutor, he 'moped' much, saw his friend Irving on his honeymoon, wrote love-letters to Annandale, where Jane Welsh lived with her mother, and during his nine months' stay wrote most of his *Life of Schiller* and translated the greater part of Goethe's *Wilhelm Meister*.

Once more, who of us happening to be in the desolate iron-country of Muirkirk of Ayr but would recall that day-long walk of Carlyle and Irving among the peat-hags of Drumclog Moss, when the younger confided to the other the secrets of his spiritual life? " These peat-hags are still pictured in me: brown bog, all pitted, and broken into heathy remnants and bare abrupt wide holes, four or six feet deep, a flat wilderness of broken bog, of quagmire not to be trusted " [the scene of many a Covenanters' meeting, and immortalised by Scott as the locality of Claver'se (Claverhouse) Skirmish] : " I know not that we talked much of this, but we did of many things . . . a colloquy the sum of which is still mournfully beautiful to me, though the details are gone. I remember us sitting on a peat-hag, the sun shining, our own voices the one sound; far, far away to westward, over our brown horizon, towered up, white and visible at the many miles of distance, a high irregular pyramid. *Ailsa Craig !* we at once guessed, and thought of the seas and oceans over yonder." Or there is that other walk by the lovely shores of Aberdour: " the summer afternoon was beautiful; beautiful exceedingly our solitary walk by Burntisland and the sands and rocks to Inverkeithing " ; or Moffatdale with its green holms and hill-ranges; or a score other such excursions, memorable in all ways, and for intimate associations above all. Many of my readers will know, some may have landed on that lonely isle of Inchkeith, and wandered among the coney-haunted grasses and over by the Russian graves, and from the same 'wild stony little bay' where Carlyle landed have looked on that scene which, he tells us in his *Reminiscences*, seemed to him the "beautifullest he had ever beheld" . . . "Sun just about setting straight in face of us, behind Ben Lomond far away, Edinburgh with its towers, the great silver mirror of the Frith, girt by such a framework of mountains, cities, rocks and fields and wavy landscape, on all hands of us; and reaching right underfoot (as I remember) came a broad pillar as of gold from the just sinking sun; burning axle, as it were, going down to the centre of the world!"

But we might traverse Scotland, highland and lowland, if we recall overmuch. After all, we must hark back to the Kirtle Water and the winding Mein, to moor-set Ecclefechan, Main-hill and Scotsbrig and Hoddam, to remote Craigenputtock.

As to Carlyle's town life, that was unequally divided between London and Edinburgh, for in the latter he spent far fewer months than the tale of years he spent in Chelsea. To Edinburgh he and his young wife went in 1826, and lived for eighteen months at 21, Comely Bank, then an isolated country-clasped suburb of Edinburgh on its north-western side, with its back to the Forth and its front towards the Hill of Corstorphine and its deep woods: our 'trim little cottage,' he wrote at the time he was contributing his first essays to the *Edinburgh* and the *Foreign Quarterly* reviews, "far from the uproar and putrescence (material and spiritual) of the reeky town, the sound of which we hear not, and only see over the knowe the reflection of its gaslights against the dusky sky." He had already had experience of Edinburgh, where, as a student at the University, he had lived in Simon Square, off Nicholson Street, then a poor and now a sordid region; and, after one or two unfortunate experiments, at No. 1, Moray Street (now Spey

Street), Leith Walk, of special interest to us, as it was here he first began in earnest that literary work which he was to carry to such a magnificent development. It is a street to be remembered of every reader of *Sartor Resartus*, all of whose Teutonically-hued pages were coloured from home-dyes. Who does not know that the German realm 'Weissnichtwo' is no other than the 'Kennaquhair' of Annandale; that 'Entepfuhl,' that centre of the world, is the homely Scottish village of Ecclefechan; and that even Blumine, that fair maiden of the famous 'Romance of Clothes,' was no Saxon *fraulein* but a winsome lass o' Kirkcaldy? For Spey Street or Moray Street, or in its ampler dignity as Leith Walk, is the 'Rue Saint Thomas de l'Enfer' of *Sartor*.

In London, also, Carlyle resided, now here, now there, before he took the house in Cheyne Row where he lived from 1834 till his death forty-seven years later. Chief of these temporary metropolitan homes was 4, Ampton Street, Gray's Inn Road. Here in the early summer of 1834 he and his wife came, after their burning of their ship of Craigenputtock behind them; here again earlier, in mid-winter of 1831-2, they were staying, with *Sartor Resartus* (on which hung so many hopes) just started on its unpopular serial course through *Fraser's*, when the news came of the death of that 'silent, strong man,' Carlyle the elder, at the farm of Scotsbrig—the famous writer's "last parental nest in beloved Annandale."

All readers of the *Reminiscences*, and of Froude and Eliot and other biographers, know how nearly Bayswater or Blooms-bury was given preference over Chelsea. No. 5 (now 24), Cheyne Row, however, carried the day. For long, even in Carlyle's lifetime, one of the chief literary shrines of the Metropolis, it is now more visited by thousands annually, from all parts of the world, than any other dwelling of the kind in London. Needless to write about a house and neighbourhood

so widely familiar, or of what may now be seen there by the
curious.   It is still the chief jewel in the crown of Chelsea.
But the unwary must not go thither expecting the pleasant
quarters of the 'thirties,' when "dear Leigh Hunt was just
round the corner." Carlyle, alas! would not to-day write of this
dull little street submerged in a part of Chelsea as now in any
wise lovely : "We lie safe at a bend of the river, away from all
the great roads, have an air and quiet hardly inferior to Craigenputtock, an outlook from the back windows into mere leafy
regions, with here and there a red high-peaked old roof looking
through ; and we see nothing of London except by day the
summits of St. Paul's Cathedral and Westminster Abbey, and
by night the gleam of the great Babylon affronting the peaceful
skies."

"An air and quiet hardly inferior to Craigenputtock " . . .
to that of remote Crag of the Hawks in far-off Nithsdale,
where, across the Water of Urr, Galloway calls to the hills of
Dumfries . . . no, alas ! not now, nor for a long time past.

Nor is it possible to dwell on Carlyle's life in London . . .
the mere 'literary geographical' part of it, I mean.   He knew
all West London, and much of every other region of the
Metropolis, with a knowledge gained through many years of
continual wayfarings afoot or on long 'bus-rides or on horseback.
Of all the many hints and pictures of this London life in Froude's
and other biographies and in his own *Reminiscences* I recall none
so delightful as that glimpse afforded in one of Miss Martineau's
few humour-touched pages.   It is where she relates how Carlyle,
dissatisfied with the house in Cheyne Row—no longer 'a London
Eden,' no longer as quiet as Craigenputtock—went forth one
morning on a black horse, with three maps of Great Britain and
two of the World in his pocket, to explore the area within
twenty miles of Chelsea !   But, as we all know, the house in
Cheyne Row remained the Carlyle home.   The first break was

when Mrs. Carlyle died one April day in Hyde Park, when driving in her carriage, her husband then in Dumfries; the second, fifteen years later, when all that was left of London's greatest man—who had refused a resting-place in Westminster Abbey (one remembers his scathing comment to Froude)—was carried north to his straggling natal village of Ecclefechan, to be buried there among his own people.

These North-country homes of Carlyle . . . how he loved them! Of course, Ecclefechan and Craigenputtock rank first, but with each of the others there are many associations for us, and for him there were many more. If in some regions bleak, if in certain districts sombre and for the greater part of the year repellent, the countryside as a whole is pleasant, is often winsome, and has sometimes a quiet beauty which is an excelling grace. It is far more diversified, more fertile, more human and kindly than Froude painted it in his famous 'Life.' In a hundred passages in his books and letters Carlyle himself depicts it in part and whole with all the sincerity of deep-ingrained love. Even in the days of his wooing Jane Welsh, when he was impatient to be elsewhere in the great world, "to make his cast in the troubled waters of earthly fortune," he could write to her, and as truly as sincerely, thus [in an invitation to her to visit his parents and himself at Hoddam Hill farm . . . Repentance Hill, as it is commonly called] : " I will show you Kirkconnell churchyard and Fair Helen's grave. I will take you to the top of Burnswark, and wander with you up and down the woods and lanes and moors. Earth, sea, and air are open to us here as well as anywhere. The Water of Milk was flowing through its simple valley as early as the brook Siloa, and poor Repentance Hill is as old as Caucasus itself. There is a majesty and mystery in Nature, take her as you will. The essence of all poetry comes breathing to a mind that feels every province of her Empire."

All these farm-homes lie near each other—Mainhill and
Scotsbrig and Hoddam and pleasant Templand—all save
Craigenputtock, in Nithsdale, just across the Galloway border.
There can be few pleasanter centres for the rambling ' literary
geographer ' than Ecclefechan itself, unattractive and now
' stranded ' village though it be.   The pleasant streamways and
wandering glens up the Kirtle Water and shadowy Mein are
full of charm, and are within easy reach ; so are the woods of
Brownmoor and Woodcockair ; beautiful Hoddam Castle and
ruined Bonshaw are but a pleasant walk.   The walk to Main-
hill itself is in all ways delightful ; that up the vale of Kirtle,
from Kirkconnell to Springkill by way of Kirkpatrick-Fleming,
is lovely enough to repay any wayfarer, apart from any association with Carlyle or with the moving old ballads of the Border
Country or the wild and romantic history of the Marshes.
From Criffel in the south to Sanquhar in the north, from
Scotsbrig in the east to Craigenputtock in the west, there is
almost every variety of lowland beauty and charm to be found.
The wayfarer need not even go far from Ecclefechan.   Let
him cross the Meinfoot Bridge and go along the beautiful
beech-shaded Annan road, and recall " the kind beech-rows of
Entepfuhl."   One may know loveliness and peace here, if not
in straggling, curious, and now ' disjaskit ' Entepfuhl-Ecclefechan
itself, where there is little for the stranger to see except the
Arch House, where Carlyle was born and where Herr Diogenes
Teufelsdröckh saw the light, hard by ' the gushing Kuhbach,'
as the pleasant Water of Mein was renamed in *Sartor*.   Alas !
Sartor or aught else of Carlyle is little read in Ecclefechan or
Annandale itself.   A great name, a famous tradition survive ;
but in the whole Anglo-Saxon world there are probably few
places where ' the Sage ' is less read, less veritably known.
Even in the so-called ' Resartus Reading Room ' there are (or
were) no copies of Carlyle's books.   So, another reason for not

lingering in Ecclefechan, but to fare abroad through a country in itself fair and nobly planned, and often quietly beautiful, sacred for many associations of history and religion and romance, and for ever dear to all who love the great heart and reverence the powerful genius of Thomas Carlyle. " Whatever else they did, the old Northmen," he said once to a friend, " their swords did not smite the air." And he, this Viking of Anglo-Saxon writers, though he lies at rest among the dust of his own kith and kin in remote Annandale, still wields a mighty sword that does not idly smite air. So, here in his own Northland . . . *Ave atque Vale !*

THE ENGLISH LAKES.

WHEN the late Grant Allen was asked once 'to say something about Paris,' he answered that he would be very glad to supply that particular 'omelette aux fines herbes' if he might be allowed to add a grain or two of salt to the familiar *plat* as turned out by nine hundred preceding chefs, and a flavouring of newly gathered herbs in the manner adopted by the ninety-nine past-masters of the most soothing of the arts. Thus only could he come forward as the thousandth of those who have had something to say about Paris.

I feel something of the same embarrassment before the task of the Literary Geography of the English Lakes. This particular omelette has been so often laid before the apparently inexhaustible appetite of an increasing public. It (the literary omelette, not the public) has known every vicissitude, from the local leatherette to the stodgier fare of the older guide-book, from the consistent Baedeker or Baddeley (excellent both, as solids to go upon) to the too highly sweetened *tome-soufflé* of Mrs. Lynn Linton, from the ponderous trifle (if the collocation be permitted) of Thomas Gray, when in October, 1769, the dapper little poet of Cambridge—with his 'parrot-shaped neb' like a headland on the coast of his pale face, and his dark eyes shining under his neat bob-wig—walked daintily, in brass-buttoned knee-breeches and glistening shoe-buckles, "by Derwent Water and Wynander Mere," to the more delicate Parisian article of Paul Bourget, who discovered much of interest in our English lakes, from 'l'Ange du Silence' to a *Doppelgänger*, or, more explicitly, a waiter-double of Lord Beaconsfield—or (finally, and to take breath) to the congested surfeit of that Lakeland chef, Canon Rawnsley.

Even before the recent crop of Descriptions and Associations there was more than enough Lakeland literature, of a descriptive and gossipy kind, to suit the not too exigent reader on a pilgrimage or sojourn along the lake-shores and among the dales betwixt Skiddaw by desolate Wastwater to Black Coomb, or between Hawes Water and distant Ennerdale or solitary Lowes or sea-swept St. Bee's, or between Shap Fell and Helvellyn, and thence to that pleasant Cockermouth where 'the poet-king of Lakeland' was born. The journals, notes, or literary reminiscences of Thomas Gray, of De Quincey and Lockhart, of Dorothy Wordsworth and Mrs. Lynn Linton, with Professor Knight's delightful little volume where poetry and topography are so happily wedded, are an ample supplement to the volume of Wordsworth that one will probably have with one and the volumes of Southey and Coleridge that one will still more probably forget. There may be advantages in this obliviousness: as in the instance of a pilgrim whom I met on the tramp from Ambleside by Thirlmere to Derwentwater, who informed me that he had never heard of Coleridge since he left school, that he had never heard of Southey at all, and that he knew Wordsworth only by repute and a few familiar quotations—exemplifying his familiarity with these by quoting Byron's hackneyed—

> Roll on, thou dark and deep blue ocean, roll !

but adding that, now, he had read Wordsworth (in heavy instalments), De Quincey o' nights, all Coleridge's poetry, and a terrible amount o' Southey. At home, he would have known none of these delights. True, he had absorbed with a dogged persistency rather than with that slow affection poetry demands; the upshot being that he decided Wordsworth had never " hit

the nail on the head," so far as descriptive poetry was concerned, as Southey had done in 'Lodore.' He little knew,
worthy man, that many another pilgrim has wilfully avoided
the Lodore waterfall, having suffered overmuch from the
Southeyan cataract set agoing in sympathy with that much
overrated 'aqueous discharge,' as an eighteenth-century topographer has it. 'Lodore' he ranked the highest achievement
of the Lake School, and next to it 'The Ancient Mariner,'
which, in a quaint directness of association, he " presumed was
suggested by some old seaman at Barrow, down yonder below
Furness Abbey." He had further imbibed, he admitted, much
interesting if useless information from De Quincey. Of
Wordsworth the utmost he could come to was, " He's a fine
poet to break up into little bits. The *bits*, and the smaller the
better, are often as fine as you'd expect." I wished my friend
could have met Professor Knight or Professor Shairp or Canon
Rawnsley! And having mentioned them, I am led on to the
following : a friend, resident in the region, told me that once
when he spoke to a respectable elderly inhabitant, with mention
of these and other enthusiasts for and authorities upon Wordsworth (whom the worthy Westmorlander 'couldn't abide'),
the response was as conclusive as it was concise—" Aye, aye,
they're just havering bodies too."

To attempt a detailed topographical tour of the Lakes
here would be a much more impracticable feat than that in
some measure accomplished in the succeeding section in
this series on the Literary Geography of the Lake of Geneva.
An enthusiast once set out to make a chart of the sea-lochs of
the Hebrides; when he heard that in Benbecula and South
Uist alone there are over two thousand lochs, fjords, and inlets,
he wisely desisted. It would be almost as foolish to attempt in
a couple of magazine articles a topographical summary of a
region of whose mountains and hills and many waters there is

hardly a swallow-flight's length that is not familiar, hardly a mile that has not some literary association, personal or enshrined in verse. The great names of Wordsworth, Coleridge, and De Quincey alone are associated with almost every by-way and locality, from Storr's Hall by Windermere to Greta Hall by Keswick, or from Morecambe Sands in the south to Cockermouth in the north. Indeed, one cannot even hope to enumerate all the personal associations. Think of the names of those who have sojourned in or visited the Lakes, apart from Wordsworth and Coleridge and De Quincey, apart from Southey and Christopher North, apart even from Ruskin and Tennyson, to mention only the foremost of those who have dwelt for brief periods or for long years by Grasmere or Derwentwater, by Coniston or Windermere; of all who have visited Lakeland since Gray and Joseph Addison and Dr. Johnson, since Keats and Shelley, since Thomas Campbell and Sir Walter Scott, since Landor and Matthew Arnold and Arthur Hugh Clough, since A. W. Faber and Arthur Hallam, Hartley Coleridge and Charles Lamb and Hazlitt, since Emerson and Carlyle, since Charlotte Brontè and Harriet Martineau and Sara Coleridge to Mrs. Hemans and Mrs. Humphry Ward (the collocation being euphonious, not critical!) and to the most Wordsworthian of living poets, Mr. William Watson—or, for a moment to leave literature, since Romney lived and painted and slowly won fame in the little capital of the Westmorland dales; or since Hogarth wandered along the Ambleside road by Low Wood (long, and to some extent still, the Honeymoon-Hall of the newly-wed) and Troutbeck, from that uncle's house in Ecclerigg which the visitor may still see; or Turner painted the sunset light on mountain-slope or glowing fell or flooding the wet sea-sands. Even if one were to give some chronicle of all these, other names would recur: as winsome Mrs. Gaskell, who, at the house called Briary Close, on the Windermere shore-road to Troutbeck, first met the famous woman whose biography she was one day to write, though the grave Charlotte Brontë of that occasion was a very different woman from the shy 'Currer Bell,' who, more than twenty years earlier, had looked to Greta Hall as a literary Mecca set in Lakeland, and to Robert Southey as its Prophet; as Felicia Hemans, so beautiful, so unhappy, once so admired and now so all but wholly forgot . . . who lived awhile not far from Briary Close and her loved Stock Ghyll Force, hard by where the good Father Faber dwelt, neighboured by Charles Lloyd, the loved friend of Charles Lamb, and within a brief walk of Elleray, where Christopher North abode in all his glory, and had many a famous man to guest, from Sir Walter Scott to the chief wrestlers of the dales—for 'the great Kit' loved feats of prowess almost as well as he loved the derring-do of the imagination; as Gerald Massey, who preceded Ruskin at Brantwood on Coniston, and dreamed so many dreams of worth, and of the things of worth of the imagination achieved so little for all his passionate effort; as Dante Gabriel Rossetti, who to a lonely house in the Vale of St. John brought with him too many shadows of sorrow and despair and weariness for the quietude of the solitary dales to solace or the peace of the hills to undo.

There are a hundred ways of viewing the Lakes. In a word, it is a matter of temperament, of training, and of mood, as well as of opportunity and means. Looking down on Windermere from the terrace at Elleray, De Quincey spoke of the view as such as one might expect 'on Athos seen from Samothrace': Emerson, on the other hand, thought the view inferior to some of the backwaters of Massachusetts. But then is that not ever the way? Did not Coleridge consider Words-worth the greatest English writer since Shakespeare and Milton, while Emerson again regarded him as a man harshly limited in thought, "with a narrow and very English mind, with opinions of his own but of no value, one who paid for his rare elevation by general tameness and conformity "? *

In opinions as to beauty in nature, as to beauty in women, or as to beauty in literature, there is not only persistent divergence; there always have been and probably always will be minds which can halt between two opinions, and so inflame the ire of the positive, who can no more understand seemingly contrarious views than Carlyle could understand Christopher North's loving poetry and at the same time caring for rizzored haddocks with whiskey-toddy. The sane way, however, is with John Wilson rather than with Thomas Carlyle: to be "fond of all stimulating things, from tragic poetry down to whiskey punch."

If one could paint as swiftly as one can write—or had the art to evoke with words what the painter can depict in form and colour—what scenes one could recall! No, Reader, I am not thus stealthily about to spring on you a variation on the well-worn themes of Wordsworth at Rydal Mount or at Dove Cottage, of Coleridge talking for three hours on end, or Southey in a waking trance at Greta Hall, of De Quincey's ' overpowering' first meeting with Wordsworth, or even of Ruskin pacing the avenue at Brantwood, and looking at the sunbloom on The Old Man, and dreaming of sunsets on Mont Blanc or Chamounix, on Pilatus or the Matterhorn. I had in mind, rather, some of those less often recorded, perhaps commonly ignored scenes which, in the mirror of memory, must at times be reflected—in the floating thought of those, at least, to whom all details of the lives of " the sons and daughters of Lakeland,"

---

* In a recent essay on Wordsworth as the Poet of Philosophy I read that "Emerson, to his discredit, stands alone in his disparagement of Wordsworth. No great English writer has thought Wordsworth 'narrow.'" But, to take one of several notable instances, what of Carlyle? He visited Wordsworth a year later than Emerson did, and wrote as follows to his brother, Dr. John Carlyle: "One finds sincerity in his speech, but for prolixity, thinness, endless dilution, it excels all the other speech I had heard from mortal. A genuine man . . . but also essentially a small genuine man "—and so forth dyspeptically

"servants of Minerva and Apollo," are matters of old knowledge and cherished interest. There is that episode of Wordsworth walking at sundown on the solitary sea-sands—that vast
tidal shore of Morecambe, of which was written "the sea saw
it, and fled " !—and suddenly descrying a man running towards
him along the deserted waste, and shouting as he ran, ' Robespierre is dead ! '   Or, to turn from that significant background
and that strange and momentous cry there in that desolate solitude, out of the passionate world that seemed so far removed, to
the domain of the *genre*-painter—one might recall a story of
Thomas Campbell at Keswick, or one of the several delightfully
incongruous tales told in connection with Coleridge.   Campbell
had a friend who lamented greatly because a valuable parrot
remained speechless, though when purchased a year back at
Barrow or Liverpool it had been reported (as though the seller
were a reviewer and the bird a popular novelist) of a fluent and
copious vocabulary.   One day a foreign sailor called at the door
for alms, and was shown into the room where Campbell and
his friend sat.   The man spoke in Spanish, and he had hardly
uttered a few words before the parrot swung to and fro in violent
excitement, then broke out into a torrent of Spanish exclama-
tions.   When the seaman turned and spoke to the bird, it burst
suddenly into screams of joy, and then abruptly fell dead.*   Or
there is the delightful episode narrated in Dorothy Wordsworth's
Journal (June 10th, 1802) : "Coleridge came in with a sackful
of books, &c., and a branch of mountain ash. He had been
attacked by a cow."   One can imagine heavy, stout, loosely-
built Coleridge, with the wildered look on his face and a dim

* I cannot remember the original source of this story, so have to give it as told me.
My informant added to this parrot story another as strange   One whom we both
knew had a parrot to which he was extremely attached, and the more so when it
became clear that the bird returned the fondness. During an absence from home our
friend unfortunately lost his reason, and hopelessly, as it proved ; but before removal
to an asylum he returned home. At the moment he entered his sitting-room the
parrot screamed with delight ; then abruptly it fell silent, sprang from his shoulder
(on which it had alighted), and flew out of the window, never to be seen again.

haze in the large grey eyes (an aspect so familiar to many who knew him), walking down Grisedale laden with his netted bag of books, and perhaps one open in his spare hand, and carrying at the same time the fruited rowan branch intended for his dear friend Dorothy Wordsworth—or, more probably, plucked for self-defence against that combative cow which had imperilled the way. Or, again, in another kind, how pleasant to re-create for oneself that scene by old Brathay Bridge over the swift hill-water, on the Windermere skirt of Ambleside, where Charles Lamb was wont to sit or lean with his friend Charles Lloyd (a man little known, even in his prime, though the translator of an excellent version of Alfieri and an accomplished student—but beloved of 'Elia,' who indeed in his affections ranked him next to Coleridge); and where on other occasions De Quincey would be the companion—listening "with profound emotion and awe, [as to] the sound of pealing anthems, as if streaming from the open portals of some illimitable cathedral; for such a sound does actually arise, in many states of the weather, from the peculiar action of the river Brathay upon its rocky bed, and many times I have heard it, of a quiet night, when no stranger could have been persuaded to believe it other than the sound of choral chanting—distant, solemn, saintly." *

* The whole of the closing part of the Charles Lloyd chapter in De Quincey's *Autobiography* should be read in connection with the Brathay, at this lovely 'sanctified' spot between the now far from 'secluded' towns of Windermere and Ambleside: for the music of this mountain stream gave birth to some of the noblest notes of the great writer's own anthem-music. "But sometimes, very early on a summer morning, when the dawn was hardly beginning to break, I have heard in that same chanting of the little mountain-river a more solemn, if a less agitated, admonition —a requiem over departed happiness, and a protestation against the thought that so many . . can have appeared for no higher purpose or prospect than simply to paint a moral, to cause a little joy and many tears, a few perishing moons of happiness and years of vain regret! No! [I believe] that the destiny of man is more in correspondence with the grandeur of his endowments, and that our own mysterious tendencies are written hieroglyphically in the vicissitudes of day and night, of winter and summer, and throughout the great alphabet of Nature. But on that theme—beware, reader! Listen to no *intellectual* argument. One argument there is, one only there is, of philosophic value . . . an argument drawn from the *moral* nature of man The rest are dust and ashes."

Or who would not offer sacrifice to the good genius who could re-create for one that scene when De Quincey and Coleridge, at a friend's house, met Lady Hamilton—"Lord Nelson's Lady Hamilton—the beautiful, the accomplished, the enchantress"; when Coleridge (" who admired her prodigiously —and she, in her turn, was fascinated with Coleridge") was, as De Quincey chronicles so tantalisingly and so sparely, 'unusually effective in his display'; and then " she, by way of expressing her acknowledgments appropriately, performed a scene as Lady Macbeth—how splendidly I cannot better express than by saying that all of us who then witnessed her performance were familiar with Mrs. Siddons's matchless execution of that scene, and yet, with such a model filling our imaginations, we could not but acknowledge the possibility of another and a different perfection, without a trace of imitation, equally original and equally astonishing.   She had Medea's beauty and Medea's power of enchantment."

What an evening indeed! . . . with Lady Hamilton, in her bewitching beauty and her ' Medea's power of enchantment,' rivalling Mrs. Siddons, ' that transcendent creature'; with Coleridge ' unusually effective in his display'!

Or, once more, for the retrospect might be indefinitely prolonged, one of those poignant if perplexing and even perturbing episodes, the outcome (as depicted by De Quincey himself) of his passionate and ideal love for little three-year-old Kate Wordsworth, the fourth child of the poet; of " a passion so profound, a grief so frantic" that, on the sudden news of her death, he fled from London to Grasmere, in a paroxysm of woe that was strange and terrifying to himself, and must have bewildered if not appalled those who witnessed it.

I know no literary episode so seldom alluded to, none I am sure more tragically passionate and more tragically futile,

Langdale Pikes.

A sketch by M. Greiffenhagen.]

A sketch by M. Greiffenhagen.]   BUTTERMERE.

A sketch by M. Greiffenhagen.]   ROSTHWAITE.

ROBERT SOUTHEY.

CHARLES LAMB.

S. T. COLERIDGE.

THOMAS GRAY.

William Wordsworth.

After a painting by H. W. Pickersgill, R.A., in the National Portrait Gallery. Photo by Walker and Cockerel.

WASTDALE HEAD AND STY HEAD PASS.

Photo by Pettitt, Keswick.]

WINDERMERE from near "Elleray."

RYDAL MOUNT, Wordsworth's House.

RUSKIN'S HOUSE, Brantwood, Coniston.

EAGLE CRAG AND STONETHWAITE.

A sketch by M. Greiffenhagen.]

THE NEEDLE ROCK, GREAT GABLE.

Photo by A. Pettitt, Keswick.]

HONISTER PASS AND CRAG.

Photo by A. Pettitt, Keswick.]

DERWENTWATER, with promontory of Friar's Crag.

"OLD MAN," from Church Town, Coniston.

Photo by J. Valentine, Dundee.]

and none perhaps of so strange psychological interest and import. But let the master of words tell his own story.

"Over and above my excess of love for her, I had "always viewed her as an impersonation of the dawn and "the spirit of infancy; and this abstraction seated in her "person, together with the visionary sort of connection which, "even in her parting hours, she assumed with the summer "sun, by timing her immersion into the cloud of death with "the rising and the setting of that fountain of life : these "combined impressions recoiled so violently into a contrast "or polar antithesis to the image of death that each exalted "and brightened the other. I returned hastily to Grasmere ; "stretched myself every night, for more than two months "running, upon her grave ; in fact, often passed the night "upon her grave, not (as may readily be supposed) in any "parade of grief; on the contrary, in that quiet valley of "simple shepherds I was secure enough from observation "until morning light began to return ; but in mere intensity "of sick, frantic yearning after neighbourhood to the darling "of my heart. . . . In many solitary fields, at a considerable "elevation above the level of the valleys—fields which in the "local dialect are called 'intacks'—my eye was haunted, at "times in broad noonday (oftener, however, in the afternoon), "with a facility, but at times also with a necessity, for "weaving, out of a few simple elements, a perfect picture of "little Kate in the attitude and onward motion of walking; ". . . usually I saw her at the opposite side of the field, "which might sometimes be at a distance of a quarter of a "mile, generally not so much. Almost always she carried a "basket on her head; and usually the first hint upon which "the figure arose commenced in wild plants, such as tall ferns, "or the purple flowers of the foxglove; but, whatever might

" be the colours or the forms, uniformly the same little full-
" formed figure arose, uniformly dressed in the little blue
" bedgown and black skirt of Westmorland, and uniformly
" with the air of advancing motion. Through part of June,
" July, and part of August, this frenzy of grief continued. It
" was reasonably to be expected that nature would avenge
" such senseless self-surrender to passion. . . ."

De Quincey then narrates what happened, including his
serious illness, although the malady was obviously of shaken
nerves, till his physical recovery and even more absolute mental
reaction in November, at Ilfracombe, whither, in weary quest
of health, he had drifted from Bath and elsewhere.

" . . . But the remarkable fact in this catastrophe of
" my illness is that all grief for little Kate Wordsworth, nay,
" all remembrance of her, had, with my malady, vanished
" from my mind. The traces of her innocent features were
" utterly washed away from my heart; she might have been
" dead for a thousand years, so entirely abolished was the last
" lingering image of her face or figure. . . . Even her little
" grassy grave, white with snow when I returned to
" Grasmere in January, was looked at almost with indiffer-
" ence; except, indeed, as now become a memorial to me
" of that dire internal physical convulsion thence arising by
" which I had been shaken and wrenched; and, in short, a
" case more entirely realising the old Pagan superstition of a
" nympholepsy in the first place, and, secondly, of a Lethe or
" river of oblivion, and the possibility, by one draught from
" this potent stream, of applying an everlasting ablution to
" all the soils and stains of human anguish, I do not suppose
" the psychological history of man affords."

So wrote De Quincey in 1840, more than a quarter of a

century after his passionate love for little three-year-old Kate
Wordsworth had so strangely lapsed to an almost callous
indifference; but we recall with a fresh emotion how in
advanced years he surrendered once more with longing affection to his memories of his child-love, devoting to her many
pages of his autobiography. Surely none can forget how, in
his mature manhood, the solitary student at Grasmere—'insu-
lated in reverie,' as he wrote of his friend Coleridge at Greta
Hall, in the days before Southey began his long residence at
that famous abode — loved this winsome little girl as 'the
impersonation of the dawn,' and yet humanly and sweetly, who
in turn gave to the wifeless and childless man her whole-hearted
love, "so that in a manner she lived with me at my solitary
cottage; as often as I could entice her from home, walked with
me, slept with me, and was my sole companion"; and, above
all, we remember that almost inexplicable extremity of grief
when little Kate died, and those 'visitations,' compelled by
longing and the imagination working together, wherein the
dreamer saw his lost love re-arising from amidst the green foam
of the fern or from out the purple mist of the foxglove.

Although Wordsworth looked at once pityingly and
unsympathetically on his friend's devotion to his baby-daughter,
and loved the child in his unemotional way (though, as De
Quincey says, she was noways a favourite with her father), it
was of 'this radiant spirit of joyousness,' as her 'lover' called
her, that the poet - father wrote in the beautiful lines
beginning—

> Loving she is and tractable, though wild.
>
> . . . . . .
>
> Even so this happy creature of herself
> Was all sufficient solitude to her
> Was blithe society, who filled the air
> With gladness and involuntary songs.

Possibly, however, Wordsworth loved with a restrained or

veiled emotion wilfully unrevealed to De Quincey. The great poet, it must be admitted, was ever more admirable than lovable; sometimes one believes that no one save his silent wife (whose sole divergence from domestic speech is said to have found unvarying and simple expression in ' God bless you '), and that remarkable woman of voiceless genius, his beloved and loving sister Dorothy, ever knew tenderness towards the somewhat harsh, uncouth, and prematurely aged " great chieftain of the Lakeland clan." Certainly De Quincey, and all who knew him intimately, admired the poet much more than they loved the man, for all the pleasant and enduring friendship about the engrossing details of which it is so pleasant to read. Wordsworth's mind may have shone

More bright than madness and the dreams of wine,

but the record of a humble contemporary is probably more faithful to the outward aspect, " It was a feäce wi'out a bit o' plesser in it." Nor was the difference between De Quincey and Wordsworth more marked than that between Southey and his successor in the Laureateship, and certainly not more than that between Wordsworth and Coleridge. In this connection one may recall a characteristic episode narrated in Dorothy Wordsworth's *Journal of a Tour in Scotland.* A turnpike-keeper in Nithsdale had offered his poor fare of oatbread and cheese and sour milk; but "William lay under the wind in a cornfield below the house, being not well enough to partake of the milk and bread. . . . Coleridge gave our host a pamphlet, *The Crisis of the Sugar Colonies !* " * In most affairs, ' William ' was apt

* By far the most vivid personal account of Wordsworth is that in De Quincey's *Autobiography*, vol. ii. (Masson Edition), pp. 242-50 ; as again, of his early years, at p. 262 *et seq.* The account begins with his complexion, and the famous remark, " His legs were pointedly condemned by all female connoisseurs in legs " and at pp. 248-50 are the passages about the premature ageing in expression of the Wordsworths, and notably the poet, and the narrative of how the latter, on the Keswick coach, was, when thirty-nine, taken to be between sixty and seventy.

to ' lie under the wind ' and be quite indifferent in consideration for others, and in most affairs Coleridge was apt to confer ' Sugar Crisis pamphlets ' on grateful but embarrassed recipients who had perhaps looked for other reward. As for that " fraternal intimacy where one had no joy in which the other did not rejoice," of which an enthusiastic biographer speaks, one is apt (perhaps in sheer contrariety of spirit !) to recall how, on the day of Wordsworth's marriage, Coleridge published in the *Morning Post* his now familiar lines entitled ' Dejection : An Ode ' !

A systematic peregrination of the Lakes ! No, I am afraid this article is far from systematic. Rather it calls, in truth, for the commentary of the unwittingly humorous Parsee candidate for professorial honours, who, on the subject of Emerson, wrote : " One must not be shy, but declare with obviousness, that his writings are often infinitely void of the subject such as we might expect, and otherwise are acceptable as fallaciously idle and even hopeless." Well, an they be but ' acceptable,' the rest may be admitted—even condoned. One need not boggle at being called fallaciously idle. Truth is stranger than fiction.

Does any one now ever read *Dr. Syntax's Tour ?* With the author of that once famous book I must remember—

> With curious eye, and active scent,
> I on the Picturesque am bent
> This is my game : I must pursue it ,
> And make it when I cannot view it.

Of the sad state of literary ethics revealed in the last line I have nothing to say, save to repudiate with indignation the idea that any one except Dr. Syntax could " make it when he cannot view it." True, one has heard that Théophile Gautier's excellent book on Russia was written in the more convenient environment of Paris, with a map of the Czar's dominions and the *Guide-Joanne* as basis for his travels. Even thus was history written by the great De Rougemont ; and some years ago a book appeared, *A Woman's Ramble through Mongolia*—or it might be *On a Motor through Thibet*—or *Up and Down the Caucasus on a Bicycle*—written by a Young Lady of Brixton (not Edward Lear's friend), whose sole qualification lay in being the industrious and ingenious possessor of a British Museum reader's ticket.

But these be daring freaks of literary conscience. There is, however, something in the idea, as in that of the sweep who told Dickens there's only one way of seeing London. If one knows the whole Lakeland region, its roads and by-roads, its hotels and inns, its becks and ghylls, its passes and forces, its meres and tarns, its seats and pikes and screes—in a word, all overlooked from the windy brows of Skiddaw or Helvellyn to where Black Coomb frowns on the sea or Ennerdale fills with the light of the west — and if in addition one is fairly familiar with the host of literary associations, the task of adequate chronicle is not for the magazine - writer but may be attempted (as it has been) by Mrs. Lynn Linton in three hundred eloquent and learned pages, or by James Payn in two large quarto volumes as 'replete' with humour and first-hand information as nowadays every hotel or boarding-house is with 'comfort,' or by the indefatigable Canon Rawnsley, whose voluminous intimacy with everything and everybody and every place in Lakeland must be a great wear-and-tear on a brain already Atlas-laden with the vastest brood of sonnets ever fathered on one parent—rumour, indeed, has it that they already number over ten thousand, and are but the playful vanguard of a great army in reserve! Canon Rawnsley (whose Lakeland books are really delightful of their kind) lives at Crosthwaite, near Keswick; and it is said that when visitors to that town or pilgrims to Greta Hall inquire as to what the local industries may be, the answer is, "The famous lead-pencil manufacture, and Canon Rawnsley's sonnets." It may not be true—I am perhaps prejudiced in credence—for the Westmorlander or Cumberlander is not of a literary turn, and is, I believe, commonly ranked with the Sussex native in the matter of poetic tastes. Still, as the Daily Mills that grind our stale and hallowed chestnuts with relentless industry remind us so frequently, the continual dropping of water will wear away a stone: and who knows what effect the ceaseless dropping of sonnets may have on . . . ? Well, enough: we can but envy others their opportunities, and go our way in peace.

How best to see Lakeland and all its sights—including the Crier of Claife and the Bottom-wind of Derwentwater? Both the individual and the phenomenon are of familiar repute to those who pass by Bowness and by the Ferry and Claife Woods of Windermere, or adventure to Friar's Crag, or along Borrowdale road by the Derwent Water; but not even among the most primitive inhabitants of Bowness (autochthones they must be by their names, Rain, Mudd, and Snow being characteristic) is the audacious person to be found to assert that he has himself heard the 'Claife-Cry,' nor is it easy to encounter the Keswickian who has himself observed the bottom-wind on calm Derwentwater throwing foaming waves towards the placid shallows, or 'had it nearer' than from 'my brother's uncle's cousin's aunt.' How best to view, how best to enter? Well, that, and what one should see or would like to see, and what the literary pilgrim should take with him, and what he should admire at given places and reflect upon at other places, and remember or quote or read or hunt up at still other places— are these not all written in the books to which allusion has been made, and in scores of good, indifferent, and bad guide-books purchaseable (with major part consisting of interesting local advertisement) from the sum of one penny upward? With these, with their amplitude of detail, and their *ex cathedrâ* method of imparting wisdom illustrated by 'the gems of modern literature,' one cannot adventure upon rivalry. But in the ensuing section

some supplementary matter to the common stock of the Literary
Geography of Lakeland may redeem the character of the present
writer as a too discursive topographer.

Meanwhile a piece of good advice from that ardent and
loving Lakelander, Mrs. Lynn Linton : " Eat then the lotus at
(Grasmere or elsewhere), but lay aside your life's armour while
there, and think of no battles to be fought and no victories to
be won."   To which may be added, " *Hic jacet* the only true
way to a proper holiday," as the Eton boy rendered a certain
classic epitaph at Windsor.

*_**

In one of the local Lakeland periodicals—the sole literary
ornament, except an old ' A B C ' and a handbook of the
Harwich route to the Continent, in an hotel-parlour on whose
glass door was engraved the euphemistic legend ' Library and
Reading-room '—I read a touching account of the last hours
and parting words of some of the famous people associated with
the Lakes.   These records of adieux were delightfully characteristic, but without even that workable basis which a famous
specialist once declared was essential to a really good lie.   Hartley
Coleridge, I recollect, was made to remark, with a clannish
adherence to the family poetry, that his life had been idle as a
painted ship upon a painted ocean.   To Edward Quillinan, who
married Wordsworth's only daughter, Dora, was imputed an
all-but-impossible four-line quotation about his father-in-law,
beginning—

> Of him the tarns and meres are eloquent.

Ruskin at the last moment exclaimed, ' I see the Alps ! '   Even
Tennyson is dragged in, though with a complication of misstatement that would seem to promise for the writer a high
place as an election-agent or auctioneer, or in some other of the
persuasive arts; for by inference one would gather that Tennyson
died at Mirehouse, near Keswick, that it was at Tent Lodge on

Coniston Lake ("where Gerald Massey had been his predecessor") he learned he was to succeed Wordsworth in the
Laureateship, that the last thing he asked for was his copy of ' In
Memoriam,' and that his dying words were, ' Crossing the Bar.'
Tennyson visited James Spedding at Mirehouse in 1850, and
never revisited it or Keswick, and it was immediately subsequent
to this stay at Derwentwater, either at Tent Lodge, Coniston, or
at Park House, that, some months after the death of Wordsworth, he heard of his succession to the Laureateship; * when
he resided at Tent Lodge (where his literary predecessor was
not Gerald Massey, who lived at Brantwood, but William
Smith, the author of *Thorndale* and *Gravenhurst*) he was not
only the official Laureate, but Laureate by the people's will;
the last book he asked for was ' Shakespeare ' (not *Cymbeline*, as
commonly stated, though it was at *Cymbeline* the volume opened,
and at a favourite passage) ; and as for that final legend, it died
years ago after a brief paragraphic ecstasy.

Another somewhat cryptic misstatement relates to Matthew
Arnold, " who called the cross-roads by his old home Armboth,
' Old Corruption.' " Armboth is a locality (it was of Armboth
Fells that Matthew Arnold wrote in his reminiscent poem
' Resignation '), not a house. Arnold's several holiday-homes
were at Brathay Hall, where as a boy he made his first acquaintance with the Lakes; Allen Bank, Grasmere; Wythburn Walk,
and Fox How. It was not Matthew Arnold, however, but his
father, Dr. Arnold, who named the three then indifferent roads
leading from Rydal to Grasmere, ' Old Corruption,' ' Bit by Bit
Reform,' and ' Radical Reform.'

But enough of these misstatements. I allude to them
mainly because in some form they permeate local Lakeland
literature. One should at all times be wary of ' last hours,' and
exceedingly circumspect as to ' dying words.' It may be

* See the somewhat vague statement in the *Life*, vol. i., p. 334.

pleasant to think of the aged Ruskin exclaiming at the moment of death, ' I see the Alps,' but one has a sense of outrage when informed that he never said anything of the kind. It is, of course, sometimes sad to lose those sentimental friends of the anecdotist.   Perhaps some day the historian of the Victorian age will deprive those who come after us of Cecil Rhodes' famous last words, " So little done, so much to do " (which by the way are not his own, but a quotation from Tennyson), as other historians have disputed Themistocles' ' Strike, but hear' and even Cæsar's ' Et tu, Brute.'   One of the saddest dispersals of legend is the instance of Pitt's pathetic " My country, how I leave my country ! " now, I understand, usurped by " I hope something will be done for Jenkins "—the implicated Jenkins being no other than Pitt's butler, who, in the disappointment of an unmentioned legacy, either invented or conveniently remembered the solemn admonition.   We have, however, Sydney Smith's avowal, I forget on what authority, that Pitt's dying words related neither to England nor to Jenkins, but were merely a husky request for barley-water.   And so all is vanity.

James Russell Lowell spoke of this region as Wordsworthshire, and a certain vogue has been given to the name.   It is a misnomer, for all save the uninformed or the fanatical.   True, Wordsworth dominates.   His is the greatest name associated with Lakeland; but that can hardly be called Wordsworthshire which also is associated with other poet-names such as Thomas Gray, Keats, Shelley, Coleridge, Tennyson, Matthew Arnold, and so many others of lesser repute but held in honourable remembrance.   Indeed, in Lakeland itself, even to this day, Wordsworth is not a name to conjure with among the natives. Christopher North is better remembered.   Tales of his physical prowess, however, have outlasted the tradition of his literary fame.   Even at Grasmere Wordsworth's name never signified to the native residents—has never become—what Ruskin's long meant, and now more than ever means, at Coniston. A friend who lives in the heart of Lakeland and has exceptional means of knowing how the Lakelanders think, assures me that Words-worth is very little read, and very little 'thought of'; in truth, he adds, there is no country in the world, except Switzerland, where poetry is so little valued or the poet as a native product so rare. And certainly in Lakeland, as in Switzerland, the observer cannot but note the singular paucity of folk-songs and ballads. Almost every alien dweller in the Lake Country has noticed this, and almost all are agreed upon the unpoetic nature of the people. Probably the general attitude is that of the gardener of a friend of the present writer: "Wordsworth and sic' like are for folk who dinna require to work for their livin', an' are no varry particular what they do *then*." My friend, finding this gardener once in a less utilitarian mood and willing to have a try at another poet associated with the Lakes, gave him Shelley, with advice as to 'The Sensitive Plant.' The gardener read no more: 'The Sensitive Plant' at once inculcated in him an emphatic distaste for and profound distrust of poetry. "A man who talked like that about a plant, whether it was sensitive or wasn't," he declared, "should never have left his father's trade, whatever that was." It has nothing to do with the question of the rural theme, or simplicity in the treatment of it; indeed, 'Peter Bell' and the like are rather resented as an imbecile presentment of the Westmorland intelligence. It is simply that poetry is 'not wanted here.' Perhaps the quantity of the imported article has dulled the native to any desire for more intimate acquaintance or to any wish for home-culture. The driver of an Ambleside coach remarked to me one day, apropos either of Wordsworth or Coleridge or of whomsoever's home we were approaching or had just passed, "the aggeravatin' thing about poetry is that it never tells you anything *straight*." There are a good many people, I fancy, who regard it in the same way. "The definite fact and no nonsense about it" is what they want. To these I can recommend a recent volume by a bard who veils his patronymic under the pseudonym 'Indicus.' It is called *The Olympiad : Classic Tales in Verse*, and here is the straightforward and sensible way in which we are instructed in the fable of Jove's love for the Spartan Leda, and his 'attempt to dissemble' by taking upon himself the semblance of a swan :—

> Finding Sparta's queen in wanton mood,
> *In course of time a pair of eggs appeared!*

But perhaps in Lakeland there is the same division as elsewhere —the majority who do not care, the few who do. And it must be admitted that they've had more than a fair allowance of poets and poetry 'up there'—and poetry, as has been chronicled, is "a gey ill thing to live wi' unless ye hev a fixt income." 'Up there,' too—and all Lakelanders in exile will recognise the brief home-phrase and the northward tilt of the head—they have their own way of estimating men and things. A Windermere lodging-house keeper remarked the other day to the friend who imparted it to me, that there is only one really important distinction among day-trippers: those with umbrellas are 'respectable'; those without, the reverse.

Of no region in the British Isles has so much high-falutin' been written as of the Lakes, though certainly much must be forgiven to enthusiasts for the lovely scenery of and around Ullswater, Derwentwater, Windermere, Wastwater, and Blea Tarn and its mountain - comrades. The eighteenth - century scribe began it with his 'horrid chasms' and 'appalling mountains.' Gray, so distinguished a poet, was not guiltless : on the contrary, he sinned so continually that now he is unread as a pleasing topographer. Even writers so recent as Mr. Dash or Miss Blank pass at times from the tolerable rhetorical to the intolerable hysterical. Here is how one of the elders in rodomontade wrote of pleasant Borrowdale valley: "Dark caverns yawn at its entrance, terrific as the wildness of a maniac, and disclose a narrow strait running up between mountains of granite, that are shook into almost every possible form of horror, and resemble the accumulations of an earthquake, splintered, shivered, piled, amassed." As Mrs. Lynn Linton, who quotes this gem, comments, Borrowdale is no more maniacal than Windsor Park.

Although Charles Lamb might be considered the last person to turn to for the corrective of simple statement of unaffected pleasure in nature (in the sense that his love was for the town and the town's ways and town-life), how delightful to turn from writing such as that quoted—and in degree still far too much indulged in—to what he says of Skiddaw (not 'shook into almost every' or any 'possible form of horror') : " Oh, its fine black head, and the bleak air atop of it ! " adding, " it was a day (the day he and his sister Mary made the ascent) that will stand out like a mountain, I am sure, in my life." Or, again, there's Keats. On his ascent of Skiddaw, he tells us, he was glad of some rum : "I took two glasses going, and one returning. . . . All felt, on arising into the cold air, that same elevation which a cold bath gives one. I felt as if I were going to a Tournament." These be human utterances, and worth lakefuls of the hill-road 'dreadfully sublime' and 'the tremendous wilds' of Mrs. Radcliffe (who made her famous journey here just two hundred years ago) and her followers. Truly, as she said of the air of Skiddaw or Helvellyn, their enthusiasm " is very thin and difficult to be inspired." One sympathises at times with the cautious tourist who, to the chagrin of coachman or guide, ignores information and responds with melancholic indifference. On one such occasion, on the beautiful drive over Furness Fells from Bowness to Coniston by way of Esthwaite Water and Hawkshead (through

the region of Wordsworth's boyhood and of the scenery and
poetry of 'The Prelude') the coach-driver, become a cynic by
bitter experience, confided to me that in a half-full coach
"there's aye some one who has seen the like elsewhere, an'
better too . . . real dampers they are, that folk." I told him,
to his keen appreciation, a story I had heard or read, somewhere, of a man of this kind, an ultra-cautious Scot, who, at
Niagara, stood silent before the 'how lovelys' and 'how magni-
ficents' and 'how stranges' of his American host, but at last
to repeated appeals brought himself to admit, "I'll no deny
but it's bonnie in its way, but as for *queerness* I once saw a
peacock at Peebles wi' a wooden leg."

But there's another breed of fellow-traveller to be regarded
askance. They come to the Lakes as the locust upon Egypt.
These are they who fall into raptures or amazements over the
most trivial things, and gather and retail these informations as
though of vital interest and significance in connection with this
or that poet—as who should say that Wordsworth's palate had
a tickling longing for sage, or that Coleridge invariably drank
a glass of small beer at dinner, or that Ruskin was wont to
partake of a single egg of a morning. The contagion thereof
is spread even unto those who ought to know better. Among
the many hardly illuminative anecdotes 'of the great departed'
which are included in Canon Rawnsley's industriously compiled
mélange of Lake-notes, for example, are some as valuable as the
'personal record' of a dalesman who confided to his listener the
important item that Wordsworth "went upo' Sundays to
church wid a girt big prayer-beuk under his arm . . . I've
seed his jaws gáán when he was saying 'I believe' manny a
time." This tells neither way, as, on the contrary, does that
excellent and characteristic anecdote which relates how a
worthy statesman (Westmorland for a yeoman-proprietor)
went miles out of his way to attend a political meeting,

attracted by the announcement that the Poet-Laureate would address the assemblage, but abruptly left in high dudgeon when he saw that the mysterious magnate was "nobbut old Wadswuth o' Rydal efter aw!"—or that of the stone-breaker who told Hartley Coleridge (apropos of Wordsworth having passed that way, 'humming' his lines as he walked) "that ald Wadsworth's brocken lowce ageean." This idea of poetic pre-occupation being nothing other than temporary mania, to be regarded more or less seriously according to the respectability and station of the sufferer, appears to have been general throughout the dales immortalised by the Lake Poets. As a contemporary of Wordsworth remarked, "I daresay he's quite sensible, whiles, if ya nobbut catch him reet." That, no doubt, is the difficulty with poets, to catch them 'reet.' Southey probably thought he had done this when he wrote to his friend Bedford one January day in 1812: "There is a man here in Keswick who acts upon me as my own ghost would do. He is just what I was in 1794. His name is Shelley." But he hadn't 'caught him reet,' as he found later: an experiment where few succeeded, though Southey (who more closely resembled Shelley in intellectual sensibility and in person than any other poet of his day or since has done) knew him as Matthew Arnold in his cold egoism never perceived him even through the light of his genius at its highest, as even the far more catholic and sympathetic Rossetti never understood him, considering him as madder than the ordinary madman.*

If one could be transported to the top of Helvellyn or

---

* Tourists to Keswick who visit Greta Hall should not forget among its Southeyan and many other associations that it was here Mrs. Southey 'confected' that buttered cake which the enraptured Shelley desired 'to eat for ever.' Strange that so much seeming interest should be taken in Southey, now so little read, while Shelley's Lakeland home, Chestnut Hill, close by, is so rarely visited. The charming cottage is still much as it was in his day, and when I last saw it, one day in May, was in a gay environment of hepatica and the yellow Cambrian poppy, that bright banneret of spring in Lakeland. This was the garden where Shelley puzzled the natives by "making flames at nights in bottles and what not, instead of going to church."

Skiddaw or Great Gavel (or Gable) or Seat Sandal, that would
be the way to see Lakeland—all the country of the poets
beneath and beyond, from Solway Water, which Scott saw
from a Cumberland height with sudden emotion and longing, to
that gleam of wet sands and lifted whiteness south of Black
Coomb, where Turner watched the sunset moving like a fading
fan of flame.   What invisible company, too, from Keats to
delicate Mary and Charles Lamb, from that brilliant and fervent
Dorothy Wordsworth and her great brother to Tennyson and
Edward Fitzgerald!   We might even be content with some
lesser height, as that 'thousand-footer' (as Mr. Payn calls it)
Golden Howe, overlooking Thirlmere and St. John's Vale—the
one and only 'elevation' (with the exception of Primrose Hill
or Hampstead Rise) ever climbed by Rossetti.   To St. John's
Vale, it will be remembered, the poet-painter came in the sad
later days of his life, but left the hoped-for Avalon of Lakeland
within a month, no longer being able (in Dorothy Wordsworth's words of William) for solitary feastings with Silence.
But on the morrow of his arrival he and his companion, Mr.
Hall Caine, made the ascent of Golden Howe.   "We sat for
an hour on that highest point from whence could be seen the
Skiddaw Range to the north, Raven's Crag to the west, Styx
Pass and Helvellyn to the east, and the Dunmail Raise to the
south, with the lake below."   But neither thoughts of grandeur
or beauty nor pleasure in these came to Rossetti, already over-
worn by life to concentration only upon his own ills and
longings.   Very different the exaltation and outlook of Wordsworth, as recorded in the second book of 'The Prelude'; or the
spiritual emotion of Carlyle, who in *Sartor Resartus* reiterates
his thoughts on that day he ascended and looked abroad from
the summit of Great Gavel: " A hundred and a hundred savage
peaks, like giant spirits of the wilderness; there in their silence,
in their solitude, even as on the night when Noah's Deluge first

dried. Beautiful, nay solemn, was the sudden aspect to our Wanderer. He gazed over those stupendous masses with wonder, almost with longing desire; never till this hour had he known Nature, that she was One, that she was his Mother and divine. . . . A murmur of Eternity and Immensity, of Death and of Life, stole through his soul; and he felt as if Death and Life were one; as if the Earth were not dead; as if the Spirit of the Earth had its throne in that splendour, and his own spirit were therewith holding communion."

From one of these heights how easy in imagination to float down at once to Greta Hall or Chestnut Hill or Mirehouse or Dove Cottage or Rydal Mount or Briery Close or Elleray or Storrs or Tent Lodge or Fox How or Brantwood, and be of the imagined company of Southey and Shelley, Wordsworth and Coleridge and De Quincey, of Charles Lamb and Charlotte Brontë and Scott, of Spedding and Arthur Hallam and Clough and Fitzgerald and Tennyson, of Christopher North (perhaps on the day of the great carnival on Windermere, for Sir Walter's delectation, as recorded by Lockhart), of the Arnolds, of the great and solitary Ruskin—so genial and fond of company and needing love as the body needs food, and yet throughout life intellectually so solitary. To which of these would we go first . . . or to yonder cottage below Skiddaw, where Keats wrote one of his lovely sonnets, or to yonder hillside inn in the Vale of St. John below Wythburn, where the author of *The House of Life* knew nothing of that peace of the hills so loved and reverenced by the greatest of English nature-poets—a peace known even to these sorrowful 'children of opium,' Coleridge and De Quincey, after a prolonged bout of poetic ecstasy handcuffed by dyspepsia on the part of the one, and an equally prolonged festival of high dreaming followed by diurnal visions of pursuing serpents on the high road on that of the other.

A score of guide-books will give the reader, more or less fragmentarily and more or less accurately, the chief details in connection with the more famous localities.   Let us glance, instead, for a moment at Mirehouse, by Bassenthwaite Water, near Keswick, about the time of Wordsworth's death, where James Spedding had for visitors 'Old Fitz' (Edward Fitzgerald) and Alfred Tennyson.   Here it was, in the summer of 1835, that Tennyson read to his friends, out of a little red book of manuscript, certain poems which he was slowly maturing for their publication when the hour was come—the 'Morte d'Arthur,' 'The Day-Dream,' 'The Gardener's Daughter,' and others.   What evenings these must have been, "when all the house was mute," as Fitzgerald says, when " mouthing deep his hollow *aes*," Tennyson read these as-yet-unknown poems in his deep billowing voice.   At times he and Fitzgerald would leave Mirehouse and go abroad: as on that day when the two spent some hours in a boat on Windermere one quiet afternoon of May, " resting on our oars, dreaming into the still water," " Alfred quoting from the lines he had lately read us from the manuscript of ' Morte d'Arthur,' about the lonely lady of the lake and Excalibur—

> Nine years she wrought it, sitting in the deeps '
> Upon the hidden bases of the hills."

" Not bad that, Fitz, is it ? " asked the poet.   And most of us surely have the same delight in it that he had, and that ' Old Fitz ' had.   Perhaps it was on this occasion that the comrades had a contest as to who could invent the weakest Wordsworthian line imaginable ; and *both* claimed the authorship of—

> A Mr. Wilkinson, a clergyman.

It was during one of Tennyson's rambles in this region that he met Hartley Coleridge, of whom all ' Lake ' reminiscences have so much to say, and the tradition of whose eccentric personality appears, among the Westmorlanders, to have outlived that of greater men with whom he is associated. Lord Tennyson told his son Hallam an anecdote about him which I do not recollect having seen chronicled elsewhere. Hartley had been asked to a luncheon or dinner at the house of some ultra-Presbyterian folk, and for a wonder had accepted, probably because his host, a minister, had ' cornered ' him. Always over-sensitive, he was habitually unable to endure the nervous strain of sustained silence among a company of strangers. In this Presbyterian household he found himself in a dreary and stiff-necked company indeed, the members of which apparently considered that a gloomy and unoccupied taciturnity was the best preparation for dinner. None spoke a word, and poor little large-eyed, pinch-faced Hartley endured it as long as he could. Suddenly, springing from his seat, he embraced the amazed daughter of the house and then abruptly decamped, leaving the company as astounded as it was scandalised.

Lord Tennyson was also fond of telling another story about Hartley Coleridge, about his having set off with three or four friends on a rambling expedition (from Low Wood on Windermere over by Troutbeck and Kirkstone Pass on the Ullswater route, a corroborative account declares) through the then unfrequented regions between the Brathay and the Lake of the Four Brothers. Suddenly it was noted that 'little Hartley' had mysteriously disappeared. The most thorough search revealed no trace of him. Some six weeks later he was observed emerging from a wayside inn, smiling gently. Tennyson, as every one else, loved him. Lovers of the prose and poetry of De Quincey and Wordsworth, of the journals of Dorothy Wordsworth, of the reminiscent pages of Coleridge and Charles Lamb and others whose names will readily recur, will need no reminder of the common love of and pity for this spirit of frail genius set in a shattered constitution in a small and enfeebled frame.

Ruskin and Tennyson, these are the two greatest of recent
names associated with the Lakes—for Carlyle and Emerson
were but passing visitors.   And what a library of books has
been written about this Lakeland region, and, to adopt a line
of Keats, the great spirits who sojourned there!   A librarian at
Windermere told me that, ' years ago,' he had counted the
hundredth novel or volume of stories relating to the Lakes.
Since that account there has been at least one notable work of
fiction among many deservedly or undeservedly forgotten novels,
Mrs. Humphry Ward's *Helbeck of Bannisdale*; but having
mentioned that I must not omit allusion to two other little-
known but delightful saga-stories, by Ruskin's good friend and
biographer, Mr. W. G. Collingwood.   For me, at least, one of
the great fascinations of Lakeland is its Kymric and Norse past,
and those who share this interest in any direction should obtain
Mr. Collingwood's Viking saga-tales of Westmorland, *Thorstein
of the Mere* (Coniston region) and *The Bondswoman* (Windermere region).   I think it is in the former, but possibly in both,
that the author has included a most interesting map of the Lake
Country, with all the Norse and Celtic names before the last
Vikings were driven from the fells, and the Anglo-Saxon
invasion compelled the Brythons to seek refuge in the Cambrian
wilds or beyond the Solway Firth.

For the Wordsworth lover—no, for the lover of poetry
(for in this book is the very quintessence of Wordsworth as a
nature-poet, and therefore of some of what is noblest and
loveliest in English literature)—I can recommend no small
volume for the pocket as companion here, there, and everywhere, better than Professor Knight's delightful little *English
Lake District: as interpreted in the Poems of Wordsworth*, in the
size and of the general appearance of the familiar *Golden Treasury*
series, though not of it.   Many a traveller in these parts must,
I am sure, have come to know and love Wordsworth through

this best of silent companions. One wishes only that it contained more of the notes and letters of Dorothy Wordsworth; better still, perhaps, that a 'Dorothy' volume should go with it. Dorothy Wordsworth and Jane Welch Carlyle—these two brilliant and original women merely 'supplemented' brother and husband, and yet even if we had no Charlotte Brontë or Jane Austen or 'George Eliot,' no Mrs. Gaskell among the chroniclers of genius or no Miss Kingsley among the chroniclers of dark countries and savage races, we could still realise that the genius of English literature has not been solely the heritage of men. And there are some who would join with these two names that of another woman of the Wordsworth day, Sara Coleridge, whose *Phantasmion* has still its fragrance and charm, though now so little remembered.

What a pity there is no small volume which would give us in connection with Ruskin somewhat in kind with what Professor Knight has given us in connection with Wordsworth! It would have to begin with Friar's Crag, that beautiful pine-clad promontory on Derwentwater, below Keswick; for it was here that John Ruskin as a child had that first unforgettable " glimpse of the beauty and wonder and charm of the English Lakes." To-day an inscribed monolith commemorates the record; and though this, and the many iron seats, and the continual coming and going of townsfolk and visitors, take away much from the charm of this enchanted spot, once so isolated in a virginal wayward loveliness, it still remains one of the most beautiful of Lakeland localities, still affords one of the loveliest and grandest of Lakeland outlooks.

And, of course, such a book would have to end with the granite obelisk in Coniston churchyard, under the shadow of that 'Old Man' upon whose vast cloud-shadowed shoulder Ruskin used to look with ceaseless affection every morning and evening while he was at Brantwood, and was wont to remember with longing when a breath of cool air came on his brows across the heats of Lugano or Como, or when the shadow of the mountain-wind rose or fell on the slopes of the Jungfrau, or among the precipices of Chamounix.

A brief while ago I stood on the Ferry Nab, halfway up Windermere, watching a rising wind turning the dark amber and blue of the water—after weeks of calm and unwonted drought—into a moaning and whispering blackness, while round every island or ' holm,' from Seamew Crag and Bee Holm and Green Love, up Ambleside way, to Lady Holm and Curwen's Isle, under Claife Woods, and so to Grass Holm and Ling Holm, beyond the dense groves of historic Storrs, a fringe of greyness widened to a tangled wind-tormented scarf of stormy white. It is not often, save in late autumn or mid-winter, that one sees a storm change the serene beauty of Windermere to the wildness of a tormented sea on a lonely coast.   At times, however, the waves that race towards the Nab are like the billows of the sea on a shallow sandy shore.   And by some subtle association I recalled an evening, many years ago—some seventeen or eighteen it must be—when, a guest at Brantwood, I stood by Mr. Ruskin's side, at a window overlooking Coniston Water.   True, the lake was calm, and there was only a continuous low whisper in the dense foliage beyond the house; but a gale was breaking itself against the granite and green slate of the ' Old Man,' and a fierce tumult came eddying down the glens.   Mr. Ruskin had been showing me some of the lovely and numerous uncut or unset gems he collected with such insatiable delight, and had been asking insistently, but as one questioning himself, "*How* were these made ?—*how* were these made ? There is genius here. Yes, genius," and then, after a spell of silence in the room, he said : "This Lake Country, it also has a genius.   And listen, look —that genius is abroad to-night.   There will be a change in everything to-morrow, for good or evil."

Yes, the Lake Country has a genius. Many must have noted this who have dwelt long by its fells and meres. Lakeland is unlike any other mountain-region. None could mistake it for Scotland; it is distinct from highland Wales; and even the Lakes of Killarney have merely accidental resemblances. The whole land is under a kind of enchantment. The mountains have a singular look, as if they were in a conscious suspense, as if in a dreaming or brooding trance, a meditation unawakened from age to age. "It may be only a matter of mist and invisible vapour," as (I think) Professor Tyndall declared, but the poets go nearer when they speak of the conscious quiescence of these lovely heights. Matthew Arnold was merely literary when in one of his poems he alluded to " the cheerful silence of the fells " ; that was the utterance of a holiday-maker in good company. No other poet before or since Wordsworth has written of this ' cheerful ' silence. From the low shores of the southward ends of Coniston and Windermere to where Bassenthwaite and Derwentwater mirror the clouds drifting from Skiddaw or Helvellyn, or where the solitary raven flies by desolate Wastwater or beautiful mountain-circt Blea Tarn or lovely Hawes Water, the same veil of a peculiar because not a sombre or even sad melancholy has been woven by that genius of the Lake Country, of which Ruskin spoke that night many years ago at Brantwood when stillness was upon the mere and a faint whisper in the woods of Coniston Fells, but when tempest was unloosed upon the forehead of that giant ' Warder at the Southern Gate ' loved by our greatest modern master of English prose with reverence in passion and with awe in delight.

And now one farewell word of advice. Let it be in the words of Southey, who wrote from long knowledge and true love. "Summer," he declares, "is not the season for this country. Coleridge says, and says well, that it is like a theatre at noon. There are no *goings-on* under a clear sky. . . . [One must know it at midwinter.] The very snow gives new varieties; it brings out the recesses of the mountains, and designates all their inequalities; it impresses a better feeling of their height; and it reflects such tints of saffron, or fawn, or rose-colour, to the evening sun. . . . The lake-side has such ten thousand charms: a fleece of snow, or of the hoar frost, lies on the fallen trees and on large stones; the grass points are powdered with diamonds; the ice on the margin with chains of crystal, and such veins and wavy lines of beauty as mock all art; and, to crown all, Coleridge and I have found out that stones thrown upon the lake, when frozen, make a noise like singing-birds; and when you whirl on it a large flake of ice, away the shivers slide, chirping and warbling like a flight of finches."

But, of course, one might keep on quoting indefinitely. I recall the solemn admonition in Dorothy Wordsworth's Journal : " To-day William wasted his mind in the magazines." And so, enough.

THE THAMES FROM OXFORD TO THE NORE.

THE literary geography of the Thames! Is not this a more hazardous undertaking than our recent itinerary of the Lake Country, or of that which follows on the long waters of Geneva? For who could number the many who have written about, or sung of, or dwelt beside, or had some abiding association with our great river—even if only unwilling baptism such as befel Mr. Verdant Green, or such undignified immersion as was the damp fate of Sir John Falstaff when, his huge bulk secured in the buck-basket, he was so ignominiously chucked into the deep flood by Datchet Mead? Since Chaucer crossed 'Thamesis' in the Tower ferry or Shakespeare recrossed from Southwark to the reedy shore of silt and mud known as the Strand, till Samuel Pepys 'took barge' (with pretty Mrs. Manuel singing all the way) to visit friends by the sequestered and rural hamlet of Putney, what a far cry! What a far cry, again, till, in Gravesend Reach, David Copperfield says good-bye to Peggotty and Mrs. Gummidge . . . or, on another occasion, Mr. Micawber and the twins pass from our ken . . . or till Mr. William Black entertains us with his house-boat on the upper reaches; or till we see William Morris, walking Hammersmith riverside in swift twilight travellings, as though to overtake some caravan beyond price, pondering ideal Thames scenes (alas, remoter now even than then, for the desecration of the jerry-builder is now on every wayside) to be limned in ' A Dream of John Ball,' or in ' News from Nowhere ' ; or till,

P

in a roomy old boat on the upper waters below Kelmscott
Manor, near Lechlade, we have a glimpse of Rossetti writing
part at least of his lovely 'Stream's Secret'; or till, 'by still
Isis,' Matthew Arnold wanders, conning the stanzas of 'The
Scholar Gypsy,' . . . in a word, from Chaucer to Milton, from
Milton to Shelley, from Shelley to the latest true poet of the
Thames, Mr Robert Bridges, what a catalogue of sounding
names !

That way, however, lies the scribe's dilemma. He must
either strive to be inclusive [an impossibility in a volume,
even, for some industrious idler would always pounce upon
something or somebody forgotten] and therefore relapse into
a graceless chronicle—as though one were to describe the
National Gallery by a transcription from the catalogue of the
names and birth-and-date particulars of all the artists represented; or else he must deal so fragmentarily with a multi-
farious theme as to disappoint the reader who wants Thames
statistics, or exasperate those who desire all the respectable old
'tags' to be trotted out in good guide-book order. And there
are some whom in any case it would be impossible to satisfy
. . . as that inquirer who wondered if Pope's Villa at
Twickenham had ever been temporarily occupied by a Holy
Father in exile.

As nothing is to be gained by repetition of the hackneyed
chronicle of Thames-side associations already so plentifully
extant, will it not be better to relinquish any attempt to take
reach by reach, parish by parish, village or town by town or
village, 'twixt Gravesend and Oxford? Books of all kinds,
dealing with the subject—literary, artistic, dramatic, political,
commercial, aquatic, natural-historic, botanic, and scandalous—
can be more or less easily consulted. There is the voluminous
tome of *Our Royal River*, with its letterpress by several able
'Thamesters' and many illustrations, or Mrs. S. C. Hall's like-

wise bulky and venerable 'stand-by'; there are the annual
cheap volumes of Dickens' *Dictionary of the Thames*, and
half a dozen booklets more or less interesting and more or less
trustworthy issued by Penny Steamboat Companies or other
enterprising publishing firms of the like unconventional kind.
Between the gaudy pamphlet of inconvenient shape and the
still more inconvenient but delightful *édition-de-luxe* of *Our
Royal River* are numberless volumes, represented in fiction by,
let us say, Mr. William Black's *Adventures of a Houseboat*,
and in pictorial art (and nothing much else of moment) by
pleasant book-making such as Mr. Leslie's *Painter's Chronicle* or
Mr. and Mrs. Pennell's *Stream of Pleasure*.

With these, and Baedeker and the local guide-books, one
cannot vie.

I propose, therefore, to take simply a rapid glance along
the great watercourse, from where the herons rise from the
reeds of often-looping Isis to where the seagulls scream about
the Nore or beat up against the east wind from the bleak
estuary shores where the gaunt Reculvers stand like wardens of
the Sea-Gate. Thereafter, to add in a more personal fashion
some notes concerning two or three great names not yet
exploited by the route-book or local manual; trusting, in doing
so, to be forgiven the egotism of reminiscence for the sake of
the men and things remembered, and for the supplement of
lesser-known literary associations to the Literary Geography of
the Thames.

But just a word first about the River. No, not a dithyramb.
Many have sung or magniloquently prosed its charms and
beauty, and at all seasons. It has had laudation at every turn,
from the Pool or Wapping Stairs at slimy ebb to the Bells of
Ouseley in odoriferous drought, when a lamb could step across
'Thames' onward-sweeping silent flood' in safety. If it can
allure poetic minds then, it may well do so at happier times

and at all points. To the true Thames-lover there is hardly a mile of it that has not its abiding spell. As for the Thames-lover who is also a familiar, has he not all the lovely and commonly ignored wintertide to delight in: the time when the frost-white boughs on eyot and hanger are lovely in their still beauty, and when in the backwaters the coots shake the snow like dust from sprays of alder and willow?

Nor, Reader, shall you have to suffer from timeworn anecdotes of Pope and Horace Walpole such as our grandfathers endured as hoary acquaintances; nay, what is more serious, not even of ' Mr. Walton '—as ' Old Izaak ' was recently named by an allusive reviewer. What microbe of ' Nomenclatururia ' is it, by the way, that makes some people invariably, in allusion to Shakespeare or Ben Jonson or Izaak Walton or Fitzgerald or Whitman, always speak of ' The Swan of Avon,' ' Rare Ben,' ' Old Izaak,' ' Old Fitz,' ' Good Old Walt '? However, that's another story, as Mr. Kipling would say.

As for one aspect of the Thames, the poets, from Spenser onwards, have been as superbly flattering as they are wont to be to their mistresses. Never trust a poet about his lady-love's beauty nor about the sea ; he is most conscious of the charms of each when he is remote from either. The folk-lorist of the future may take this as a wise saw among the common people of the Edwardian epoch.

That aspect is the illusion conveyed in the familiar epithet silvery. There has been enough epithetical silver lavished on the mud-saturated flood of Thames to have exhausted any other mint than that adjacent to the Fount of Eternal Ink. We love Spenser's ' silver-streaming Thames,' and Herrick's ' silver-footed Thamesis' is a delightful image ; but it is a pity that when every successive Mr. Brown brings out a new volume of sonnets, or every successive Miss Jones a new effusion of 'miscellaneous pieces,' there should not be some variation in this metallic *cliché*. Besides, it isn't true. The rain of sunshine and the ripple of wind would make the sluice of a maltster 'silvery.' Thames-water ceases from such refinement as soon as Isis, Churn, Coln, and Leach have travelled from the Cotswolds, and speed together east of Oxford *en route* to grasp the tired hand of the upreaching sea-tide that slips under Richmond Hill and wavers and falls away at Teddington.

Some day, perhaps, a new Michael Drayton or Water-Poet successor to Taylor will attempt the epic of Thames, as the great Provençal poet Mistral has achieved the epic of the Rhone. He will have to sing also the beauty and charm of the tributary waters that swell its flood, from pastoral Churn to the moist discharge that oozes from Medway flats. There are some of us who love the Mole and the Loddon, the Kennet and the Windrush almost as we love their 'eternal bourne.' By the way, it is by no means commonly known that the Thames is not really entitled to the royal name till Dorchester, near which the Thame joins the Isis-cum-Churn-cum-Coln-cum-Leach (or Lech). As for the name 'Isis,' the old idea that it is a survival of *Thamesis* is no longer admitted. Learned dwellers by the stream which laves Oxford's meadows tell us that 'Isis' is a quasi-classical form of 'Ouse.' It is at least more reasonable than Mr. Verdant Green's idea that it had something to do with the great goddess of the Egyptians.

The very names of these tributaries and upper reaches and backwaters, how they thrill one, at a distance, in remembrance! And their associations—especially by the banks of the Cherwell, and the Isis meadows beyond Oxford. But Oxford! . . . that would require an article to itself, merely to enumerate names. It is a task not to be attempted. Even a chronicle of modern days is impracticable. But all lovers of much of what is loveliest in our Victorian literature will think of how so many poets walked and roamed by these waters, what vivid impulses arose or were discussed within sight of the towers of Oxford. Here was Matthew Arnold's 'waterway to Eden.' Here the two young undergraduates, William Morris and Edward Burne-Jones, went their first walk with a young poet and painter of whom they had heard much, Dante Gabriel Rossetti—who had come to Oxford to paint those strange, crude, but potently new and significant frescoes for the 'Union,' which became the torch that set on fire the modern decorative movement, with all deeper and beyond what the phrase carries. Here the youthful Swinburne — "the man who knows the Greek dramatists like an old Athenian, and has hair like flame blown upon by the wind," as a contemporary described him—began, in his swift, impatient, solitary walks, the first working out in poetic drama of the tragical history of Mary Queen of Scots. Here the most famous of the Masters of Balliol was fond of walking with a friend, with his lips sweet with honey of old wisdom, and his eyes alert and smiling at the aspect of young and unwise life on the river-reaches. Here Walter Pater thought out many of his essays, composed many of those sentences of amber and pale gold which link the flawless chain of 'Marius the Epicurean.' But one might go on with name after name—and besides, we are coming near the cohort of the living !

   " Spenser and Sir John Denham and Pope are good enough as literary associations," some may think.   Well, for those who love the old just because it is the old, and never find the out-worn other than the pleasanter for being threadbare and infirm with age, let joy be had where it can be obtained.   For all the great authority of Dryden, who considered Sir John's 'Cooper's Hill' then, and for ever, " for the majesty of its style, the standard of exact writing," one degenerate at least must admit that, except as a sedative on a day of dull rain, when no riverine exercise is to be enjoyed, the famous masterpiece of the Caroline poet is a most deadly weariness. Every guide-book, every chronicler of 'A Day on the River,' 'Up the Thames,' 'Down the Thames,' 'On the Thames,' and so on in prepositional accumulation, alludes at more or less length, and with more or less ample quotation, to this 'great English poem'—which probably not three in a score of the scribes alluded to have ever read. Admittedly the finest lines in 'Cooper's Hill' are those of a quatrain added after years of recovery from the giant effort of the original production. They appear to have won the worshipful regard of the eighteenth century, and to have maintained their spell till the present year of grace.

> O could I flow like thee, and make thy stream
> My great example, as it is my theme !
> Though deep yet clear, though gentle yet not dull,
> Strong without rage, without o'erflowing full.

Excellent commonplace, and kindly good sense. But is it more than a rhymed copybook tag? As for its flawlessness, neither Mr. Gilbert nor Mr. Adrian Ross, these passed masters in modern metrical flights, has ever tried to join in wedlock terminals as innocent of rhyme as 'dull' and 'full.' There was (perhaps is) a bard of minor degree of whom Rossetti would never hear a word in favour, because in actual speech as well as in his written verse, he invariably (being Yorkshire-bred, I expect) pronounced 'full' and 'pull' and 'push' as though rhyming to 'hull' and 'gull' and 'hush.' As inconsequential, perhaps, as Heine, when he delighted in a graceless acquaintance, whom he ever recalled with a glow of pleasure, just because of the singular way in which he (or she) 'turned over' the letter *r*.

Well, 'tis a far cry now, anyway, back to 'Cooper's Hill'

—written, it is strange to think, within a quarter of a century of Shakespeare's death. All the same, the dweller in Egham and its neighbourhood, both on the Surrey bank and opposite, will find faithful portraiture in the 'harmonious numbers' of this famous poem:

> *Though short, yet long, of gentle* ennui *full,*
> *Without a rival picturesquely dull!*

But we have slipped past I know not how many miles, 'without o'erflowing full' of literary associations—and have not even delayed at Great Marlow, with its memories of Shelley, where the young poet, afterwards to become so great, wrote 'The Revolt of Islam,' and pondered how best to assist the Almighty to reconstitute a mismanaged universe. Here Shelley spent so many happy days, sailing far up or down the winding river, or cloud-shadow hunting, or drifting under the lower trees of Cliveden woods, which 'Alastor' loved so well, and William Morris thought of indifferently as 'rather artificial.'

I remember hearing, but cannot recollect where or from whom—possibly Dr. Furnivall, whose father lived at Great Marlow, and was both friend and physician to the young poet —an anecdote of Shelley akin to a delightful story given to the world on the authority of Mr. Andrew Carnegie. Two fishermen in a punt were drifting down stream, when they caught sight of a boat ahead of them, with a slim figure crouching at the bows and staring into the water as though spell-bound, and apparently by horror rather than by piscatorial frenzy. One angler thought the young gentleman intended suicide, while his companion fancied that the man's transfixed despair indicated the loss of his flask. But, when they came close, Shelley—for it was he—answered their inquiry blandly to the effect that he was simply watching his own corpse, as 'the thing in the water' unquestionably seemed to resemble him closely. The two anglers did not wait to drag 'the thing':

A Corner of the Pool.

BATTERSEA

BLACKFRIARS.

A peep at Tilbury Fort

Folly Bridge, Oxford.

Looking up from Wapping. Pelican Stairs

LIMEHOUSE: High water.

MAGDALEN BRIDGE, OXFORD.

before they got far, they saw Shelley hoist his little lateen sail and go off happily and imperturbably before the wind.

However, for imperturbability, the story that Mr. Carnegie is fond of relating to his friends is unsurpassable in kind. An American cyclist was skirting the shore of a solitary Highland loch, and noticed a boat in which was a man languidly examining the depths with a water-telescope. Now and again he would pause and chat with a friend who sat on the bank reading a newspaper; or he would lay down the telescope and light his pipe. The American, who had dismounted, could not restrain his curiosity, and at last asked the idler on the bank, "What is your friend looking for? Oysters?" 'No,' was the matter-of-fact reply,—' my brother-in-law.'

Well, we must leave Great Marlow and Shelley, though both invite to tie-up awhile in beautiful Maidenhead Reach or under Cliveden's gigantic green shadow. It was here, if I remember aright, that the poet of revolution and social reformation, and other -*tions* and -*isms*, projected that ideal marital union whereto the consenting parties should be not two but three. Alas, we have fallen back again into our old ways, and the Revolt of the Married Poet is still *in esse* an unconstitutional performance! As has been sagely remarked, moreover, the highest tides of feeling do not visit the coasts of triangular alliances! *A propos*, if any reader has visited or should visit pleasant Bisham, a short way above Great Marlow, he may remember or newly note with gentle pleasure the touching tombstone-lines of a Mrs. Hoby, staunch upholder of the good old doctrine that Marriage is *not* a Failure :—

> Give me, O God! a husband *like* unto Thomas,
> Or else *restore* to me my husband Thomas.

Hopeless, alas, to attempt even the most superficial exploitation of the Windsor neighbourhood. One place, in

particular, however, is hallowed ground.   At Horton, near
Wraysbury, on the Colne, is where Milton lived for the first
five or six years of his fruitful early manhood after he left
Cambridge.   Here he wrote that supreme threnody 'Lycidas,'
here also he wrote 'Comus' and the 'Arcades,' and possibly
'L'Allegro' and 'Il Penseroso.'   As we drift down Windsor
way, coming from Maidenhead, or whence westward we come,
many must recall his—

> Towers and battlements . . .
> Bosom'd high in tufted trees

Then Chertsey, Hampton, Laleham, Datchet, with associations
of Cowley, Garrick, Dr. Arnold of Rugby, Sir Henry Wotton
and Izaak Walton—places recalled at random, with names
recollected at hazard : but what a wealth of association all down
the waterway of this region of our love and pride! Above all,
when Eton meadows and the elms of Windsor Park come into
view . . . who does not thrill then if perchance remembering
that here some three hundred years ago (*i.e.* in 1593)—because
of the Plague in London—*The Merry Wives of Windsor* was
first acted before Queen Elizabeth!   What would one give to
see that woodland cavalcade and laughing processional array,
with Shakespeare, it may be, walking by the Queen's palfrey to
the spot where the play was to be acted.   It is said—it is a legend
only, but we can credit it—that Elizabeth wanted to see the
great Falstaff worsted in a new way, and thus (by command, as
we should say now) Shakespeare wrote for the delectation of
the royal lady and her court his delightful *Merry Wives*.

After Windsor is left, the lower reaches simply swarm
with 'associations.'   But among the many famous names that
need not be specified, as doubtless familiar, and certainly
chronicled in full by river-manual or local guide-book, let the
wayfarer recall for a moment at Mortlake (which Turner so

loved) that unfortunate Partridge (the astrologer, not 'September's fowl') whom Swift and Steele tormented so sorely. The poor man lies here at peace at last, after those exasperating later years when Steele would write his obituary, and on his indignant protest that he was alive and prophesying still, was informed that he *must* be dead, as his own almanac had foretold the event. The unfortunate man made a desperate final attempt not to be shelved to the shades while still in the portly flesh, but the attempt failed, and he had to endure a fresh obituary article about himself with added picturesque details of the funeral.

At Twickenham, as already promised, we shall not linger, though it was the Ferney of the eighteenth-century literary world, as Pope was the English Voltaire. As for Horace Walpole, was not he the artificial sinner who outraged every tradition of genuine English poetry or prose, from Chaucer to William Morris, by writing of 'enamelled meadows with filigree hedges'?

And so we slip on down stream, past Richmond . . . so 'replete,' it, the Park, and the 'Star and Garter,' with Georgian anecdote and early Victorian reminiscence ! . . . to Barn Elms. "Mighty pleasant," wrote Pepys, "the supping here under the trees by the waterside." Here that ever genial old youth came, on a memorable occasion, on a barge from the Tower, 'a mighty long way,' with Mistress Pepys and maid and page, and dames Corbet, Pierce, and Manuel, "singing all the way, and Mistress Manuel very finely." Here he and his strolled and scandalised and laughed under the elms by moonshine . . . "and then to barge again and more singing." 'Tis a Watteau picture. Would we could look on its like again! Now the route is by the crowded excursion-steamer, and 'Arry and 'Arriet do the rest. Pepys and Evelyn and all of that blithe company would sniff 'mightily' now, I fear, at all riverside resorts, from the

Bells of Ouseley, fragrant of tea and buttered buns, down to remote Gravesend, where still, as of yore, at Mrs. Brambles' of Hogarth's day, tea and shrimps inevitably concur.

As we pass Putney and Hammersmith and Chelsea, what memories of great names past and present! Beyond the old bridge at Putney the great Gibbon was born and 'had his schoolings'; and a short way up the Rise is the house where Mr. Swinburne has so long resided, and with him, at The Pines, Mr. Theodore Watts-Dunton. The famous poet-critic-romancist has so many visitors that it is rumoured the High Street will soon be renamed Aylwin Avenue! At Hammersmith, as every one knows, William Morris had the London home of his later years. To a mean little house in a poor neighbourhood, here, the great American romancist, Nathaniel Hawthorne, made a pilgrimage, in order to pay homage to Leigh Hunt, when in his silver-haired, beautiful old age that sunny-hearted poet and prince of delicate things lived there in poverty and isolation.* As for Chelsea, is not 'the sage of Chelsea' already a byword and a phrase? But fewer know that a short way from Cheyne Row, where the great philosopher-historian lived so long, is the house (16, Cheyne Walk) occupied during the latter part of his life by the poet-painter Dante Gabriel Rossetti. To this house came, gladly and proudly, all who could win the privilege of entry; here, as has been said, many of the most famous pictures and many of the most famous books of our time were discussed in advance, and in some instances projected. Rossetti's house, in a word, was from 1871 till 1881 the Mecca of the 'romantic' devotee in both pictorial and literary art. We are not dealing with the artistic associations of the Thames—to use the word in its common significance—or Mr. Whistler and others would delay us. The

---

* Hawthorne contributed a long and interesting account of this visit to the *Atlantic Monthly* about thirty years ago (1874, I think).

literary and artistic history of Chelsea, indeed, would be of more interest and importance than that of any other part of London, in connection with the study of the literary and artistic history of the later Victorian epoch.

Well, down stream we go, past Blackfriars, where once Rossetti and Mr. George Meredith in early days had rooms, and where both Dickens and Thackeray found a never-ceasing fascination. Below the vast new bridge and past the Tower, with a glimpse of Traitor's Gate,

> . . . through which before
> Went Essex, Raleigh, Sidney, Cranmer, More,

and so through The Pool, the maelstrom heart of London. How painters, from Turner to Whistler, have loved this grimy but ever inspiring and wonderful water-heart, whence all the countries of the world may bring tribute to London, and in which London sees as in a crystal (alas! that it is but a metaphor!) all lands and nations from California to Cathay. One living painter has, in ' Wapping Old Stairs,' seized the poetry of The Pool, and fortunately Mr. W. L. Wyllie's picture is now a national possession. It goes without saying that Dickens, Marryat, Clark Russell loved The Pool only this side of idolatry. Readers of this series of Literary Geography will recollect how the heroine of Charlotte Brontë's *Villette* set off alone and friendless one wet and stormy night from here, and the strong, vivid etching of the scene. What lovers of *Our Mutual Friend* and *Great Expectations* do not know intimately all this haunted region, from where The Pool becomes The Port, till the great tower of Westminster recedes from view, and the river—with hoys swinging sideways, and barges veering wildly, and every kind of craft as seemingly at the mercy of malicious river-sprites—sweeps on to the Isle of Dogs (once the Isle of Ducks . . . in days when the bittern was common in Plumstead Marshes, and when the curlew and the lapwing wailed over waste places where now the electric tram screeches or the coster howls)?

But before the City is left, who will not remember that great sonnet of Wordsworth, composed at early morning upon Westminster Bridge, when

> This city now doth like a garment wear
> The beauty ot the morning . . .
>   . . . the very houses seem asleep,
> And all that mighty heart is lying still.

As for Southwark, are not its associations among the greatest we have? Chaucer, Shakespeare, these two names alone make this (now, alack, far from attractive) region supreme among all the boroughs of London. Here was the Globe Theatre, where, so to speak, the banner of the Elizabethan drama flew so gallantly at the peak. Many will recall the fact of the sudden conflagration of the Globe, three years before Shakespeare's death, during a performance of 'Henry VIII.' Not far from the old theatre, in the High Street, was the Tabard Inn, whence adult English literature set forth upon its first high adventure. In the old church of St. Saviour's (anciently St. Mary Overies) lie the remains of learned John Gower, Chaucer's contemporary, and those of Chaucer himself; of Edmund Shakespeare, the brother of our great poet; of Philip Massinger, not the least dramatist of that marvellous period; and of John Fletcher, poet and dramatist, whose name, with that of his colleague Francis Beaumont, stands so high in the admiration of all who love the best literature of the great Elizabethans.

Thence, to the meeting of the sea-wind coming over Plumstead Marshes, or slumping the tide-wash against the ebb at Tilbury Fort, or causing the famous 'Thames Dance' at the Nore, or bearing inland the heavy booming of the guns of Shoeburyness, or making the grey-green seas surge like a mill-

race across the eighteen-mile reach from Whitstable to Foulness
Point . . . this is a journey indeed! And of Rotherhithe
(where still are inns bearing the old heroic Elizabethan designa-
tions of 'The Ship Argo' and 'The Swallow Galley'); of
Rosherville, of Greenwich and its park (Scots readers will recall
a great scene in Sir Walter Scott's one London romance, *The
Fortunes of Nigel*), of Gravesend and 'Farewell Haven' (lovers
of Dickens, Marryat, Clark Russell, of many from Smollett to
W. W. Jacobs, will regret so cursory a mention)—of these and
of every mile from The Port and the great wilderness of the
Docks, to where the solitary Reculvers watch the last dispersed
flood of Thames swallowed up by the sea . . . what a
chronicle might be written!

Truly, Thames-flood carries one on unwitting of the rapid
flow. I am come almost to an end of my space, and yet have
not even touched those more personal recollections which I had
in mind to commit. Well, some other time, perhaps. Meanwhile, they can be but alluded to. And then, too, the many
persons and episodes one has forgotten to chronicle! Sheridan,
for instance · how few think of him as 'a literary association'
of the Thames! Yet what reader of that delightful comedy,
'The Critic,' can have forgotten the inimitable scene at Tilbury
Fort, where the Governor's daughter genteelly goes mad in white
satin, and is accompanied into lunacy by the 'umble friend and
companion who, as becomes her meaner condition, respectfully
and discreetly goes out of her senses in ordinary white linen!

It is a far cry back from Tilbury to remote Lechlade, and
yet I would like to be there again, and starting with the
sympathetic reader on a new waterway pilgrimage. How well
I recollect the Trout Inn there, one May day, with its great
sycamore rustling in the lightsome west wind! In the sunny
little garden and orchard behind, under the fragrant shadow of
a great walnut-tree, a friend was seated, reading. Pale, some-

what heavily built, a student and thinker (as the least observant
could not but have discerned), low-voiced, sensitive as a leaf,
and yet with a restful composure all his own, Walter Pater read
a recently written and one of the loveliest chapters of a book,
from the first conceived in beauty, and to the end in beauty
achieved . . . the book now so surely gathered into English
literature, and known to all who care for what is finest and
rarest therein as *Marius the Epicurean.*

Then as to Kelmscott Manor, a cuckoo's flight away: a
whole article might well be given to this beautiful old riverside
place and its many associations.   The country home of William
Morris for twenty-five years, it has also many associations with
Rossetti, who for a year or two from 1871 was fellow-tenant
with and, as to occupancy, preponderant partner with Morris;
as also with Mr. Swinburne, Mr. Theodore Watts-Dunton,
Burne-Jones, and many others.   "Kelmscott Manor," wrote
Morris, and characteristically, in a letter in 1882, "has come
to be to me the type of the pleasant places of the earth, and of
the homes of harmless, simple people not overburdened with
the intricacies of life; and as others love the race of man
through their lovers or their children, so I love the earth
through that small space of it."   That, of course, was long after
the Rossetti-Morris days at this beautiful old riverside home:
indeed, it was written in the sad year of that great poet and
painter's death. There is a little island formed by the backwater
close to the house, and in spring this was always an Eden of
songbirds in a region which was and is the songbirds' paradise.
Here, and at the Manor, Rossetti wrote many of his loveliest
lyrics and sonnets, and the long and noble poem 'Rose Mary.'
Who has forgotten the music of 'Down Stream'?—

> *Between Holmscote and Hurstcote*
> *The river reaches wind,*
> *The whispering trees accept the breeze,*
> *The ripple's cool and kind*

At Kelmscott, also, he wrote (or rewrote from an earlier version) that lovely poem of some nine-score stanzas, ' The Bride's Prelude.' I recall how once, at Kelmscott, Morris turned to me, after he had been speaking of Tennyson and Browning and Matthew Arnold, as also of the poetry of Mr. George Meredith and of Mr. Swinburne — and, speaking generally, for the work of any of these poets he did not really at heart care much—and said abruptly, " Poetry has spoken only once in *absolute* beauty since Keats." Then, turning a volume in his hand and glancing once in a way at the page he opened, he recited, in that strange sing-song sea-sounding chant of his, the following lines, which open the poem of ' The Bride's Chamber' (as he called it, and as Rossetti had originally entitled it) :

'Sister,' said busy Amelotte
    To listless Aloyse;
'Along the wedding-road the wheat
Bends as to hear your horse's feet,
And the noonday stands still for heat.'

Amelotte laughed into the air
    With eyes that sought the sun
But where the walls in long brocade
Were screened, as one who is afraid
Sat Aloyse within the shade.

And even in shade was gleam enough
    To shut out full repose
From the bride's 'tiring chamber, which
Was like the inner altar-niche
Whose dimness worship has made rich.

Within the window's heaped recess
    The light was counterchanged
In blent reflexes manifold
From perfume caskets of wrought gold
And gems the bride's hair could not hold

Q

> All thrust together: and with these
> A slim-curved lute, which now,
> At Amelotte's sudden passing there,
> Was swept in somewise unaware,
> And shook to music the close air.

"There," he said, "there you have the unadulterated article. That's *poetry*. As for the rest of us, for the most part we write verse poetically."

Morris's likings in poetry were singular. Wordsworth he actually disliked: Milton, save in rare lines and on rarer occasions, had little appeal for him. For a little of Chaucer he would have relinquished all of Tennyson's work save his earlier verse: and Browning he considered "to have stopped climbing the hill" when he forsook the method and manner of his early manhood—though there was none whom he more loved to quote and extol in those far-off Oxford years, when, as one of his biographers has chronicled, the Morris of "the purple trousers of the Oxford days" had not matured to "the great simplicity and untidiness" of his middle age.

The last time I saw Morris at Kelmscott Manor was just such a day as that on which a year or two later he was buried in the little churchyard close by: a day of chill October, with a rainy wind soughing among the alders, and the damp chrysanthemum-petals blown about the garden-ways beneath a low grey sky. I think this was in 1894: at any rate, I recollect it was on a day when he had just received a welcome letter from Mr. Swinburne, relative to the publication by the Kelmscott Press of certain old thirteenth-century reprints of French prose. I remember the latest (or one of the later) volumes was lying on the table, near the window, against which a sleety rain pattered—the *Violier des Histoires romaines*—and in his letter about it Mr. Swinburne recalled their mutual delight in these old French prose-poems "in the days when we first foregathered in Oxford," . . . that is, forty years earlier, for it was in January, 1856, that, there, the young undergraduate Algernon Charles Swinburne first met Morris and Rossetti.

It was not at his beloved Kelmscott Manor, however, that William Morris died, though buried in the village graveyard; but at Kelmscott House, his London home in Hammersmith.

With him passed away one of the most fervent of Thames-lovers and one of the greatest of those who have set their seal upon the Royal River.

THE LAKE OF GENEVA.

Toi, notre amour, vieille Genève,
Dont l'Acropole a double autel,
Qui tiens la Bible et ceins le glaive,
Cité du droit, temple immortel ;
Toi, lac d'azur, dont l'eau profonde
Baigne l'Eden créé pour nous,
Sous quels cieux trouver, en ce monde,
Aïeux plus grands, berceau plus doux ?

AMIEL.—*Hymne à Genève.*

ET the travelled as well as the untravelled reader rest assured : I have not written of Lac Léman in order to describe Chillon and quote the deadly-familiar lines of Byron, nor to record the fact that a considerable change has come upon Lausanne since that innumerably chronicled hour, when, in an alley overlooking the lake, near midnight, Gibbon walked slowly to and fro alone, having just written the last lines of his great life-work—'his monumental masterpiece,' as the guide-book writers call it, as though it were the *chef d'œuvre* of an 'artist in funereal stone,' to quote the delightful designation of a proud Marylebonian. These things have been done to death. I am sure many tourists to the eastern end of the Lake of Geneva refrain at Vevey, or stand fast at Territet, because of this exploited Chillon, these exhausted associations, these paralysing quotations. It is a point of honour among residents at Montreux to ignore Bonnivard, and to become distant at any mention of Byron. Sometimes, on the steamer from Montreux to Villeneuve, or on the top of the electric Vevey-Territet car, when a group of tourists stare, some hungrily, some shamefacedly, upon Chillon, an uncontrolled mind breaks out in the timeworn Byronic quotation. It is always done with an air of new

discovery or of lightly-carried erudition, without pity for the sufferings of others. Then there is that island, wedded hopelessly to an inane couplet. No, if one wish to 'Byronise' (as a serious French writer has it), let it rather be at Ouchy, where, at the Anchor Inn, the poet spent pleasant days, or at the Villa Diodati on the Geneva shore, opposite Coppet, where 'Manfred' was written, and where Byron the poet is much more interesting than Byron the sentimentalist.

Of course they must be mentioned. As a matter of fact one could not sail eastern Geneva without a heard, read, or remembered Byron quotation or association; as a matter of surety one could not visit Lausanne without a real quickening at the thought of Gibbon as not last nor least among its 'associations.' True, the quickening slacks off considerably when one penetrates the Hôtel Gibbon, and particularly if one stays or has a meal, when the bill is apt to suffer of a dropsy because the visitor is a Briton and because (as an imported cockney-Swiss waiter may confide): "'Ere, sir, yessir, it was 'ere, sir, that the great Mr. Gibbon wrote 'is 'istory. View from the window, sir, when you 'ave your coffee. Wine list, sir?"

But the time is past to dwell upon them. Many scores, many hundreds belike, have, in connection with the Lake of Geneva, exploited these two great names. By Léman shores there is a contagious ailment, to Byronise, to Gibbonate. To read most guide-books and kindred chronicles, one would think the Lake had no other associations; that at most these are shared, though in lesser degree, by Voltaire and Rousseau only. And what a deal of eloquence always accompanies those reminiscences! I take up one familiar volume, and read that in the pleasant hotel-gardens are " the harmonious sounds of an almost invisible orchestra in the fleecy foliage of the glades, whose melodies mingle with, etc., etc.—delicious rocking of the soul and the senses in an immaterial atmosphere." The same enthusiast states that Annecy is the nurse of passion. Alas! my soul was never, along these lovely shores, deliciously rocked in an immaterial atmosphere; and, a conscientious St. Anthony *en voyage*, I avoided Annecy. The reader, therefore, must be content with little of Gibbon and less of Byron, and nothing of dithyrambic. A simple directness must be my humbler aim—if not quite the same simple directness as that of the American translator of Voltaire's *Princesse de Babylon*, who makes the Pharaoh of Egypt address the Princess Formo-

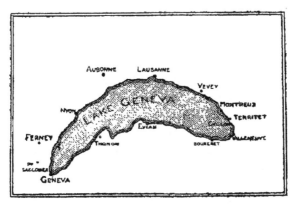

GENEVA AND ITS ENVIRONS

santa as "Miss, you are the lady I was in quest of"; or, again, "Miss," replied the King of Egypt, "I know life too well," etc.

This same Formosanta, by the way, has always struck me as a most delightful character and a veritable Princess Charming among the *princesses lointaines* of modern literature. Why is she not better known? How naïve her continual delightful reverie —as when she ponders profoundly on the certainly puzzling problem as to why the young man of her fancy should choose to ride a unicorn. Unicorns, it may be added, are for some singular reason as common in *La Princesse de Babylon* as are wicked baronets and dishonourable honourables in contemporary fiction. One is surprised that when the Pharaoh approaches Formosanta with select wooing-gifts he omits this useful animal in his present of two crocodiles, two sea-horses, two zebras, two Nile rats, and two mummies in prime condition. On the other hand, those who have read the tale will remember that, in an emergency, the obliging Phœnix forthwith ordered a coach with six unicorns. And what a Phœnix! What words of wisdom it communicates in and out of season! How far from Maeterlinckian in its freedom from mysticism, as when it remarks " Resurrection ? Why, resurrection is one of the most simple things in the world; there is nothing more in being born twice than once."

All which is not so inapposite as it may seem. For *La Princesse de Babylon* was written by the same waters where Calvin· brooded, where Amiel sadly pondered, where Dumas laughed and Tartarin gasconaded, etc., etc., etc.; yes, where Gibbon historiographed, and where Byron immortalised Bonnivard, and where Lady Rose's Daughter has been a recent visitor.

It would be impracticable to give a complete list of all the famous folk in art and literature in one way or another associated with the shores and towns of Lac Léman.* It is a kind of shore-set Cosmopolis. Julius Cæsar is a long way off, and Mrs. Humphry Ward is very much of to-day, but between these two scribes is an army of poets and novelists, essayists and philosophers, 'Alpestriens' like De Saussure (and, let us add, Tartarin), 'word-painters' like Rousseau and Amiel and our own great Ruskin. Switzerland itself gives many names, from the great

---

* I think it is Amiel who remonstrates somewhere on the habitual foreign and even French misuse of *Lac Léman* for *Lac du Léman*, but use and wont have now made the article obsolete, and even purists like M. Anatole France and M. Paul Bourget have concurred in the vulgarisation.

Jean Jacques to the much-loved romancist Töpffer and the still living Victor Cherbuliez—'this young conqueror,' "this young wizard of erudition and charm," as Henri Frédéric Amiel wrote of him more than forty years ago in the famous *Journal*. But it is France, with Voltaire, De Senancour, Stendhal, Mme. de Staël, George Sand, Dumas, Daudet, and others ; England, with Byron, Gibbon, Dickens, and a score more, from Ruskin, the literary high-priest of Switzerland, to more than one eminent novelist of to-day ; America with Longfellow and Mark Twain, Russia with Turgéniev, Germany with a battalion led by Goethe, Italy with Edmondo de Amicis and others, which contribute collectively far more to the roll-call than does the Helvetian Republic. Indeed, the chief Swiss critics themselves recognise that their country does not excel in literature and the arts, though they can say with pride that the most influential of all modern authors, Jean Jacques Rousseau, was not only born a Swiss, but lived the better part of his years and wrote the better part of his immense achievement in his native country. The one regret we have, said a Freiburg professor whom I met on a ' Nouvelle Héloïse' pilgrimage in the pleasant hill-country between Montreux and Vevey, "is that Rousseau lies at Ermenonville, in France, instead of at Geneva or Lausanne, Vevey or Clarens, Neuchatel or Berne, or best perhaps at that Ile de la Motte, on the beautiful Lake of Bienne, where he spent some of his happiest days."

For a moment I was puzzled, for I remembered somewhat vaguely having read in the *Confessions* or elsewhere that Rousseau had recorded his happiest memories as connected with the Isle of Saint-Pierre. However, my companion of the hour informed me that the Ile de Saint-Pierre and the Ile de la Motte are one and the same, and obliged me further by quoting Jean Jacques' own words : "de toutes les habitations où j'ai demeuré, et j'en ai eu de charmantes, aucune ne m'a rendu si véritablement

Madame Recamier.

The 'Rousseau' (Montreux) end of Lake Geneva.

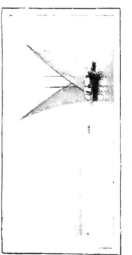

GENEVA.

A Genevese Craft

VOLTAIRE.

J. J. ROUSSEAU.

J. M. W. TURNER, R.A.

GEORGE SAND.

MADAME RECAMIER.

MONT BLANC.

CALVIN.

GIBBON.

Madame de Stael.

Chateau de Voltaire à Ferney.

Madame de Staël's House at Coppet.

COPPET.

heureux et ne m'a laissé de si tendres regrets que l'île de Saint-Pierre au milieu du lac de Bienne "—(which I trust are correctly given; if not, the fault is mine, not the good Freiburger's).

But as it does not do for a foreigner to make sweeping statements about the literature of another country, let me translate a passage from M. Joèl Cherbuliez's excellent monograph *Genève.** After recounting some of the more or less celebrated Swiss names since Rousseau and Madame de Staël—*e.g.*, the publicist, Mallet Du Pan; the historian Bérenger; the philosophic writer P. Prévost, who made known in France the works of Dugald Stewart, and had (according to the point of view) a good or bad influence as the French populariser of the doctrines of Malthus on the regulation of population; Sismondi, the historian of the Italian Republics; and Chr. V. de Bonstetter, a name once so familiar in the literary circles of Geneva, Lausanne, Paris, London, and Berlin, but now almost forgotten, though to our disadvantage, I thought, after reading one day at Lausanne this spring his excellent *Voyage dans le Latium*, and suggestive *L'Homme du Midi et l'Homme du Nord*—M. Cherbuliez adds: "As to light literature, it has never flourished among the Genevese. As yet Geneva has not been fertile in poets; she can claim but a very small number of writers of fiction, and not a single dramatic author of any renown. It is her weak side."

I was about to add that there is hope, none the less, for verse and *belles-lettres* in Geneva, for the city, like London, has its Mr. Gosse; on inquiry, however, I discovered that the Swiss variety is an authority only on the Turkish bath.

It may be admitted, of course, on the principle of quality and importance rather than quantity and promiscuity, that to

---

* M. Joël Cherbuliez, one of the heads of the great Paris and Geneva publishing firm of the Cherbuliez, was (possibly is a still surviving) brother of the famous novelist and art-writer, Victor Cherbuliez, the most eminent living Swiss.

have produced Rousseau and Madame de Staël—the one a great
writer, whose genius blew over the minds of men as an irresistible wind, and whose thought descended in fertilising rain
upon waste regions, or upon places become or becoming arid;
the other, one of the few women who have shown the way
and seized the passes of new regions for the curious mind and
the eager imagination—is, perhaps, adequate distinction for a
country so small and language-severed as Switzerland.

Ah, that fatal handicap of the absence of a national
language! "Where am I," writes Mark Twain somewhere:
"where am I, in this unhappy land, where one citizen speaks
German, and the next fellow-citizen speaks French, and the
third speaks Italian—to say nothing of the Swiss waiter, who
speaks everything from Chinese to Choctaw?"

"Is there a Switzerland!" wrote Dumas in one of his
delightful reminiscences of travel: "or is it only a geographical
expression for an international playground snipped off from
France, Germany, and Italy?"

And lovers of the immortal Tartarin and Bompard will
recall their pregnant summary:—

"'What a queer country this Switzerland is!' exclaimed
Tartarin.

"Bompard began to laugh.

"'Ah, vaï! Switzerland? In the first place there is
nothing Swiss in it!'"

Every visitor to the Lake of Geneva will, *en route* or on
the spot, have learned all that his 'Baedeker' or 'Joanne' or
other guide-book has to tell, as to the physical geography of
Lac Léman or Genfer-See, as French and Germans respectively
call this mountain-circled inland sea, which stretches from
Geneva along French shores by Yvoire and Thonon and Evian
to Saint-Gingolph, a townlet in the valley of the Rhone where
one may sleep in France, but at the post-office across the road

is in Switzerland; and from Eaux-vives, on the Genevese left bank, by Coppet to Lausanne and Vevey, to the three towns of Montreux, and to the final shores at Chillon and Villeneuve. There is not a locality on either side that has not some association of literary interest. In this respect, indeed, there is truth in Voltaire's verse, when in a moment of rare enthusiasm he exclaimed, ' My lake ranks foremost.' Even small unnoticed districts, as St. Saphorin on the north and Des Allinges on the south bank, have their added interests of association with Amiel and Saint François de Sales.

Also, he will read all the hackneyed particulars about Bonnivard at Chillon, and Byron's lines; about Calvin at Geneva; and the distinct waters of the Arve and the Rhone when they have become one river—with the usual commentary that it is like life, like fate, like marriage, or like something else to which it bears a painfully obvious symbolical or other resemblance.

So, rather, let us seek other company, be content to linger or turn aside, and not hurry through from Geneva to Territet by boat, or let a glimpse of Geneva and Lausanne suffice for this section of the Canton de Vaud. It would be delightful to wander upon the mountain-lands with a De Saussure; along the hill-pastures and lake-meadows with a De Candolle or Huber; to study with Bouvet those unexpected aliens, descendants of a remote sea-ancestry, the laughing-gull, the sea-swallow, and the wild swan, lovely habitants which give a note of wildness and strangeness to Geneva waters; to stroll by shore-roads and highland ways with the often mournful but oftener eloquent and moving pages of the *Journal Intime*, for that is the way to realise to the full the subtle charm of Amiel; to wake in a Vevey dawn, as De Senancour chronicles in that often beautiful but most *triste* of books, *Obermann*, " to the exquisite fragrance of new-mown hay, cut during the cool freshness of the falling dews, in the

light of the moon"; or to go to the scenes painted by
Delacroix, to visit Chartran at his island-studio off Clarens, to
watch this or that deft French artist painting the picturesque
felucca-rigged boats and sailing-barges which, inimitably graceful, inimitably lovely, are an untiring pleasure for the eyes, or
watch this or that Swede or Norwegian (the Scandinavian and the
Russ are almost as frequent now as the English and German, and
in art have many more representatives) painting the seemingly
motionless highlands and vast capes of cloudland reflected in the
moveless blue depths; to spend hours adrift in a sailing-boat,
in hazy mornings, in dreamlike afternoons, in moonlit nights,
sometimes dreaming, sometimes reading a few winged and
lovely words of those beautiful pages where Ruskin's heart
overflows in a grave ecstasy—it would be delightful to do all
this vicariously as well as directly to enjoy it, but, alack, the
adequate chronicling of it would need a volume.   These
delights can only be indicated.   And are they not, in truth,
of the kind which the few will find out for themselves,
if time and the occasions permit?   To the many, Calvin's
pulpit in Geneva and Bonnivard's damp quarters in Chillon
seem the paramount attraction of a visit to French-
Switzerland.

Besides, I should like to unburden all my accumulated
lore!   Meanwhile, with the vagrant New Englander in *A
Tramp Abroad*, I must perforce content myself with "I know
more about this lake than the fishes in it!"

Most visitors approach by way of Geneva itself.   And
this is the right way.   It is not to discredit the City of the
Faith to say that other places along these shores will seem
better after it; that is, to go to other places on the Lake first
and then to visit Geneva is to come upon disappointment.
It is difficult to say why this is so; and of course the impression may not be general, may for all I know be merely personal.

With all its spaciousness, with its magnificent quays, its city divided into two beautiful towns, its many buildings of interest, its quick and active life, its whole-hearted eagerness to spoil the Egyptian, and every other admitted and unadmitted attraction, from Rousseau's Isle ('Who was he, anyway?' remarked a Cook-conducted American one day) to the Calvinium and the Model of Jerusalem, where the travelling evangelical mightily rejoiceth—with all this, and all that Baedeker indicates and the local guide welters in, Geneva remains a dull place for other than a brief stay. Something of its old hard Calvinistic *régime* endures. It has no French gaiety, though it is so near France and is in many things so French. Nor, despite its size and importance, does it vie with Lausanne as an intellectual centre. Perhaps one reason why the city is somewhat in disfavour with foreign residents now is conveyed in a remark made to me by a depressed hotel-proprietor : "Too many anarchists and such-like come here to live, and too few watchmakers go away. People nowadays think Geneva does nothing but turn out millions of watches, and then at odd times makes bombs to meet the international demand." As for the anarchists, however, I think the Genevese have little affection for their company, though it is pleasant to be told at regular intervals that one's town is the true Cosmopolis, and that the Genevese are the 'Birds o' Freedom' of Europe. "And then," said one expostulating restaurateur indignantly, "they're teetotallers to a man. Why, the worst of the lot, that Russian what writes above a red dagger an' a bomb as his signature, *he* feeds on milk and sardines."

The abiding attraction at Geneva is the magnificent outlook, from the superb rush of the azure Rhone between the two towns, to the ever-beautiful vicinage of hills and mountains and snow-white Alps, with the crowning glory of Mont Blanc visible from many a busy thoroughfare as well as from the fascinating quays, the Rhone-spanning bridges, and the lovely promenades and environs.

In the town itself, visitors who combine a literary pilgrimage with the pursuit of pleasure commonly divide allegiance between Rousseau and Calvin . . . 'those two disagreeable people,' the remark with which Mr. Clemens casually introduces and summarily dismisses them, in that humorous classic of his. Certainly one should go and see (the somewhat moulty eagles of Geneva, like the bears of Berne, must be 'done' first, I am told, if one would be in the run of popular taste—so let one see, and then leave, the Place Bel Air) that venerable cathedral of St. Peter whose towers rise so impressively from old Geneva, where Calvin preached and whence John Knox went to Scotland. And one must visit, of course, the steep and somewhat malodorous Grande Rue, and look at the uninteresting house-block, on one floor of which the great Jean Jacques was born (for the drift of evidence is against the more picturesque house on the right bank of the Rhone, now known as No. 27, Rue Rousseau . . . where, certainly, Rousseau's grandfather lived). But perhaps for most visitors there is more significance in the simple chronicle that here, in Geneva, Calvin died and Rousseau was born; the harvest was spent, the new seed was sown.

Calvin made Geneva the Mecca of the Protestant world. But it is safe to say that if the Geneva of to-day were the least like the Geneva of the Calvinistic *régime*, Messrs. Thos. Cook and Co. might close their much-frequented office in the Rue du Rhône. For were not all citizens imperatively required by that *régime* to be out of bed at 4 a.m. in summer and at 6 in winter? And was not the cuisine ordained to the hard-and-fast extreme of two dishes, "one of animal, one of vegetable food," and no pastry? As for wine, it was anathema. Meanwhile, the 'Consistoire' looked after 'the other morals.'

To-day, however — by way of revenge, I suppose—Geneva
'rises later' than Paris or any other large French town, and is
become gastronomic, not to say *gourmandisiac* in its tastes ;
while as for pastry, that lyrical effervescence, the *vers-de-société*,
the exquisite poetry of the culinary art (mixed metaphor goes
well with the mixed mysteries of the confectioner), one may
seek and find none to surpass it between the Boulevard St.
Germain of Paris and the Via Vittorio Emanuele of Milan.
And this, the grateful visitor must recollect, is in great
part due to Voltaire, who laughed away so many drear
absurdities. "When I shake my wig," he wrote from
Ferney, "its powder dusts the whole republic." And
more powder fell at Geneva than anywhere else. Here,
and in these respects at least, the most confirmed anti-
Voltairian will admit the justice of that famous summing-up
of his own achievement, "*J'ai fait un peu de bien: c'est mon
meilleur ouvrage.*"

But before we take the electric car out beyond the pretty
village of Grand Seconnex, close by which the French frontier
runs, a mile or two from Ferney, to Voltaire's home, a
reminiscence or two of another kind. The visitor will have had
more than sufficient of Calvin; there is little enough interest
in seeing the more or less authentic house where 'that impu-
dent fellow, Jean Jacques,' was born, or the square or *place*
where 'Candide' and the 'Dictionnaire philosophique' of 'the
old devil of Ferney' were publicly burned; and I doubt if
there are many visitors who care to find out where Amiel was
born some eighty years or more ago. One literary tourist,
indeed, who was "working up Voltaire and that lot" (a rival,
I thought at first, and imitated Brer Rabbit when Brer Fox
was around), remarked to me in surprise that he thought Amiel
was a book written by Stendhal or somebody, or perhaps (he
added, as an afterthought) was "the pseudonym of Obermann

or Henri Beyle or one of those fellows." But in those lovely environs of Geneva one (if that way inclined) could not do better than take the *Journal Intime* as companion: much of it was written there, notably at Lancy and Vandœuvres—from which latter, I may add for music-lovers, Frederic Amiel went one May-day in 1857 to hear the first performance of 'Tannhäuser' given out of Germany, performed at the Geneva theatre by a passing German company, and wrote that night perhaps the subtlest criticism of Wagner's music yet given in these ensuing five-and-forty years. Either by the hill-pastures or on the calm waters of the lake, no 'literary companion' wears so well as the *Journal* of this famous Swiss, who knew and could describe the mountains as well as De Saussure, and the Rhone-stretch and Rhone-lake as well as Ruskin, and the whole of " this symphony of mountains, this cantata of sunny Alps," as well as "our common ancestor in modern literature," Rousseau.* But if one's tastes are not that way, a delightful walk or sail along the right shore may be made from Geneva to the Villa Diodati, where, as well as 'Manfred' (as already mentioned), Byron wrote the third canto of 'Childe Harold.' As for Geneva itself and its immediate vicinage I can think of nothing for the reader able to understand French comparable to the fifty-seven delightful stanzas which in an almost unknown book of verse Amiel himself calls *Guide du Touriste à Genève*, where everything of interest is mentioned, from the Plainpalais to the site of La Tour Maîtresse, from " nos quais, lignes de flamme

---

* "Rousseau is an ancestor in all things. It was he who inaugurated the literary pilgrimage afoot before Töpffer, reverie before René, literary botany before George Sand, the worship of nature before Bernardin St. Pierre, the democratic theory before the Revolution of 1789, political discussion and theological discussion before Mirabeau and Renan, the science of teaching before Pestalozzi, and Alpine description before De Saussure [and Ruskin]. He formed a new French style, the close, chastened, passionate, interwoven style we know so well. Nobody has had more influence than he upon the nineteenth century, for Byron, Chateaubriand, Mme. de Staël, and George Sand all descend from him."—AMIEL · *Journal Intime.*

et d'eau " to the Rocher du Niton, off the lake-embankment of the Eaux Vives,

> Où l'on sacrifia, dit-on,
> Au dieu Neptune . . . .

from the Salève to the joining of the turbid Arve and the azure Rhone,

> . . le lieu
> Où l'Arve gris, le Rhône bleu,
> Hymen étrange,
> Joignent, par un destin brutal,
> Sans les mêler, l'un son cristal,
> L'autre sa fange.

Of more modern and unfamiliar associations than those connected with Calvin and Rousseau, with Voltaire and Byron, I recall none more interesting than those wed to the names of George Sand and Liszt.

In the tenth of her published *Lettres d'un Voyageur*, George Sand gives us a delightful account of her sudden departure from Nohant, her rapid journey across Eastern France in August of 1837, in order to join the Abbé Liszt and his sister at Geneva, who had arrived there a year before and ever since been daily awaiting her! Arrived, astonishing people by her " blouse bleue et ses bottes crottées," she told the postillion to drive ' chez M. Liszt,' when ensued the following dialogue :

" Liszt ? Who's he ? What does he do ? What's his business ? "

" *Artiste* "—(this shortly and conclusively).

" Veterinary ? "

" Bah, you must be in need of such yourself, animal ! "

At this point, when France and Switzerland were at loggerheads, a passer-by intervened, with the remark, " Ah, I know whom you're after. . . . He is a fiddle-merchant. . . . I can show you where he lodges."

The quest, however, was not at an end. At the first place the weary traveller was told that M. Liszt was in Paris; at the next, London was specified; at the next, Italy.   Finally, at the latest place of call, the lady found a note from the musician's sister, la Comtesse d'Agoult (George Sand's 'Princesse Mirabelle'), saying briefly : " We have long waited you ; you take your own time ; and now we're wearied out.   It is now your turn to seek us out, for we're gone."

The weary and disgusted traveller posted on as soon as possible, and ultimately found herself at the Hôtel Union at Chamounix.   This time, instead of asking for Liszt by name, she gave a description of the person she sought : " A man in a short blouse, with long and dishevelled hair, a cravat tied in a knot, more or less limping at present, and habitually humming the *Dies Iræ* in a light agreeable fashion!"   The description was unmistakable, and the fugitive was tracked.

With all their mutual affection and admiration, each doubtless found the other somewhat trying at times : the lady, certainly, had her ways.   For example, in her *Impressions et Souvenirs* there is an entry : " Midnight, January.—A. has just raised a scene because of the open window.   This excellent man cannot understand that it is better to have a cold in his head than to deprive his soul of a sublime joy (*i.e.* contemplation of the moon).   I try in vain to describe to him this quiet enjoyment arising from contemplation.   He is enraged. . . ."

It was in this hotel that Liszt wrote in the visitors' book under the statutory headings :

QUALITY : *Musician-philosopher.*
PLACE OF BIRTH : *On Parnassus.*
WHENCE COME : *From Doubt.*
WHERE GOING : *To Truth—*

and that George Sand described herself and party as ' *la famille Piffoëls* ' in this fashion :

NAME OF TRAVELLERS : *The Piffle Family.*

DOMICILE: *Nature.*

WHENCE COME: *God.*

WHERE GOING: *Heaven.*

PLACE OF BIRTH: *Europe.*

QUALITY: *Idlers.*

DATE OF PASSPORT: *For Ever.*

(lit *titre*, meaning Voucher and Claim, as well as its other meanings.)

BY WHOM GRANTED: *Public Opinion.*

Neither, it will be seen, suffered from excessive modesty.

At Geneva itself we may enjoy a delightful reminiscence of these two great ones when they lived in an hotel by the Rhone-side, which we owe to Mme. Lina Ramann. "Here," she chronicles, "the Abbé Liszt used often to extemporise, when his hands wandered over the white keys with that delicate mother-o'-pearl touch of his, while George Sand would sit near the fire, listening attentively, or turning with dreaming eyes and looking out on the magnificent landscape seen through the window, while her mind transformed the master's harmonies into her own poetic visions."

It was here, and thus, that Liszt composed, on a Spanish air, his 'Rondo Fantastique,' which he dedicated to George Sand. "Shortly after he had composed it, the Abbé played it one autumn evening to George Sand, who was seated in the twilight at a couch by the window, smoking her cigarette. Moved by the music," adds Mme. Lina Ramann, "and by the murmurous wash of the lake-water along its narrow beaches, she gradually let her mind weave other fantasies born of the 'Rondo,' and that night took up her pen and wrote *Le Contrebandier : Conte lyrique. Paraphrase fantastique sur un Rondo fantastique de Franz Liszt.*"

* *

But now for Voltaire-land and the lake-side home of Mme. de Staël.

The former means an expedition across the frontier. Ferney (or *Fernex* as generally printed in Switzerland) used to be somewhat inaccessible for the ordinary tourist ; now it can be reached swiftly and frequently by an electric car, which leaves Geneva from just off the Rue du Mont Blanc, opposite the new General Post Office. A pleasanter way still, however, is to drive, or, except in the summer heats, to walk. But to those unhurried, and with a preference for the unbeaten track, I would recommend that the morning or forenoon steamer be taken to Coppet, when, after a stroll through the sleepy, charming village-town and a visit to Mme. de Staël's old home, one can strike across a charming region, visit by a detour the Villa des Délices, where Voltaire had his first home in these parts, and so come upon Ferney.

To the lover of French literature, and of genius that knows no geographical limit, a visit to Coppet cannot but give a moving pleasure. What a wonderful woman this Mme. de Staël was : so brilliant, so charming, so great a captain of the intellectual forces of modern Europe ! One may turn to-day from *Delphine* and its fellows ; even *Corinne* may seem outworn now, with all the revelation become commonplace and the quick life gone away on the wind. But her influence, which was so great, endured as an awakening, a moulding, and even a directing force ; though it is, perhaps, only since Georg Brandes' fine study of the intellectual achievement of this princess of letters that, in this country at least, she has won anything like adequate recognition.

To-day, the Coppet manor-house, with its two grey towers, and the near-by chapel where her impatient spirit knew rest at last, has relatively few pilgrims ; but these go in reverence and love.

To some it may be new that Mme. de Staël's mother, when Suzanne Curchod, knew Gibbon well, fell in love with him indeed, and even fascinated that somewhat cold and irresponsive student. During his four years of absence in England, between his first and second sojourn in Lausanne, she remained constant; but, on his return, not even Rousseau's mediation brought the callous historian ' to reason ' ; not even when the lady finally pleaded that at least they might remain friends did Gibbon relent, for he declined the compromise as ' dangerous for both.'

We may deplore the gentleman's philosophic calm, but cannot regret the fair Suzanne's disappointment, for in a fit of the blues she married M. Necker, afterwards to become Louis XVI.'s famous Minister of Finance; went to Coppet; and bore to her husband and the literary world of Europe the beautiful girl and enchanted mind whom it was long the wont to allude to as ' Corinne.' There can be no doubt that in gaining a Mlle. Germaine Necker by losing a Miss Gibbon we owe a big debt to the Destinies.

She had her faults, of course, this brilliant woman, and in her work as in her life. Particularly in her earlier writings she is like her own heroine in the *Histoire de Pauline*, " apt to pour out the feelings of her young and tender soul in an incorrect but extraordinary style." On the other hand, I can recall no youthful critical effort more mature in thought and expression than her admirable Essay on Fiction, prefaced to the two volumes of *Zulma, and Other Tales*, all written before she was twenty.

It was here, in Coppet, that, in the perilous days of the Revolution, Mme. de Staël was visited by so many famous people, from Sismondi to Byron. Here the brilliant Benjamin Constant first met Mme. Récamier, that woman so beautiful that at forty-three she had as ardent lovers as at twenty-three, and even

when seventy and blind was found by the great Chateaubriand
'still lovely and still charming.'   Mme. de Staël herself had
this unpassing beauty, this undying youth and unfading charm;
and has herself chronicled her "passionate and inappeasable
desire to be loved."   She was forty-five when she fell in love
with and married the successor to M. de Staël-Holstein —
M. Rocca, a handsome youth of three-and-twenty, who had
first attracted her attention and admiration by pirouetting and
leaping his black Andalusian stallion under the windows of the
house in Geneva where she was then staying.

But, poor thing, she was a *mondaine,* and longed ever for
Paris and the excitements of life. To her, too often, this lovely
view that we look at from Coppet to-day "oppressed her with
its inexorable beauty and maddening calm."

One wonders, though, if she was really happier in Paris or
London, or here,

Où Corinne repose au bruit des eaux plaintives.

For she was of those in whom life is intensified to the double.
But Mme. de Staël and London! . . . some will wonder. Yes,
for a while, she had her *salon* here. It was in Argyll Place,
Regent Street (No. 30, near the present Union Bank), that in
her hour of exile she 'received' such mixed if brilliant society,
that Byron said it reminded him of the grave, as all distinctions
were levelled in it!

But what about "le vieux diable de Ferney . . . où est
cette âme infernale," as a contemporary chronicler politely
alludes to Voltaire?

Well, Voltaire and Rousseau, Gibbon and Dickens, the
gay Dumas and the irresistible Tartarin, and company, must
now be diligently sought.

Besides, I bear in mind the apposite words of an anonymous scribe of 1785, writing upon 'that singular man
Rousseau': "There is scarcely any prejudice more general

than that which inclines us to believe that whatever is pleasing
to ourselves must necessarily be so to the rest of the world.
This desire, *improperly indulged*, not only fails of producing the
wished-for effect, but is often followed by one quite contrary."

Again, I recollect the warning of that objectionable elderly
Miss from Chicago, in *A Tramp Abroad*, who, on the Geneva
steamer, remarked incidentally: " If a person starts in to
jabber-jabber-jabber about scenery and history and all sorts of
tiresome things, I get the fan-tods mighty soon."

And no self-respecting writer would inflict ' the fan-tods '
even on that most genial of collective beings, the Reader.

**

Switzerland a crammed caravanserai in August? Yes, no
doubt.   And yet it is constantly maintained that English visitors
are not nearly so numerous as formerly, except perhaps at Easter
and other popular holiday seasons.   This, however, is partly
because that seventy or a hundred years ago comparatively few
' ordinary ' people travelled for pleasure, except English ; to-day
the German outnumbers the Britisher, not only in Switzerland
but along the Italian Riviera and North Italy, and even as far
south as Sicily.   There is at least one gain in this : it is not
' the inevitable English' one hears of now, but ' these Germans' ;
and it is some consolation to know that, in every country, the
change is hailed with most sincere regret, for the Teuton, especially the Prussian variety, is nowhere loved, and for the most
part is scrupulously avoided.   ' The English invasion ' began
with the freeing of Europe after Waterloo : once Napoleon was
secure in St. Helena, the British tourist spread in a fertilising
(if often exasperating) flood over Western Europe.   It is amusing
to find that even then ' the superior people ' resented the crowd.
In the delightful record of the 1819 Journey of Earl-Spencer-
All-the-Talents and his lively Lady Lavinia, recently given us
from the dame's letters, we find the complaint, early in October,

that " Geneva is as full as it can stick with English " ; while at the next stopping-place the sprightly correspondent writes: ". . . When we all arrived, extenuated with fatigue, we were favoured with a thunderstorm. . . . Quantities of English everywhere. *One family of nineteen,* ten children, here yester-day." The lively Lady Lavinia must have been an amusing person to travel with, though she had her tempers (when her language was more emphatic than refined) and sometimes must have tried the patience of her courtly but pedantic lord. " Ld S. has made some extraordinary acquisitions of curiositys, which I have heard discussed over and over, with an eagerness which always surprises me, for the duce a bit can I recollect the name of one of these Treasures." And Rome found her no more amenable than Geneva. It was the time when 'the antiquarian circles' were much excited over the excavations in the Forum, and the leading part taken by the Duchess of Devonshire; but Lady Spencer showed as little respect for the first as for the second, writing of the lady as 'that witch of Endor,' and of the treasure trove as ' old horrors.'

To adapt Gibbon, my readers will, I trust, excuse this short digression: "the practice of celebrated moralists is so often at variance with their precepts." For I had meant to begin this article with Voltaire, and to lead off with that admirable motto of his: " Precision in thought; concision in style; decision in life."

Yes, it is time we were at Ferney. Not that the Voltaire associations with Geneva itself have been adequately touched upon: it would take a volume to exploit that theme. And then those lovely vicinage walks, especially that by the Salève, Lamartine's ' Salève aux flancs azurés,' and its memories of the great French poet, its association with those Thursday walks recorded by Edmond Scherer when he and Amiel and Victor Cherbuliez and others devoted themselves to ' débauches

platoniciennes.'   Here it was that Amiel found those ceaseless
metaphors of beauty which give so great a charm to his prose
—as this, at the tumultuous town-weir of the Rhone, where
the river pours like a melted avalanche—"This standpoint (of ideal vision) whence, as it were, one hears the
impetuous passage of time, rushing and foaming as it flows
out into the changeless ocean of eternity,"—where he wrote
so many of those lovely if almost wholly ignored poems, of
which I give one, adventuring by its side a poor translation :—

APAISEMENT.

Partout le regret ou l'inquiétude,
  Partout le souci :
Toujours la tristesse et la solitude,
  Et le deuil aussi !
Où fleurit l'espoir ? où verdit la palme ?
  Où croît le bonheur ?
Où cueillir la joie ? Où trouver le calme ?
  Où poser son cœur ?
L'or ni le savoir, le vin ni les roses,
  L'art ni le ciel bleu,
N'emplissent le cœur ; et deux seules choses
  L'apaisent un peu :
C'est d'abord un cœur fait pour lui, qui l'aime
  Et qu'il nomme sien,
Et puis une voix au fond de lui-même
  Qui lui dise Bien !

SOLACE.

Regret, disquietude
  And weary care :
Grief, melancholy, solitude
  Everywhere !
Where blossoms Hope ?
  Where blooms Life's palm ? .   .
Happiness . .   joy . .
  O heart . . . or calm ?
Nor wine nor gold
  Nor art nor the blue sky
Bring peace to this sad fold,
  Bring but this quiet sigh—
A heart to hold my love,
  A heart its love to tell ! .   .
Then from the depths shall this low whisper move,
  "Soul, it is well."

Well, when ' Obermann ' came back one July from Paris or Fontainebleau to Switzerland, he begins his letter, " Il n'y a pas l'ombre de sens dans la manière dont je vis ici ": and in like fashion, when I consider what extent of ' literary geography ' I have to cover in this article, I say to myself that there is no shadow of sense in the manner in which I hark back to Geneva!

As I wrote a few pages back, one may come upon Ferney either from Geneva by the frontier village of Grand Seconnex, or by the lake-steamer to Coppet, and thence afoot by way of Voltaire's earlier residence, the Villa des Délices, and Les Charmilles.

To approach the home-farm, so to say, of this great agriculturist of the mind, this strenuous, mocking, earnest, laughing, eager, jibing sower of good and evil seed, is indeed an experience for any one versed in the great ways of literature. Voltaire the man may no longer wear that aureole woven of the wonder and admiration of a startled, scandalised, but fascinated Europe: Voltaire the publicist may be ignored, Voltaire the romancist be spoken of rather than read, Voltaire the dramatist be (deservedly) forgotten, Voltaire the historian be shelved, Voltaire the autocrat of letters be discredited. There is enough left to keep his fame alive, apart from the great, the unparalleled tradition of the supreme place and influence he won and so long held. If everything else of his perished, the volumes of his correspondence would suffice to justify the legend of his supremacy. What a wonderful old man, this, who laughed at everything, and yet had unselfish enthusiasms impossible to the Gibbon who decried him and the Napoleon who hated him! And apart from all else, Voltaire lives as an abiding quality, as an intellectual tradition. He is the high-priest of irony. " Always walk laughing in the road of truth," he writes in one of his letters to D'Alembert. Once it was the fashion, and in this country in particular, to class him with Mephistopheles ["why drag in Mephistopheles?—Voltaire is the original Satanic name," was doubtless the unexpressed thought of many]; but later and fuller knowledge reveals 'le vieux diable de Ferney' as a man who wore a mocking smile as our forefathers wore a wig, and carried the air of the cynic and the infidel as the beau of that day carried a cane: at heart sound, a giant mind, a nature perverse but fundamentally fine.

Among the innumerable books written about Voltaire, I doubt if any affords more revelation of the man than the little volume published in the Year X (*i.e.* 1802), entitled *Soirées de Ferney*. I re-read this delightful book one wet and stormy spring evening at Ferney, at the amusing if neither particularly clean nor comfortable Hôtel de la Truite. As the rain came in sudden noisy whispers, with the wind-eddies abruptly rising or falling, I fancied I heard the ghosts of many old laughters, many cries of anger, and half-real, half-mocking lamentations, many half-solemn, half-blasphemous derisions. And looking in the leaping flame of the wood-fire I dreamed I saw a withered old face—cynical, ironical, vain, great in intellect, and behind the mocking eyes a spirit of love and charity and good-will.

"A good deal of it all was tomfoolery" (*c'était de la petite charlatanerie*). There we have Voltaire. "Below all my raillery there has ever been the anger at evil, the cry for justice, the passion of an idea." There also we have Voltaire. And he sums up both when he says somewhere, "For all that, I was not born more wicked than any one else, and at bottom I'm not a bad fellow" (*quoique je ne sois pas né plus malin qu'un autre, et que dans le fond je suis bonhomme*). But he would not be Voltaire if his last words were not, "For some thirty or forty years I took everything seriously, and was a fool for my pains. I have finished by laughing at everything."

"What *is* the Voltairian spirit in ordinary life?" some one asked me the other day.

"Audacity that hits the mark," I answered.

"Such as . . . ?"

But not remembering at the moment ' la phrase juste,' and recollecting an apposite anecdote, I answered: "A great lady once replied to the third Napoleon, shortly before he appropriated the vacant throne of France, when he had with an ironical smile asked her to explain the difference she drew between ' an accident' and 'a misfortune':—'If,' she said, 'you were to fall into the Seine, that would be an accident; if they pulled you out again, that would be a misfortune.'"

An American transcriber published a volume of the *Humour of Voltaire*. But humour, as we understand it, is no characteristic of his. His wit is keen, poignant, sometimes cruel, generally a lash—even when it laughs it bites. When he is alluding somewhere to ' the soul' and our hope of immortality, he adds, "I am persuaded that if the peacock could speak he would boast of his soul, and would affirm that it inhabited his magnificent tail." He is nearer humour when, in a well-known tale, he has : "'A little wine, drunk in moderation, comforts the heart of God and man.' So reasoned Memnon the philosopher; and he became intoxicated." Of wit his very spirit was made; fun he had in plenty—not of Dumas' or Dickens' genial kind, not of Daudet's brilliant burlesque, not of Mark Twain's sly drollery, but a perverse, amusing, often convincing and always fascinating fun of his own. But he had nothing of that pawky humour which we consider so essentially northern, as, for example, that story of the unco'-cautious Scot who always emptied his glass at a gulp because he ' once had one knocked over.'

Not that ' the ecstasy of the incongruous ' did not appeal
to him.   One can imagine his sarcastic reticence if, in writing
on heroism in modern life, he had lived long enough to be able
to illustrate the narrative with that duel between Dumas and
Jules Janin—when Janin would not fight with swords because
he knew an infallible thrust, and Dumas refused pistols because
he could kill a fly at forty paces, and so the foes embraced ! Or
his mocking delight if, in writing on the sincerity of ideals, he
had lived long enough to supplement that wicked 'Conversation'
of his, concerning *Ossian*, between an Oxford professor, a
Florentine, and a Scot, at Lord Chesterfield's, with the episode
of how, under the Directory, persons near the Bois de Boulogne
were one day alarmed to see a great blaze among the trees, and
on coming close perceived some men ' attired in Scandinavian
fashion ' endeavouring to set fire to a pine tree, and singing to
the accompaniment of a guitar with an air of inspiration—
merely admirers, as it proved, of *Ossian*, who intended to sleep
in the open air, and to set a tree alight in order to keep themselves warm, and thus emulate the people of Caledonia ! (Thus
Mons. Texte, in his able and suggestive work on *The Cosmopolitan
Spirit in Literature*.)

Voltaire had pre-eminently the genius of repartee. None
more than he would have rejoiced in that cutting rejoinder of
the elder Dumas to Balzac, when the two great men were
brought together at the house of a well-meaning friend.   After
neither had spoken a word to the other, Balzac was about to
leave, when he said viciously : " When I am written out I too
shall take to writing dramas."

To which Dumas at once replied : " You'd better begin
at once, then ! "

But . . . Well, no; this has become a series of ' buts,
like that dialogue of ' buts ' between Don Inigo-y-Medroso-y-
Comodios-y-Papalamiendos and the Englishman (whom the

good Bachelor Don Papalamiendos imagined an anthropagus) in our great man's tale of *The Sage and the Atheist.*

Some time ago a doubtless worthy but certainly bigoted individual perpetrated a booklet on Voltaire. One of the deadly sins he adduced was that 'this Scoffer incarnate' stole his name, 'like all else.' It is quite true that François Marie Arouet, in a crude anagram, evolved the name his genius adopted and made immortal. But to keep on speaking of Mons. Arouet is more pedantic than to allude invariably to Bacon as Lord Verulam. As for Voltaire's standing unique in this iniquity, it is enough to cite, among other famous instances, Montesquieu, whom no one knows now as Charles Secondat, Jean Chauvin, known to us as Calvin, or Molière, whose actual name of Jean Baptiste Pocquelin is long forgotten.

When one thinks—at Lausanne (Monrion), at Tournay, and still more at Aux Délices, and above all at Ferney—of what Voltaire achieved merely in quantity of work, one stands amazed. Even at an age when most men are content to (or at least eager to) 'cultivate their cabbages,' Voltaire maintained lightly and set himself heroically to tasks overmuch for ninety-nine men out of a hundred in the fulness of youth. Some idea of this may be gathered from the fact that after he was sixty-four he published some forty volumes; or, to put it another way, he issued in the last twenty years of his long life some twenty-eight works, apart from many long and short tales, pieces in verse, miscellanies.* However, we cannot dwell upon his achievements: we are but pilgrims to where he lived and

* The reader interested in Voltaire may care for these particulars : 8 vols. of the *Dictionnaire philosophique,* and 5½ of the 6 of the *Philosophie;* more than a vol of the *Mélanges littéraires,* 2 vols. of the *Mél. historiques,* and 2 of the *Dialogues;* 1 vol. of the *Hist. de Parlements de Paris;* the several vols of the *Facetiæ;* 2½ of the 3 of *La Politique et la Législation;* 3 vols. of *Comments sur les Œuvres Dramatiques; Peter the Great; The Age of Louis XV.;* 8 vols. *Correspondence.*

worked. If one is alert to the irony of changing circumstance one may stand on the shore at Coppet, or on the high road to Grand Seconnex, and look over or back to Geneva, and recognise that the same town burned Voltaire's most famous books, and received him with adulation when he drove city-wards in his coach-and-six; for long sedulously decried him as an evil, and now as sedulously cultivates him as an important commercial asset. The value of his work and the extent of his influence have been exaggerated by many who have written about both; they have been more grossly underrated by the ignorant and the prejudiced. In one direction, at least, I think no one has so keenly perceived and tersely stated the relative distinctions as the great historian Michelet, when he wrote, " Montesquieu écrit, interprète le droit; Voltaire pleure et crie pour le droit; et Rousseau le fonde."

When I was at Coppet on a previous occasion I found in the salon-de-lecture of the Hôtel du Lac the discarded or lost MS. diary of ' a travelling miss.' I copied one entry: " Madame de Stael was *a dear*. Her portrait as Sappho, by David, at the chateau, *is sweet*. Voltaire is an old horror. He's always laughing at one, and looks a wicked old fright, and Dan says he's the same in his books."

The effervescent miss and the more reserved Dan represent the great public. The sentimentalism of ' Corinne ' keeps her memory sweet, and there are tears and sighs at Coppet. The continual irony of Voltaire discomposes, and refuge is taken in the first available car back to Geneva.

At the Hôtel de la Truite in Ferney I asked if many foreigners came to ' Voltaireville ' to stay. Very few, I was told; many bicyclists, hundreds by car every week during the summer seasons, but few to stay overnight.

' Many English and American ? ' I asked.

' Yes, a good number. But '—and this enigmatic afterthought was propounded with an air of gloom—'mostly aërated waters.'

The Villa aux Délices of Voltaire's day is not the Villa aux Délices of to-day. The beautiful site is the same, near the confluence of the Rhone and the Arve, with, as Voltaire wrote, twenty leagues of Alp beyond, and Geneva on the lake-side across the narrowing waters :—"And I can see from my window, as I write, the quarters where Jean Chauvin, the Picard called Calvin, reigned, and the spot where he burned Soret for the good of his soul."

Here and at Ferney Voltaire entertained royally : "for nearly a quarter of a century," he wrote, "I have been the *aubergiste* of Europe." Condorcet, D'Alembert, Diderot— everybody visited him who was anybody: kings, princes, philo- sophers, poets, writers of all kinds and every nation, statesmen, women of genius, women with beauty, women without either genius or beauty but uplifted by this fad or that vogue, exiles, patriots, rogues, the sorrowful and hopeless, the hopeful and unprincipled: "All ways lead to Ferney, as to Rome." In his correspondence we see him in all his Protean changes, from modesty (rare)—as when, from Tournay, he wrote to M. de Prégny, "I, a labourer, a shepherd, a rat retired from the world into a Swiss cheese"—to fantastic grandiosity, as when he wrote to the Duc de Richelieu, "I have succeeded in con- verting a miserable and unknown hamlet into a charming town, and in founding a commerce which embraces America, Africa, and Asia" ! All the same, he worked wonders at Ferney. The place bloomed. Here Voltaire wrote, talked, read, posed, corresponded almost beyond credible limits ; but here also he lived the life of a country squire, interested in agriculture, forestry, breeding, dairy-produce, farm-produce. He desired to be a French Virgil, and wrote, "I enjoy my tranquil occupations, my ploughs, my bulls, my cows." Not a day passes, writes a friend, one Bachaumont, that M. Voltaire does not 'put out children to nurse,' which is his expression for planting trees. He even bred horses, with the comment that "as so much has been written about population I will at least people the country with horses, not expecting the honour of propagating my own species."

"I am going to reside at Ferney a few weeks," wrote Voltaire to D'Alembert in November, 1758. The stay extended till February, 1778, nearly twenty years. To-day Ferney is all Voltaire: his memory is its sustenance. The village-town is pleasant; the environs are delightful, the near hills lovely, the lake and the Alps are within easy reach. But to enjoy Ferney one must be *Voltairien*. He smiles, mocks, allures, enchants, repels, amuses, wearies, at every step—one cannot escape him. The kitchen wench and the boots at the Hôtel de France or the Hôtel de la Truite are in a Voltairian conspiracy. One has one's lake-trout *à la Candide*, chicken-legs *au diable de Ferney, Rosbif au Pierre le Grand, Tarte aux Délices;* one goes to sleep with the murmur of 'The Sage and the Atheist'—one wakes to the whisper of 'Memnon the Philosopher.' The château, where he lived and worked, the chapel (now, alack! fallen from its holy estate) with its famous inscription, 'Deo erexit Voltaire,' the room where he slept, the study where he wrote so many of his twenty-eight tragedies and twelve or more comedies, the shrine which is said to enclose his heart ("His Spirit is everywhere, but his heart is here"), the avenues wherein he walked, the village church where once he appeared as Mahomet cursing the superstitious Savoyards of the Rhone (as Pastor Gaberel relates), the garden, of which little remains now save his hedge of evergreens, where he strolled as the Autocrat of the Metropolis of Esprit, as the Public Exasperator and the private good genius and generous benefactor, as the Thinker and Poet, as the Pope of Literature, and as (for a brief season, to the laughing amazement of Paris) 'Brother François, unworthy Capuchin '—one may see all these, and look at the quaint, old, smiling, ironical face of the bronze bust in the *Place*, or at that of Lambert's statue erected in 1890, and think one has 'done it all.' But there is no escape from Voltaire till one has fled from Ferney. 'He is in the air,' as Mark Twain remarks of the thousand-odoured smell of Cologne.

True, much is gone. The chapel is in disuse, and the famous theatre (beyond Les Délices and Les Charmilles, at the hamlet of Châtelaine) is now a store. Nevertheless, we may draw the line at the remark of a Plymouth Brother, who by some wild irony of fate wrote an account of a visit to Ferney: " Ruin and desolation sit around, and we wondered how many Abels have fallen victims to this one bold, bad man."

Well, Voltaire would have smiled genially, and we may follow his example. How could our Plymouth Brother understand an elderly gentleman, who, instead of being a pillar and a churchwarden, admitted, " It is true I laugh and quiz a good deal: it does one good, and holds a man up in his old age."

And now for Lausanne, an hour or two away through a charming region. But having written so much of Voltaire I must say no more of his residence here and at Tournay; nay, I find I must make pemmican of the ' as much and more ' I had noted in connection with Rousseau. On the other hand, like Gibbon at Lausanne and Bonnivard at Chillon, Rousseau is the prey of the guidebooker. ' La Nouvelle Héloïse ' is exploited by Baedeker, Joanne and Company with the methodical monotony of the chronicle of hotels and pensions, ' objects of interest,' and ' walks in the neighbourhood.' From Lausanne to Vevey, from Vevey to Montreux, and above all at Clarens, the unwary tourist is caught in a Rousseau net, wanders in a Héloïsian maze. He hears (generally for the first time) of Saint Preux and Milord Edouard, of the heart-adventures of Claire and Julie, and he makes pathetically arduous efforts to visit the scenes 'immortalised' by these persons of whom he may never have heard, in whom he takes no interest, and of whom he hopes in his soul never to hear again.

To know Rousseau aright one must know the history of modern literature. He is, above all other 'moderns,' "the sower of ideas, a discoverer of sources"—"and observe," adds Amiel (that close and unprejudiced thinker) "that all the ideas sown by Rousseau have come to flower." But, with Amiel in the instance of *Emile*, one will often return to him or first come to him with disappointment, for much that he wrote is bald and jejune, no grace, no distinction, the accent of good company wanting.

Rousseau, of course, is king of the countryside from Lausanne to Montreux; and with old or recent knowledge of his writings, and notably the *Confessions* and *La Nouvelle Héloïse*, the visitors to this end of Geneva-lake may have many days of delightful hill-side and shore-way rambles, and particularly in the lovely inlands reaching behind Vevey, Clarens, and Charnex. At Vevey, if the Rousseau - pilgrim will penetrate behind the Market, he will see a house known as 'At the Sign of the Key' ('A la Clef') with the inscription that the great Jean Jacques resided here in 1732; while readers of the *Confessions* will remember his writing, "J'allai à Vevey, loger à la Clef. . . . Je pris pour cette ville un amour qui m'a suivi dans tous mes voyages." There may be many who agree with Jean Jacques in his love for this much-visited place; for myself, it seems to me the least attractive of the Geneva-side resorts, for all its glorious views. "It is stuffy, dusty, and *triste*," wrote Turgéniev once, and I fancy a good many will endorse the 'impression' of the great Russian writer. Perhaps the spirit of *Obermann, triste* enough in all conscience, has taken possession of the place; for here and in the neighbourhood De Senancour wrote much of that famous but now practically-ignored book, remembered by English readers rather for Matthew Arnold's fine poem inspired by it than for itself.   He, too, as Amiel, as Rousseau, found Vevey a place of charm: " It is at Vevey, Clarens, Chillon to Villeneuve," he writes, " that I find the lake in all its charm and beauty."   For one, I do not feel that the sadness of the author of *Obermann* was the controlled sadness of sanity, but an intellectual dyspepsia.   His mind needed open windows, sunlight and fresh air, vistas; his spirit like his body needed exercise, a variegated diet, a little dissipation perhaps. We are repelled by the incessancy of that ' intolerable void ' which in the fourth section of his most famous book he says he finds everywhere ; and surely most of his readers can have but half-hearted sympathy with one who of set purpose seeks " that condition of tolerable well-being mixed with sadness which I prefer to happiness."   *Obermann* has been called " the brooding spirit of the Vaud."   I do not think the Canton de Vaud would relish the compliment.   It is the liveliest and brightest of the Swiss cantons, and though a learned philologist has demonstrated that *Vaud* is at the root identical with *Wales* and *Walloon*, it will generally be admitted that the Swiss claimant to the old Celtic name has more of Walloon light-heartedness and Welsh love of song and company than of Welsh gloom and Walloon melancholy.

At Lausanne itself the chief literary association, of course —for the Anglo-Saxon traveller at least—is Gibbon. But, apart from what has been already written of him in this Geneva chronicle, is not every visitor ' primed ' with Gibbon before the train slides midway into the hillside town ? Does he not know all that he cares about the life of Gibbon there, and the whole story of ' the closing scene ' of the great history ?   He can purchase a ' Gibbon pen ' or ' Gibbon pipe,' he can have coffee at the sign of the ' Philosopher,' or dine at the sign of the 'Historian': the youngest generation of Lausannians (Lausonians, Lausannèges—an ignorant outsider, I would not discriminate among these and others) have even a hard and perilous 'lollipop' called, for some mysterious reason, *boules-à-Gibbon*.

So, rather, let me guide a few to the pleasant eastern residential quarter, where there is now a Dickens Avenue or Street, and the house where our great novelist lived for a time, and wrote all or the greater part of *Dombey and Son*, longing the while for the life and movement and inspiration of the London streets, feeling, with an aching nostalgia, that a hundred hours of Cockaigne were better than a cycle of the Canton de Vaud.

Coming to Lausanne by the waterway, one lands at Ouchy, its port—a charming place, and, as many think, superior to Vevey, though each has its own advantages and disadvantages. Byron enjoyed his stay at the Anchor Inn here : and many a wit and poet and famous scribe, from Voltaire and Rousseau to Gibbon and Goethe, from Dumas, that great laugher, to our own genial Dickens and the smiling creator of Tartarin, have lingered at this out-of-the-season-delightful spot. There is a local legend that a great French wit died here in a feverish delirium induced by his own witticisms. I sought in vain the tomb of the great unknown; in vain, even, for any authentic trace of the legend. But we all know the delightful floating foam of anonymous wit on the wide sea of the French genius; and who can affirm that a lord of irony did not take refuge here, and perished nobly (and unfortunately in silence) as indicated? Many must have long desired to know the source of anonymous modern aphoristic wisdom such as, "Marriage is *ennui* felt by two persons instead of one." . . . "There is a magic in the word duty, which sustains magistrates, inflames warriors, and cools married people." . . . "For one Orpheus who went to Hell to seek his wife, how many widowers who

would not even go to Paradise to find theirs!" . . . "Of all
heavy bodies, the heaviest is the woman we have ceased to
love." . . . "The last Census of France embraced nearly
twenty millions of women. Happy rascal!" And perhaps the
infamous wretch lies unhonoured and unsung at Ouchy !

Does the lover of the impressionable Dumas remember his
pleasure when, on landing at Ouchy, with a touch of that
home-sickness on arrival at new places so characteristic of the
French, he was greeted with proud delight by a compatriot, in
whom at last he recognised a young exile named Allier, who
thenceforth acted as his cicerone at Lausanne and the neighbourhood? 'Le grand et cher Alexandre' was welcome
everywhere, and no wonder : he radiated good-humour wherever
he went, was 'bon camarade' with the host, the head waiter,
the cook, the chambermaid, and the 'boots' at every hotel he
visited. Of his many experiences in this region but a single
citation, however, can be made here. Scene, Martigny, across
the lake beyond Villeneuve, up the Rhone valley. It was at
the hotel here that he made those surprising economies of his,
the thought of which beforehand made travel seem so feasible,
the recollection of which after return to Paris made him re-echo
the lament of *Ecclesiastes*, "Vanity of vanities; all is vanity."
One plan was to economise with dinner, then at Swiss hotels
usually four francs. He achieved this by invariably eating
six francs worth, and so bringing the final outlay down to
two francs! And above all there is the famous episode of the
bear-steak ! The landlord gave him a table apart, and solemnly
informed him that he was to have all to himself 'a beefsteak
of bear.' But even Dumas, after 'preliminaries,' was startled
by the magnitude of the viand placed before him, and at first
had a qualm or two. Then he set to, and, later, summoned
the landlord to express his satisfaction. It was then he learned
that the 'bifsteck d'ours' *ought* to be even better than usual, for

. . . had it not been nourished by the huntsman Guillaume Mona, who had recently found his quiet grave in the interior of Bruin! From that landlord and that table Dumas precipitately fled.

But at the Vevey-Montreux side of the lake an even greater than Dumas the voyageur is to be remembered—who but the immortal Tartarin! Chillon is again a shrine for the pilgrims who follow in the steps of the mighty. Just as Bonnivard's damp cell was almost becoming 'a devil without the tail,' as the Spaniards say, and Byron's lines apt to be met by the same complacent smirk as greets the evidence of Rizzio's remaining blood-spot at Holyrood, Alphonse Daudet came to the rescue with Monsieur Tartarin of Tarascon. Among the inimitable things of modern humour is the account of the arrest of 'the killer of lions' and that Provençal Ananias, Bompard ; their imprisonment in Chillon, and how Tartarin conducted himself there ; and the subsequent adventures of the pair till the supreme irony of their unexpected meeting at Tarascon.

But, alack! there must be an end. And just as Dumas and Tartarin were a welcome relief after De Senancour and *Obermann*, so again it is a pleasure to recur to the graver note of that deepest and most abiding of all the modern influences associated with the Lake of Geneva—the sometimes too saddening, the often melancholy, but always beautiful and fascinating masterpiece of Amiel, written by these lovely shores during the long, outwardly silent life of one of the most remarkable of modern spiritual and intellectual types. His tomb is at Clarens, where perhaps it will be visited when the *Nouvelle Héloïse* is at last faded from the minds of men.

CE QUI SUFFIT.
Paix et peu
L'ombre et Dieu,
Calme et rêve,
N'est ce pas, O mon cœur,
N'est ce pas le bonheur,
Et le bonheur sans trêve ?

There we have Amiel himself, in his lifelong desire.   And in these closing words, also, as well as in the finer breath of this lovely lake, these sentinel Alps, a message for one and all:—" A last look at this blue night and boundless landscape. Jupiter is just setting on the counterscarp of the Dent du Midi. From the starry vault descends an invisible snow-shower of dreams.   Nothing of voluptuous or enervating in this nature. All is strong, austere, and pure.   Good-night to all the world! . . . to the unfortunate and to the happy.   Rest and refreshment, renewal and hope : a day is dead—*vive le lendemain !* "

PRINTED AT THE " PALL MALL PUBLICATIONS " OFFICES,
NEWTON STREET, HOLBORN, LONDON, W.C

Lightning Source UK Ltd.
Milton Keynes UK
UKHW020640060223
416537UK00012B/2521